Elvis
my best man

Elvis
my best man

RADIO DAYS, ROCK 'N' ROLL NIGHTS, &
MY LIFELONG FRIENDSHIP WITH ELVIS PRESLEY

GEORGE KLEIN
with CHUCK CRISAFULLI

2 4 6 8 10 9 7 5 3 1

Published in 2010 by Virgin Books, an imprint of Ebury Publishing
A Random House Group Company

First published in the United States in 2010 by Crown Publishers, an imprint
of the Crown Publishing Group, a division of Random House, Inc., New York

Design by Kay Schuckhart/Blond on Pond

Frontispiece: George Klein Collection

The Random House Group Limited Reg. No. 954009

Addresses for companies within the Random House Group can be found at:
www.randomhouse.co.uk

A CIP catalogue record for this book is available from the British Library

Image on page 4 (top) of picture section courtesy of
Landov/Press Association Images

The Random House Group Limited supports The Forest Stewardship Council
(FSC), the leading international forest certification organisation. All our titles
that are printed on Greenpeace-approved FSC-certified paper carry
the FSC logo. Our paper procurement policy can be found at:
www.rbooks.co.uk/environment

FSC — Mixed Sources
Product group from well-managed
forests and other controlled sources
www.fsc.org Cert no. TT-COC-2139
© 1996 Forest Stewardship Council

Printed in the UK by Clays

ISBN 9780753539507

To buy books by your favourite authors and register for offers visit
www.rbooks.co.uk

To Dara
Some things are meant to be. . . .

CONTENTS

I suppose I've been talking about Elvis since the day I met him as an eighth grader at North Memphis's Humes High School in 1948. Back then, I was amazed that this new kid in town had the talent and confidence to bring a guitar to school and sing "Old Shep" for our music class. From that moment on, in all the years I knew Elvis, he never stopped amazing me.

And the truth is, I've never really said goodbye to Elvis Presley.

It's been over thirty years since I last got to spend time with the man I was fortunate enough to consider my closest friend, but he's still a part of each and every day of my life. In my work in radio and television, I do all I can to keep his legacy alive, playing his music and speaking of his life to old fans and, I hope, new ones, too. I'm happy to promote that legacy by organizing and participating in many of the annual events that commemorate Elvis's life and music. And every day, without fail, I wear the jeweled gold ring he gave me as a birthday present.

So much has been written and said about Elvis Presley that for a long time I didn't feel the need to add my own book to the clamor. After Elvis's death, I was offered a fair amount of money to write a "tell-all," but that wasn't the story I had to tell. Now, though, I'm old enough to know that I won't always be around to speak of the Elvis I knew, and so it feels right to set my memories down in a more permanent form. I also feel that, as much as Elvis has been examined as a pop-culture icon, some important things about him have been missed.

The Elvis I knew wasn't an icon. He was a real guy, and a real friend. He was also one of the smartest men I've ever met, and his deep, natural intelligence is something that doesn't get discussed nearly enough. The other thing that's often overlooked is how funny he was, and how much fun he was to be with. His life came to a tragic end, but I spent every moment I could with him because, simply, he was a fantastic guy to be around. The people who have been touched by his music are innumerable, but there are really only a very few of us who knew him as a friend. Having been one of his closest friends is an honor I'll always feel proud and lucky to have had. I miss him every day.

In writing this book, I've had to rely on memory, and I've made every effort possible to make sure my memory lined up with the well-documented facts of Elvis's life. Quoted material in this book may not be a literal transcription of what was spoken, but it's what I remember hearing or saying. I hope I've been able to give the reader a vivid sense of what life alongside Elvis was like, from those first days at Humes to the last days at Graceland. I want this book to give readers a full, honest look at the talented, generous, intelligent, and ultimately human Elvis Presley that I knew. I want this book to stand as a tribute to a man who was a founding rock 'n' roller and a phenomenal entertainer.

Most of all, I want to offer this book as a heartfelt and lasting "thank you" to Elvis, because the best moments of my life would not have been possible if he had not allowed me to be a part of his.

George Klein
Memphis, Tennessee
January 2010

ELVIS

MY BEST MAN

All the Way from Memphis

"GK, my man."

Elvis was in a good mood. And when Elvis was in a good mood, everybody around Elvis was in a good mood.

"Hey, Elvis. Hey, everybody," I answered.

"Get over here, GK," he said. "Sit down and stay a while."

He was looking relaxed, happy, and cool as could be sitting at the head of the table in the Graceland dining room. He gestured to the empty chair next to him on his right, so that's where I took my seat, saying my hellos to some of the other folks at the table: Priscilla, Joe Esposito, Charlie Hodge, Richard Davis. It was a couple of days into the new year of 1969, and Joe, Charlie, and Richard were all working for Elvis—familiar members of our so-called "Memphis Mafia"—so it was no surprise to see them at this informal, post-holiday dinner. There were a few faces down at the other end of the table that weren't seen as often at Graceland, faces that represented more of the business side of Elvis's world: record producer Felton Jarvis, who'd become a trusted musical ally after working some of Elvis's Nashville sessions a few years before; Freddy Bienstock, liaison to the Hill and Range Publishing company that supplied and administered almost all of the songs Elvis recorded; and Tom Diskin, the right-hand man to Elvis's longtime manager, Colonel Tom Parker.

Elvis had been making me a welcome guest at Graceland since he'd bought the place back in 1957. In fact, I'd been with him when he looked at the property before he purchased it. I was comfortable enough at Graceland that, like most of us close to Elvis, I didn't really think of it as Graceland—it was simply "the house." But as many times as I'd been welcomed in, there was still something especially wonderful about being in Elvis's home during the holiday season.

This year, Elvis had gotten back to Memphis just before Christmas, having finished work on one of his Hollywood films, and I'd been happy to spend as much time with him as I could through the holidays. As always, Elvis and Priscilla had turned the Graceland grounds into a kind of winter wonderland, with sparkling lights strung up all through the property's magnificent oak trees, and a beautiful Christmas tree set up in the dining room. He loved the season, and this Christmas had been a particularly sweet one—it was his first as a father. On Christmas Eve a few of us had gathered at the house for a very warm and happy holiday party (with Elvis's father, Vernon, dressing up to play Santa Claus for the benefit of ten-month-old Lisa Marie). In the week between Christmas and New Year's we'd enjoyed several nights of private movie screenings at the Memphian Theater (Elvis liked the crazy comedy *Candy* with Marlon Brando), and we all rang in 1969 with a private party at the Thunderbird Lounge in midtown Memphis.

In the days after New Year's, Graceland returned to its natural rhythms—Elvis would come downstairs to have his dinner around ten P.M., and whoever was around was more than welcome to sit down and join him. This night, the table was laid out with some of his Southern favorites—meat loaf, greens, mashed potatoes, cornbread. I'd learned years before that midnight meat loaf did not sit very well with me, so I'd gotten in the habit of eating before I came over, and then just nursing a Pepsi or having a little dessert when I sat with Elvis for his late supper. This night, I wasn't thinking about the meal at all, though. When I'd heard that Felton and Tom and Freddy were coming over, I knew business was going to be discussed. And I wanted to be a part of that conversation. I wasn't sure yet how I was going to say what I wanted to say, but I knew it had to be said.

Elvis was still feeling extremely proud and pleased with the *Elvis* TV special that had just aired on NBC at the beginning of December. After years of feeling stuck in mediocre films and stuck with mediocre material to sing, he had fought hard to make the kind of television show he'd wanted to make. He'd shaken off the advice of the not-so-easily-shaken Colonel Parker, who wanted his star client to make something along the lines of an hour of cozy Christmas carols.

Instead, Elvis had put together an incredibly exciting hour that paid tribute to his real rock 'n' roll roots while also showing himself to be an artist and entertainer still in his fighting prime: Elvis looking lean and mean in black leather. Elvis strapping on a guitar to jam with old band-mates Scotty Moore and D. J. Fontana. Elvis looking dangerous and pow-erful and relevant all over again. Elvis putting his heart into his perfor-mances and truly enjoying himself. That's the Elvis that so many of us around him had wanted to see again for so long, and that's what he gave us in that TV special. Apparently a good portion of the country had been feeling the way we did about Elvis, because his show was watched by almost half the nation's TV viewers the night it aired and wound up with some of the year's highest ratings for any kind of program.

Elvis had gotten some rave reviews in the press, too, and the only thing that bothered him about the response to the show was that some people referred to it as a "Comeback Special." He felt he'd never stopped working hard at what he was doing, and even if the movies and soundtrack albums he'd put his energies into weren't always inspired, he didn't consider that he'd gone anywhere that he had to "come back" from. Still, he knew he'd done some exceptional work, and I was thrilled that this good friend of mine, the most talented man I knew, had really put those talents to use again, rocking and rolling like only he could.

There was more good rockin' to come in the new year, too. The Colonel had just worked out a tremendous deal for Elvis to make his return to live concert performances, with a month's run of shows at Las Vegas's brand-new International Hotel scheduled for the summer. Elvis was excited about getting in front of audiences again, and he liked to joke that the hotel and its showroom were being built just for him. For the first time in a long time, Elvis was feeling energized and optimistic about the path his career was taking.

On this particular night, when the group in the Graceland dining room had just about finished eating, Elvis pulled a small Hav-a-Tampa cigarillo from his shirt pocket. He'd become very fond of the thin, sweet, wooden-tipped cigars, though more often than not he'd just hold a cigar without lighting it up. The conversation slowly shifted from talk of the TV special to talk about the recent movies we'd seen and then toward some actual business. Felton mentioned that it was about time to start putting together Elvis's next recording session for an RCA album.

"Yeah, I know it," said Elvis, rolling the cigar through his fingers. "We'll get it worked out."

The session was supposed to happen soon at the RCA studios in either Nashville or Los Angeles, and Felton started going over which session players would be available in the upcoming weeks. Elvis always wanted to work with a strong rhythm section, and there was a bit of concern that L.A.'s top session drummer, Hal Blaine, was booked up and wouldn't be available for the recording dates. Felton had a few suggestions about suitable replacements, and went on to discuss other players who were or weren't available. Freddy Bienstock said that Hill and Range had plenty of new material to present to Elvis.

I sensed a dip in Elvis's happy mood. For all that had been going well recently, it'd been a long time since he'd had a real hit record, and at that point the thought of going to work in a recording studio probably seemed like just that—going to work. The more the session plans were discussed, the more that happy holiday mood seemed to be slipping away. Elvis had done so well with the TV special and was so excited about the upcoming concerts, it just seemed a crying shame that making great records couldn't be a part of his newfound satisfaction as well.

To me, it was not a question of ability or desire. Elvis had just shown us he was in top form, and though we didn't talk about it much, I knew he'd like nothing more than to be at the top of the charts again. I'd come to believe that getting there was simply a matter of where he recorded and what he recorded. He could certainly make any studio his own—he'd done that right from the start, cutting his first Sun records with Sam Phillips at the small, cozy Memphis Recording Service studio. But he'd never really enjoyed the bigger, fancier studios he'd worked in. It didn't matter how new the recording gear was or how expensive-looking the facilities were, Elvis worked by feel, and it'd been a while since he'd recorded in a place that had the right feel. On top of that, Elvis had a terrific ear for selecting great material to perform, but there'd been too many sessions lately where there just wasn't anything great for him to pick from what Freddy Bienstock and Hill and Range presented him with.

I knew exactly where he could find the feel and the material he was after.

But I also knew very well that it wasn't wise to come at him with some big career-related suggestion in front of a lot of other people, especially a mix of business associates and Memphis Mafia guys. As open and generous as Elvis was, he had a strong sense of pride, and you didn't ever want to do anything to embarrass him. That was a surefire way to find yourself permanently standing on the wrong side of the Graceland gates. If you had something important to say to him, especially about his work, the smart thing to do was to ask him if you could speak in private, and then soft-sell him on whatever suggestion you were making. You had to keep things subtle enough so that he could feel he was making his own decisions. He never tried to make the rest of us feel small, but the fact was that he was the superstar, not us. You had to keep in mind that as much as Elvis loved and respected his friends, he didn't want to be pushed around by them either.

I knew all that, but maybe I was feeling a little cocky at the table that night because my own career was bringing me everything I'd ever wanted from a life in broadcasting. I was the red-hot, number-one rock 'n' roll disc jockey in Memphis, and I had a popular TV show called *Talent Party* that was Memphis's answer to *American Bandstand* and *Shindig!* I made my living maintaining a feel for the pulse of what was going on in music, and I knew that Elvis appreciated that. When it came to rock 'n' roll, I had a damn good ear for what was hot and what wasn't.

Now I was sitting as close to Elvis as I could possibly be, with our chairs just about six inches apart. As Felton and Tom and Freddy talked up the plans for the upcoming session, I watched Elvis flip his cigar around in his fingers with nervous energy, his face tighter and his expression darker than it had been before. I knew the smart way to approach Elvis, but I decided not to be so smart.

I raised my hand and said softly, "Elvis, can I say something?"

The table quieted. Elvis looked over at me with a slightly puzzled expression. "Yeah, GK. Say whatever you want."

So I said it.

"Elvis, you are the greatest star who ever lived. You define what a superstar is. Your popularity is worldwide and you've got more star power and more talent than anybody. You're the most versatile singer I've ever heard. You can sing anything."

Just out of the corner of my eye I saw Elvis raise his eyebrow a bit, wondering what I was getting at. He was smart enough to know I didn't raise my hand just to tell him how great he was.

"Elvis, you know you can sing anything. But it just makes me sick that you are getting nothing but B-side material to work with. You're the greatest singer in the world, you could have the greatest writers writing for you, but you're only getting lousy B-side crap material because writers are being told they have to give up a part of the publishing and ownership of the songs to get anything through to you. The top writers today aren't going to go for that anymore, Elvis. They won't give it up, and they shouldn't. Elvis, you can't be at your greatest if you're not getting great material. And it's a shame, because if you got your hands on some great songs, you'd have number-one records."

I paused a moment to get my breath. Elvis was still and quiet, and there was dead silence at the table. I figured I might as well go all the way now.

"Elvis, getting good material is just half of it. You're sitting here, a superstar, being told which musicians you can or can't get and being told when and where you should record. Elvis, just ten miles north of here is American Sound Studios, where they're cutting the greatest hits in the world right now. It's in North Memphis, a mile and a half from our old Humes High, near the corner of Thomas and Chelsea. It's a small funky studio with the kind of feeling I know you like. It's not fancy, it's not state-of-the-art, but they're cutting fantastic records there. 'The Letter' by the Box Tops. B. J. Thomas's 'Hooked on a Feeling.' 'Angel of the Morning' by Merrilee Rush. All hits. Wilson Pickett's recorded there, so has Neil Diamond. Dusty Springfield just cut 'Son of a Preacher Man' at American— she came all the way from England to record right there in North Memphis, Elvis. And it would be a dream come true for the guys at American if you'd record over there. With some great songs to work with at American, I know you'd have yourself some hit records, Elvis. It's what you deserve."

I don't know if it's possible to get deader than dead silence, but it was awful quiet around that table.

For the first time, I got real nervous. I'd seen people get close to Elvis and then get shut out because they crossed a line with him. It would be so easy for him now to pretend that nothing had just happened, to make some kind of joke to the rest of the table and then shut me out. The thought of not being welcome in Elvis's home was terrifying. I loved this guy more than any friend I'd ever had, and I couldn't imagine anything much worse than losing my friendship with him. But it truly felt worth the gamble to try to do everything I could to help him get back on top.

There still wasn't a damn sound at the table, though I was sure everyone could hear my heart pounding through my chest.

Elvis slowly flipped that little cigar around in his fingers, then his eyes went up and he kind of squinted like he was looking at something beyond the ceiling. He turned to me, looked at me hard, and pointed an index finger right at me.

"GK's right," he said. He turned to the others at the table. "George is right."

Those sounded like just about the sweetest words I'd ever heard, and I was overcome by such a mixture of happiness and relief that it took me a moment to register another sound I was hearing: Priscilla and the guys around the table were cheering. Charlie Hodge reached over to high-five me, and Felton jumped out of his seat with a whoop. "I can get you into American, Elvis. I can get you songs by Jerry Reed, Mac Davis—whatever you want. We can make it happen."

"I've got a line to Neil Diamond," I told Elvis. "I know for a fact he'd be honored to write something for you."

Elvis nodded, then put the cigar in his mouth and bit hard on it. "I don't give a damn where the material comes from," he said. "I don't care about publishing or percentages or what the writers get or what we have to pay for. I just want some great goddamn songs."

Everyone around the table whooped again. Well, almost everyone. While I'd been speaking my piece I'd been very careful not to make any eye contact with Tom Diskin or Freddy Bienstock. I didn't dislike either of them personally, but both of them represented a way of doing business that treated Elvis like a product rather than a true entertainer—like an act to be hyped rather than an artist to be supported. Now, with a couple glances in their direction, I could tell from their tight smiles that they were not happy with the turn the evening had taken. And I knew they'd be reporting every word that had been said back to the Colonel just as soon as they could get to a hotel phone.

I knew it wasn't smart to get on the wrong side of the Colonel, but this night I didn't care. I felt I had done right by my friend Elvis.

I got a nudge from Elvis's elbow and turned to look at him. He looked back at me for just a beat and then gave me a wink. That said everything I needed to hear.

We all got up from the table and started to move to the back den off the kitchen, everyone still talking excitedly about what might happen when Elvis got his hands on some great songs. Marty Lacker, another Memphis Mafia member, was in the den, and he was equally excited by the news. He'd done some work for American Studios and also thought it would be a perfect spot for Elvis. Felton Jarvis came up to me with a huge smile on his face and before I could say a word he grabbed me and gave me a bear hug. "George, I've been thinking exactly what you were saying, but I could never say it. I always feel I'm between a rock and a hard place trying to please Elvis and the Colonel and RCA. I always figured if I spoke up, I'd lose my job. But you said it, man, you said it."

I barely had time to thank him for the support when he called over my shoulder. "Elvis, I can call American right now. We can really make this happen."

"Well, make the call," said Elvis. "The sooner the better."

Felton left to use the phone in the kitchen, and I went over to stand by Elvis. He looked at me, with that hint of smile creeping on his face again.

"Shoot, GK—you look a mess. You got your nerves in the dirt."

"Phew, Elvis. I took a hell of a chance. But you know it was from the heart."

"I know it, George," he said. "You were right, though. And when you're right, you're right."

I stood there, breathing a little easier now, as the rest of the guys talked and kidded with each other. Then Felton stepped back into the room.

"Hey, Elvis. We're booked into American Studios. Next Monday night."

Another cheer went up. Elvis was heading back to North Memphis. Back to our old neighborhood.

Back to where it all began . . .

CHAPTER ONE

The Kid Who Sang

Humes High School was a great big brick building on North Manassas Street in North Memphis—the biggest building around in that part of town—and it served as the junior and senior high school for kids in our working-class neighborhood. In the fall of 1948 I was ready to start eighth grade, my second year at Humes, and frankly I was looking forward to it. I liked being in the big building, moving from class to class, having my own locker, and being a part of a big group of kids—a group that included quite a few pretty girls. There was just one problem in going back to school, and that was a particular class on my fall semester schedule that I desperately wanted to get out of: Miss Marmann's music-appreciation class.

Humes had plenty of tough teachers, but Miss Marmann was one of the toughest, and in a school full of some pretty tough kids, the ones who were troublemakers in other classes always sat up straight in Miss Marmann's class and took care not to get caught chewing gum. Even by the standards of '48, Miss Marmann was "old school"—rumor had it that she was extremely prone to whacking inattentive students with a special ruler she kept on her desk.

I appreciated music well enough, but I wasn't too crazy about getting whacked, so before classes began that fall I looked for a way out. The rule at Humes was that if you were a member of the marching band, you didn't have to take the music-appreciation class, so I signed up for band tryouts and said I was interested in taking up the drums. I discovered that there were a lot of kids trying out for band just to get out of Miss Marmann's class—and I guess in that way she really did encourage music appreciation. But the tryouts consisted of a fairly complicated written test and music test, and apparently I didn't do too well on either one, because I was quickly judged not to be marching band material.

But, you know, if I could have played drums worth a lick, I might not have met Elvis Presley.

School began and Miss Marmann certainly lived up to her reputation. She really did wield a ruler, but as it turned out, she and I got along okay. It seems we both felt that much of the popular music of the day was dull, repetitive, and without merit. One afternoon when she was complaining about how our exposure to music was limited to a few hit songs, I raised my hand and chimed in that "Dance, Ballerina, Dance" by Vaughn Monroe was getting played over and over again on the radio, and it drove me nuts. Rather than reach for her ruler, Miss Marmann actually smiled a little and said, "That's a very good example, George."

Our lack of interest in songs from the hit parade was probably the only thing Miss Marmann and I agreed on when it came to music, though. She felt we'd all be better off listening to Bach, Brahms, and Beethoven. I didn't really know yet what the music I wanted to hear on the radio might sound like, but I was pretty sure it wouldn't be played by an orchestra.

In November, Miss Marmann's class was joined by a new kid whose family had just moved up to Memphis from Tupelo, Mississippi. I'm sure the teacher said his name and introduced him to the rest of us, but he didn't really stand out much and I didn't take much notice of him. Didn't take much notice, that is, until a few weeks later, on a Friday, when Miss Marmann announced that since Christmas was coming up soon, instead of doing regular music lessons the following week we would have a "special treat": we'd get to sing Christmas carols together. This didn't sound too "special" to me, but the new kid raised his hand right away.

"Miss Marmann?" he called out.

"Yes, Elvis?"

"Do you mind if I bring my guitar to class and sing?"

There were a few little snickers and laughs. Back in 1948 there wasn't anything cool about a thirteen-year-old kid playing a "country" instrument like a guitar. Cool would have been bringing your football or your boxing gloves to school. But this kid wanted to bring in his guitar, and he wanted to sing. He was over on the left-hand side of the classroom, and I was all the way on the right side, but I found myself staring across the rows of desks at this new kid. Elvis Presley was his name.

Miss Marmann hushed the snickerers in the class, though she also seemed a little surprised at the request. "Yes, Elvis—that'd be fine," she said. "Bring your guitar to class."

The next Monday we all took our seats in music class and sure enough, there was Elvis Presley with his guitar. When Miss Marmann called on him, he picked up that guitar, walked to the front of the classroom, and sang us two songs, neither one a Christmas carol. First was "Old Shep," a heartbreaker about a boy and his dog, and then "Cold Icy Fingers," a funny sort of ghost song. As he strummed his last chord, there was a moment of shocked silence, then just a smattering of applause.

I think our classmates had probably been expecting something outright awful—something they could laugh at. But the kid really could sing and play, and frankly, I was blown away. First of all, it was impressive that this kid had some talent, but to see him get up in front of a class—in the classroom of one of the strictest teachers in school—and sing out so strongly and easily, I'd just never seen anything like it. I'd been going to the movies and half-daydreaming about a life in showbiz, but I didn't really know how I'd ever get there. Right here at Humes High, though, was a kid unafraid to put himself in the spotlight. That amazed me and affected me.

For the first of many, many times in my life, I thought, "Damn, that guy's cool."

It'd be nice to say that Elvis Presley and I were inseparable buddies from that moment forward, but that wasn't quite the case. I introduced myself to him at some point, and we talked a little when we had the chance, becoming two guys who were happy to see each other in the halls. I do remember him saying that he'd also tried out for the marching band but had been rejected. (I'm still not sure why a guy with his talent didn't get in, but I'm thankful for it.)

Elvis and his family were then living in a rooming house on Poplar Street, though they soon moved to the government-sponsored housing projects at Lauderdale Courts. I lived right across the street from Humes with my mom and sister, and when we kids got out of school at three-fifteen, Elvis would head his way and I'd go mine. Looking back, I know he and his family had been dirt-poor in Tupelo and were trying hard to fit in and make things work in their new hometown.

My family had come from a little farther away, but was working just as hard to get by. My mother and father were both Orthodox Jews. She was from Russia, he was from Poland, and they both fled their homes in the twenties as anti-Semitism flared across Eastern Europe. My mother had relatives in Chicago, but her passage to the U.S. was sponsored by a Jewish lawyer in Memphis, and it was through him that she met my father. They settled into a little home on Leath Street in North Memphis, had my sister Rosie, then my sister Dorothy, and then me. My parents had escaped before the rise of Hitler and had begun to build a new, better life in America, but things took an unfortunate turn when my dad got very ill. In fact, I barely remember him as a part of my childhood, and to be honest I'm not even sure what he suffered from. I just have a few vague memories of going to visit him at a special hospital in Hot Springs, Arkansas, where he was laid up for the last couple years of his life.

We weren't ever wealthy, but we did well enough that I wore clean clothes and always had something to eat for dinner. My dad had started a produce business before he got sick, buying fruits and vegetables from farmers and selling them to grocery stores, and with the money he made he bought two small houses in North Memphis—one for us to live in and one to rent out. After he passed away, we lived partly on that rent money, and my mom also worked as a seamstress, altering suits at one of the nicer tailor shops in downtown Memphis. As soon as I was old enough I began working, too: I took on a paper route and hustled up extra money any way I could, doing things like selling balloons at parades.

There weren't a lot of Jews in North Memphis, and I know there are some places in the South where my family would not have felt welcomed, especially given the high tensions during World War II. But my family was so easily accepted and got so used to fitting in that the one time I came face-to-face with prejudice, I didn't know what it was. When I was in seventh grade, my first year at Humes, an older kid walked up to me one afternoon and called me a "Jew baby." Maybe he expected me to burst into tears or take a swing at him, but I just stood there staring at him because, frankly, I didn't know if "Jew baby" was supposed to be a bad thing or a good thing. So I asked the kid, "What's a 'Jew baby'?" The question kind of threw him off, and, as it turned out, he couldn't come up with an answer. He just shrugged and walked away, and I never heard words like that again.

By the time I was in school at Humes, I had a routine I followed almost every day after school: I made a quick stop at a local snack shop for a cold drink or a piece of candy, then I rushed home to spend some time with the one luxury item in my home: a great big floor-model console radio. As a little kid, I'd rarely missed an episode of the adventures of the Green Hornet, the Lone Ranger, or Superman. Now I listened to Bill Gordon, the afternoon disc jockey on Memphis's biggest station, WHBQ. Gordon played the hits of the day—the kind of stuff that left Miss Marmann unimpressed—but he was a funny, energetic on-air personality, and he was the first guy I ever heard who would talk over records and make jokes about what he was playing.

For more excitement, sometimes I'd give the radio dial a spin from WHBQ at 560 up to WDIA 1070. In 1949, WDIA became the first radio station in the South to hire black on-air talent, beginning with disc jockey Nat D. Williams. Williams, and later fellow deejays such as Rufus Thomas and a very young B. B. King, would play a very different-sounding music for the city's sizable black audience. It was by tuning in to WDIA that I started to hear music unlike anything I'd ever heard on the hit parade: songs by Big Joe Turner, the Clovers, Fats Domino, Ruth Brown, and Johnny Ace. This stuff sounded wild and a little dangerous, and I couldn't get enough of it—even if I didn't always understand the things that were being sung about. Quite a few of my classmates felt the same way, and it became kind of a fad to try to write down the words we could catch when a new song was played on WDIA and then bring them into school the next day and try to figure out exactly what we'd heard.

I know that in some homes, kids caught listening to "race music" would have been grounded or worse. But my mother never saw any point in getting upset about what I was listening to. She'd seen some real troubles over in Russia and was happy to have what she had in the United States. As long as I wasn't getting into fights, wasn't being brought home by the police, and was pulling decent grades, she wasn't going to get too upset about where I set the radio dial.

As I moved through Humes High, Elvis and I ended up having quite a few classes together, including a typing class that I think we both barely passed. I'd occasionally see him around town, too. When the Mid-South Fair came to the Memphis Fairgrounds in 1950, a few buddies and I figured out that there was a spot behind some carnival tents where you could climb a cyclone fence to sneak in and save yourself the fifty-cent admission charge. One night, I was halfway up the fence when I felt something give it a shake. I looked to my left and there was Elvis, halfway up his section of fence and just as happy to be saving his fifty cents.

I guess everybody in high school is looking for some way to be their own person—to gain a little bit of notoriety. Back then, the common ways to get noticed were by being an athlete or a cheerleader or a part of school politics, and I took the political route. I became editor of the school paper, editor of the yearbook, and by senior year I was the class president. I kind of enjoyed being able to get along with all sorts of classmates—the athletes, the brains, and the ones who were a little different. By tenth and eleventh grade Elvis was bringing his guitar in more and more often to sing at little class events like a homeroom party. By senior year, Elvis was very clearly different.

The most obvious thing about him was that he dressed differently. Most of us were wearing jeans and plain, collared shirts. But you never saw Elvis in jeans. (I'd learn later that he hated them—they reminded him of the work clothes his family had worn at their poorest.) Instead, he'd wear black slacks with a pink stripe down the side and a black sport coat with the collar turned up. He'd let his hair grow out and had it combed back high. And he had those sideburns. What's amazing to me now is that the look he had back then wasn't the fashion of the day for anybody else in any part of Memphis I knew about—it was just pure Elvis. But at the same time, as distinctive as his look was, he was low-key about it and never seemed to be angling for any special attention. He got his notoriety in a quiet but unmistakable way. Like a velvet hammer.

Elvis wasn't quite as handsome in those years as he would become—he hadn't quite grown into his looks yet. So most Humes girls weren't sure what to make of this very different classmate. On the other hand, some of the guys at Humes felt that someone so different deserved to be given a hard time. One day he was cornered in a Humes bathroom by a tough group who brandished a pair of scissors and said they were going to cut off his hair. He tried to fight them off, but his pompadour was only saved when one of the strongest, most fearless guys at Humes, Red West, happened to walk into that bathroom and saw what was going on. Red told the would-be barbers that if they wanted to cut Elvis's hair they'd have to cut his first, and that was the end of that.

The crowning moment of my time at Humes came at graduation, when, as class president, I got to make a speech to the whole school. For Elvis, I think the highlight came during our yearly senior-sponsored talent show, when he got up in front of a packed auditorium and sang Teresa Brewer's "Till I Waltz Again with You." I remember being struck by the fact that some of the roughneck football guys who had given Elvis the hardest time applauded and whistled their support for him at this performance.

I said to one of them, "You're clapping like crazy—I thought you didn't like Elvis."

"Aww, Elvis is okay," the kid said. "We messed with him a little but he took it just fine. Besides, he's part of our class and he's the best singer up there."

I couldn't argue with that.

Throughout my Humes High days, the more I listened to WDIA, the more I became infatuated with the music I heard there, and the less interest I had in the smooth, vanilla-type pop records that were being put out by the likes of Doris Day, the Ames Brothers, and Mitch Miller. DIA signed off at sundown, though, so the place to hear new sounds at night was WHBQ. The station had a late-night show called *Red, Hot and Blue* that was hosted by a wild, one-of-a-kind madman named Dewey "Daddy-O" Phillips.

Dewey had started out as a salesman in the record department at Grant's department store in Memphis, where he'd taken to moving the merchandise by getting on the store's PA system and hawking his favorite records with a speedy, wild patter that was part hillbilly, part jive cat, part auctioneer, and part lunatic. Customers flocked in just to hear him at work, record sales in the store shot up, and it wasn't long before WHBQ decided to take a chance by putting the completely untrained and inexperienced Dewey on the air. He was a hit there, too, and by 1951 his tremendously popular show was on the air from nine P.M. to midnight six nights a week. *Red, Hot and Blue* was where we kids turned to hear the fresher, more exciting sounds of doo-wop, jump blues, deep country, and, especially, what was being called "rhythm and blues."

"Look out now," you'd hear Dewey yell, "I'm telling you good people I got the nerves tonight—I'm as nervous as a frog on the freeway with his hopper busted." There'd be a shriek of feedback as he tried to cue up the next record, then he'd shout out a favorite catchphrase, "Awww—better call Sam," over the record's intro. He filled his show with a cast of crazy characters all voiced by him—Dizzy Dean, scatterbrained Grandma, man-hungry Lucy Mae—and sometimes posed questions to his supposed sidekick, a cow named Myrtle, who would respond with a somber "Moo." Even the commercials for the show's sponsors were fair game for Dewey—he'd improvise his way to some pretty wild slogans. ("Falstaff beer—if you don't want to drink it, just freeze it, slice it up, and eat it," or "Falstaff—open up a rib and pour it in.")

Listening to Dewey, I became more infatuated with radio than I'd ever been and I was driven to do whatever I could to become a part of the radio world. I got a break in my senior year at Humes when I landed a job as an assistant to the announcers who did the local radio broadcasts of our high school football games. I worked as a spotter, pointing out the names and numbers of the players involved in each play on a big roster board so that the announcers could call the game in a smooth, steady flow. When one of those announcers got a job at WHBQ the following spring, he brought me along to work as an assistant during play-by-play re-creations of Memphis Chicks baseball games.

For those games, a reporter at the stadium would report the game by way of Western Union ticker tape. At the WHBQ studios, on the mezzanine level of the Chisca Hotel, I'd feed the ticker tape to the announcer, who would call the game using recordings of cheers and boos and other crowd sounds to create atmosphere. If a ball was well hit, the announcer had a little wooden mallet he'd pound next to the mike. If the batter swung and missed, the announcer would slap his leather wallet with a ruler to create the sound of a fastball smacking into a catcher's mitt. It was odd work, but it was real radio work.

After graduating from Humes, I enrolled in Memphis State College as a business major with a minor in speech and drama, and I continued to work at WHBQ. I was still listening to *Red, Hot and Blue* at night, and working at the station taught me that Mr. Dewey Phillips was as wild a character in person as he sounded on the air. Dewey was so hard on the station's studio gear in the course of his show that the engineers had set up a separate control room just for him to use, where he could thrash away as he saw fit. Station management wanted somebody a little calmer and more responsible than Dewey to help him get through his night shifts and stop him from breaking anything so badly that it couldn't be patched up again. They thought Dewey Phillips needed a babysitter, right-hand man, and all-around gofer.

He got me.

Dewey and I hit it off right away. He was wild, but he was also a great, generous spirit, and he was very happy to have someone around him who was just as excited about the music he was playing. It was sometimes a challenge for me to keep his show running smoothly, but I got it done, doing everything from helping to run the tape machines to fetching the coffee. Pretty soon I was spending a lot of time with Dewey outside of the studio, and I knew I was "in" with him when he started calling me "Mother"—short for a less polite slang term that was starting to become popular among certain crowds.

On his radio show, Dewey casually and happily ignored the issue of race—he never said he was playing black music or white music, it was just "good music for good people." He lived by that principle, too. Dewey didn't think twice about taking me out to Martin Stadium to watch the Memphis Red Sox—our city's Negro League baseball team—and he loved watching the all-star exhibition games that would be played after the regular season was over. I don't know what I was supposed to feel about "crossing the color line," but I went home thrilled that I'd been able to get an up-close look at great players like Roy Campanella and Don Newcombe.

One weekend night, Dewey and I were the only white faces in the crowd at the Hippodrome on Beale Street, there to see a big package tour of "colored" music acts. The venue was a skating rink that also got used for concerts, so it held several hundred, and the moment Dewey walked in he was treated like royalty—in a flash it became quite clear to me how many black listeners tuned into *Red, Hot and Blue,* and how deeply they appreciated what Dewey was doing. It was an amazing lineup that night: Roy Hamilton, LaVern Baker, the Drifters, and the Clovers all in one show. It seemed like a great night until a little after the last act finished, when a horrendous fight broke out. People around me were throwing bottles and chairs and jumping on tables, and I did the only thing I could think to do—I scooted away, staying as low as possible, and squeezed myself behind the roller-rink jukebox. I stayed there even after I could hear that the cops had shown up and were clearing people out. I stayed hidden right where I was until I finally heard Dewey's voice calling out, "GK, where you at?"

"I'm over here behind the damned jukebox," I called back. "Is it safe to come out?"

Dewey answered with a cackle of laughter. "Yeah, yeah, it's safe. Get on out of there, you little mother."

In those days, if an act wanted to play for white and black fans, they had to book two shows—a "whites-only" show and a "colored" show. But Dewey had a hand in bringing together one of the first mixed audiences in Memphis. He liked playing some gospel music on his *Red, Hot and Blue* shows, and he began raving to his audience about the quality of the music at the Sunday-night services held at Memphis's East Trigg Baptist Church. The church had an all-black congregation but, at Dewey's urging, and with the consent of Reverend W. Herbert Brewster, a crowd of young whites began showing up on Sunday nights. Those services were broadcast over WHBQ, so when the opportunity arose for me to join Dewey's former assistant Bob Lewis as part of the two-man crew that handled the live radio remote setup at the church, I jumped at the chance.

The scene was incredible, not least because it was the only place in town where you saw discrimination in reverse—at the church, it was the whites who had to sit in the back. Reverend Brewster was a passionate speaker, but what really took hold of you was the music. The orthodox synagogue I'd attended with my family didn't even have an organ, and I'd certainly never seen a church band like the one East Trigg had. It was a full lineup with guitars and drums, and they were playing spiritual songs that weaved in and out of the Reverend's sermon. And, church or not, that East Trigg band played harder and stronger than any band I'd ever heard. I didn't always recognize many of the white faces in the back pews, but one stood out: my Humes classmate Elvis Presley.

As much as I loved working with Dewey, I knew there wasn't much future in being his gofer, and I decided to do everything I could to land a real job in front of a radio microphone. At WHBQ, I put together some airchecks—the voice recordings that worked for a disc jockey the way a headshot worked for an actor. I knew it would be tough to get any real work at WHBQ even as a fill-in jock, so I sent my airchecks out to all the smaller stations I could think of.

They liked me at KOSE, in Osceola, Arkansas, so as soon as my freshman year's spring semester was over in May, I headed fifty miles upriver to introduce Osceola listeners to *The George Klein Show*. Through the summer of 1954, I worked as a long-shift afternoon disc jockey, playing a mix of country and rhythm and blues records for an audience of both white and black listeners. As small as Osceola was, it had a reputation for being a pretty cool music town—plenty of musicians played their way through as they traveled between Chicago and the Southern towns and cities along the Mississippi.

I was very happy to be spinning the records I chose on my own show, and I felt I was getting a little better at my craft each and every workday. But when the weekends came, I missed Memphis. So, just about every Saturday evening after I wrapped up my shift at the station, I'd step out into the hot night air of the Arkansas Delta, and, with a small overnight bag in hand, I'd walk a few blocks along where Highway 61 turned into Osceola's Walnut Street, stick out a thumb, and hope it wouldn't take too long to hitch a ride back home.

My mother was still in North Memphis in the house across from Humes High that I'd grown up in, and I'd stay with her when I was in town. But before I headed back up that way, I liked to drop in on Dewey at the Chisca Hotel and sit with him as he did his Saturday-night broadcast of *Red, Hot and Blue*. Afterward, I could always count on him to take me out for some kind of crazy, Dewey-style adventure.

I remember one particular July evening when I got a ride down the river and over the Memphis-Arkansas bridge, finally arriving at the doors of the Chisca. I headed inside and bounded up to the mezzanine level (for some reason Dewey always announced on air that he was broadcasting "live from the magazine level"). Dewey spotted me as I stepped into his studio, and before I could get out a "Hey, Dewey," he spoke.

"Come here, Mother."

"What's up, Dewey?"

"I got something you need to hear. Come on."

Dewey squeezed past me and walked down the hall in an uneven gait—he had a limp from a broken leg that had never healed right after a car accident. Dewey was usually an excitable character, but as he led me to another control room with a turntable and speaker system, he seemed particularly intense and focused. Very gently, he took a disc from the top of a stack of records, holding it with much more care than he normally did on his show. He was also very careful to keep his hand over the label as he put the record on the turntable so that I couldn't see what he was playing.

He started the song and sat back with a smile, staring at me with wide eyes. There was a strummed guitar, then a steady bass line, and when the vocals came in I recognized the song as a version of Arthur "Big Boy" Crudup's "That's All Right, Mama," which had been out earlier that year. But while Crudup's tune had been a straight-ahead, high-energy rhythm and blues tune, this version had a beat and a sound that was harder to define. It was a little bit country, a little bit pop, and a little bluesy without being any one thing. And those strong vocals just got a hold of me like nothing I'd heard before.

The voice was just getting to the second verse when Dewey grinned a little harder and said, "Who's that singing?"

As an up-and-coming deejay, I prided myself on my ability to recognize a group or a singer or a song. But I couldn't place this singer at all.

"Shit—I don't know who it is, Dewey."

"Well, you oughta know." His grin took up most of his face now.

"What do you mean, 'I oughta know'?"

"Well," Dewey shrugged a little. "You went to school with him."

There was only one guy I knew from Humes High who could possibly sing like that. A guy who looked a little different, and dressed a little different, and who was the only person I'd ever seen carrying a guitar around school. A guy I'd always been friendly with, but hadn't seen much of lately. The guy who'd sung in Miss Marmann's class.

"Damn, Dewey—you mean that's Elvis?"

Dewey just nodded.

I listened to the song even more intently now. It almost seemed impossible that this could be the voice of the guy I knew at Humes, now coming through the control-room speakers at the city's biggest radio station.

"You mean to tell me Elvis Presley has a record out?" I asked Dewey.

He laughed. "Hell, you're watching it spin right there. Sam Phillips brought it over two nights ago. Soon as I played it the phones lit up, so I played it again and again. We got Elvis up here in the studio and interviewed him, then played it some more. I played it seven times that night. Man, I love it. People are still calling for it."

I was new to radio, but I knew that it was unheard of to play a record seven times in one night. If a record was a smash hit you might play it once an hour, but Dewey had broken all the rules to play this debut record from my Humes High classmate Elvis Presley.

"Man, that's pretty good," I said. It already felt like a serious understatement.

"Yeah, it's pretty good, all right," laughed Dewey. "I think this kid Elvis has a shot at something. Here . . ." He handed me a copy of the record from the stack near the turntable. "Take that back to Arkansas and give 'em a taste."

I took the disc and looked down at the label. There it was—his name spelled out as clear as could be.

Elvis Presley.

My schoolmate, Humes High class of '53, had a record out.

"Hey, Dewey," I said.

"Yeah, Mother?"

"Play it again."

CHAPTER TWO

On the Radio

My first big moment behind a microphone in Memphis was not exactly the classiest of gigs: On a sunny afternoon in the fall of 1954, I was up inside the belly of a thirty-foot-tall wooden Indian who stood in the parking lot of Katz's Drug Store.

The Indian's roomy plywood belly had been turned into a temporary broadcast booth, and from that lofty position I was emceeing the grand opening of the Lamar Airways Shopping Center in East Memphis—the first big strip mall to be built in the Memphis area. I'd left Osceola at the end of the summer and returned to my hometown to continue studies at Memphis State. While I hadn't expected my next career opportunity to come in the form of a wooden Indian, an advertising agency hired me to work the mall's grand opening as a live, on-the-spot disc jockey, a two-day job that required me to play records for the crowd of shoppers while mixing in commercials and announcements that touted the new businesses:

"Hi, ladies and gentlemen, this is 'GK' George Klein, and that was Big Joe Turner with 'Shake, Rattle and Roll'—and don't forget to shake your way down to Jimmy Jones's Paint Store, where they've got a special today on gallons of latex paint . . ."

The shopping center had also lined up some live entertainment for the second day of festivities: my classmate Elvis Presley, along with his backup musicians, guitarist Scotty Moore and bassist Bill Black. I'd played my copy of "That's All Right, Mama" in Osceola two days after Dewey had played it for me (I think I can safely say that I'm the second disc jockey to play Elvis Presley on the radio). I'd been excited to see Elvis's second single, "Blue Moon of Kentucky," climb up the country charts, and I'd heard that he and his band had stirred things up when they performed both songs as part of a concert bill at Memphis's Overton Park bandshell. Now, as a part of my MC duties, I was going to introduce Elvis before he gave his first headlining public performance, and I could hardly wait to see my old Humes High friend in person again.

From where I was working inside the Indian, I couldn't be seen by the crowd, but I had a slot to look out of, and when I saw Scotty and Bill arrive out in the parking lot I took a break and headed down the steps out the back of my Indian to go say hello to them. (I knew Scotty a little bit from the session work he'd been doing for producer Sam Phillips over at Sun Records.) We'd just started making some small talk when I saw a familiar face approaching—a face that lit up with surprise when it got a look at me.

"GK—what are you doing here?"

"I'm here to tell 'em about you, Elvis. I've been talking you up all day."

We laughed and shook hands and quickly caught up with each other; I told him how much I liked his records and he told me he'd heard I'd been working with Dewey. We still weren't what I'd consider really close friends, so it was almost strange how good it was to see him, and how good it felt to know that he was happy to see me.

I wasn't the only person working under unusual circumstances that day—instead of being on a stage, Elvis, Scotty, and Bill had to play up on a flatbed truck parked in back of Katz's. When they were ready, I climbed up on the truck and made my introduction:

"Ladies and gentlemen, here's the moment you've been waiting for. By popular demand, the hottest new talent on the *Billboard* charts, the pride of Humes High School, the one they call the Hillbilly Cat: Ladies and gentlemen, Memphis's own Elvis Presley, with Scotty and Bill!"

As I stepped off the makeshift stage, the trio kicked into "That's All Right, Mama," which was followed by a few other cover tunes they'd been working up and finally "Blue Moon of Kentucky"—a performance that lasted a total of maybe thirty minutes. Elvis didn't move around quite as much as he might have because, after all, he was standing on the back of a truck, but still the energy that he and the guys generated was intense.

I can't say for sure that after watching Elvis perform that day I knew he was going to be a star, but I was sure he was going to make a living doing what he was doing, and that alone seemed pretty huge at the time. The other thing I was sure of that day was that it gets awfully hot inside a wooden Indian. I wanted to do what I could to get back to a real studio.

My next job in Memphis was real radio work, though it didn't last as long as even the shopping center gig: I worked for one day at WDIA, the pioneering station that put black talent on the air and turned so many of us white kids on to the power of rhythm and blues. All the disc jockeys at WDIA were black, but the board operators were white, and those guys worked the controls while the jocks were on and then read the news on-air at the top of the hour. I'd dropped off some of my airchecks at the studio, and a program director named David James apparently felt I deserved a chance at a job. He had me do the news during Rufus Thomas's afternoon *Hoot and Holler* show. I'm still not sure if I sounded too young, too white, or just not "newsy" enough, but by the end of the day I was told the station higher-ups didn't need me to come back the next day. Mr. James helped soften the blow when he told me, "Don't let it discourage you, George. You're just starting out and you've got talent. Keep at this and you've got a real shot at something."

I took those words to heart, and just a few weeks later I did get a shot, though not exactly doing the kind of radio show I'd had in mind. A little station called KWEM hired me to handle their religious broadcasting on Sundays. After having so many crazy nights with Dewey, it felt odd to be up early on Sunday morning in the Quonset hut where the station was housed, playing spiritual music, overseeing remote broadcasts from churches, playing tapes of sermons, and even having preachers join me in the hut to do their preaching live on-air. There was one preacher who was paying for his radio time by selling his listeners "prayer cloths." I remember him reading what he said was a testimonial from a soldier who'd been in the Korean War, claiming that a bullet had bounced off the soldier's chest because he had his prayer cloth in his shirt pocket next to his heart. I had my doubts, but the preacher did sell quite a few of those cloths.

When KWEM offered me a country-music hour on Saturdays, I jumped at it and became a quick study of country sounds. That job also required me to stick around Saturday afternoons, when the station allowed just about anybody with twenty-five dollars to buy a fifteen-minute block of airtime for themselves. One afternoon I answered a knock at the studio door to find a tall, imposing, dark-haired fellow with a guitar who politely introduced himself to me. His name was Johnny Cash, and his employer—the Home Equipment Company—had put up the money for him to perform with his band, the Tennessee Two (Luther Perkins and Marshall Grant). So, not too long after emceeing Elvis's flatbed-truck appearance, I got to be a part of what would turn out to be another moment of music history—putting Johnny Cash on the air for the very first time.

Johnny and his group played some of their earliest original songs such as "Wide Open Road" and "Belshazzar," and in between each musical number, Johnny put in pitches for the awnings, porch screens, and wire fences available from Home Equipment Company. Within a year, Johnny and I would renew our acquaintance over at Sam Phillips's studio when Johnny began recording for Sun, and Johnny let me know how appreciative he was of my early encouragement over at KWEM.

Finally, I got a shot at hosting the station's rhythm and blues program, *The Jack the Bellboy Morning Show*. Having seen Dewey at work, I knew it was crucial to do something that would make me more than just a voice between songs—something that would make me stand out as a personality. I'd spent enough time around musicians to pick up some of the hipster slang that was coming into style—phrases like "Everything's cool, baby" actually sounded fresh off the streets back then. I started talking that style of bop talk on the air, and quickly discovered that I had a knack for making up rhymes on the spot: "Hey, this is DJ GK coming your crazy way on a Monday with records to play, on the scene with my rock 'n' roll record machine. Baby, don't mean maybe, hang with me cuz it's just me and you and Memphis, Tennessee—"

Believe it or not, it caught on, and within six months I was considered a "hot jock." My station was too small to afford subscribing to the ratings services that told you how big your audience was, but we measured our success by the amount of mail we got. It wasn't long before I was getting over a hundred letters a day along with a pile of telegrams, and I had to come in a couple of hours early just to go through the mail. While reading some of those request letters on the air, I developed my own special radio nickname. A lot of mail was addressed to me as "DJ GK," but when I read it during the show, I sometimes paused as I scanned ahead to see what song was being asked for, so that it came out with a little stammer: "Dear DJ—uh—GK." It happened enough that listeners came to expect it, so I stopped trying to correct it, and "DJ-uh-GK" became my tag. (When I'd see Elvis around town, he'd address me by shortening it even further to "DJ Uh.")

I was feeling good about my morning show, but things soon changed in a big way. One morning, I got a phone call from Bill Grumbles, a fellow who had been the general manager at WHBQ when I worked with Dewey, and who was now managing WMC, an NBC station across the street from the Chisca Hotel. "George, are you aware that you're number two in the morning?"

"What do you mean, 'number two,' Mr. Grumbles?"

"You've got the number-two-rated morning show in all of Memphis. The whole city. Congratulations."

He wasn't calling just to be nice. He offered to double my salary if I'd host the afternoon rock 'n' roll show on WMC. He had a name in mind for that show—*George Klein's Rock 'n' Roll Ballroom*. I liked the sound of that.

By the fall of 1955, "rock and roll" was a big deal. That phrase was used more and more to describe the new kind of music being made by the likes of Chuck Berry, Little Richard, Fats Domino, and Bo Diddley, and it became a hipper description of their sound than "rhythm and blues." Probably the one record that really announced the arrival of rock 'n' roll was Bill Haley's "Rock Around the Clock," which became hugely popular in '55 after it was used during the opening credits of the film *Blackboard Jungle,* and became the first rock 'n' roll song to hit number one on the national record charts.

Of course, not everybody was happy about rock 'n' roll's arrival. All across the country, all sorts of authorities—professors, preachers, mayors—were condemning the music's "primitive rhythms," "raw emotions," and "sexual content." Rock 'n' roll music was seen as a promoter of immorality, a surefire path to juvenile delinquency, and, more ominously, as an encouragement to an unacceptable mixing of the races.

Those who saw rock 'n' roll as a gathering force of change for the worse thought it had to be battled back at every turn. Schools cracked down on dress codes, dances were canceled, and, with every new rock 'n' roll hit on the charts, there was a flurry of anti–rock 'n' roll editorials in newspapers. In an attempt to soften rock 'n' roll's influence, there was even a small cottage industry of white cover versions of some of the great songs recorded by black artists—but it became clear pretty quickly that if kids wanted to hear "Ain't That a Shame," they wanted to hear Fats Domino sing it, not Pat Boone. Frankly, a lot of us were too busy enjoying rock 'n' roll to spend much time worrying about the backlash.

Elvis was certainly a pioneering rock 'n' roller, making his case strongly with great Sun singles like "Good Rockin' Tonight." And as he started to get more popular, he started taking a lot of heat for the "threat" he posed to the nation's youth. But in 1955 he was still mixing up country, blues, gospel, and pop in his sound, and was actually considered a country act by many due to his appearances throughout the year on the *Louisiana Hayride* radio shows. I actually have a sharp memory of a bit of conversation I had with Elvis that year, on a night when we both ended up at WHBQ again, waiting to goof around with Dewey after his show. I knew Elvis had been a huge success on those *Louisiana Hayride* broadcasts and was quickly moving up the bill from an opening act to a featured star to a headliner.

"Elvis, it looks like you're in competition with Webb Pierce and Ferlin Husky and Hank Snow," I said, citing some of the top country stars he had appeared with.

He shook his head and let out a little snort of a laugh.

"No, George. I'm shooting for Bill Haley."

We didn't know it, but in just a few quick months, Elvis would in fact be rockin' at the top of the charts, with nobody mistaking him for a country crooner anymore.

I was well aware that rock 'n' roll had the power to offend as well as excite when I kicked off my first day at WMC with my first broadcast of *The Rock 'n' Roll Ballroom*. But I decided that if I was going to be offensive, I'd do it in a big way. I introduced myself to WMC listeners by playing the loudest, hardest rock 'n' roll record I could think of: Little Richard's newest single, "Tutti Frutti." I was officially rocking and rolling.

I continued playing the loud, hard rock 'n' roll records I loved on WMC, and pretty quickly mail started pouring in just the way it had at KWEM. And it wasn't long before the letter writers themselves were showing up. A lot of stations back then would let kids come watch a disc jockey broadcast, but there wasn't much room at the WMC studios, so the station made the decision to give me a real ballroom-sized space: a three-hundred-seat auditorium in the Goodwyn Institute building, where WMC had its studios. I'd be up on stage in the special broadcast booth the station built me, working away doing my regular show, and kids could come and take a seat and watch just the way they would at a live concert. Some radio guys might not have enjoyed being turned into a live performer that way, but frankly I loved it. It was really a kick to feed off the energy of a live crowd, and nothing made me happier than to play a song that got people dancing in the auditorium aisles.

Elvis had a bunch of singles out on Sam Phillips's Sun Records now, and I made a point of playing them, always impressed that his music just seemed to get better and better. (Actually, I always thought "Milk Cow Boogie" was a little corny, but songs like "Mystery Train" and "Baby Let's Play House" were killers.) Occasionally, Elvis himself would show up during my show to drop off a new record and hang out in the booth with me, just the same way he had with Dewey. He seemed to get a big kick out of listening to me put together my crazy rhymes introducing a record, and, in addition to "DJ Uh," he came up with a new teasing nickname for me: "the rhyming fool on the stool."

He particularly liked one of the rhymes I began using to introduce his records: "Here's the King to sing." I can't say for sure that I was the first jock to call Elvis "the King," but neither he nor I had heard anybody else use it before then.

As a guy playing mostly black rock 'n' roll records for mostly white kids, I should have been right in the middle of the music's cultural conflict, but to be honest, I don't think I ever got an angry letter from a preacher or a teacher or a parent. I was living in the undeniably segregated South, but I really think there was something special about Memphis that allowed people to come together through music in ways that they wouldn't otherwise. It would be unthinkable to see a black face at Jack's, the hamburger joint and teen hangout just down the street from Humes High (and it didn't really occur to us that a black person might want to have a hamburger at Jack's). But when I went down to the record shops, there'd be a mix of black and white faces that seemed to get along just fine. For a lot of us, a love of great music was simply more important than any difference in skin color—a lesson I learned by example watching Dewey and Sam Phillips at work.

I saw the famous news clips of radio station managers around the country breaking rock 'n' roll records and declaring that they wouldn't play any "n——" music on their station, but I never heard that kind of talk at the stations I was at. And even out around town in Memphis, you might hear people use the n-word, but it wasn't considered cool to speak that way by anyone I knew, and the word was generally considered to be something that would come out of the mouth of someone who just wasn't too bright.

Folks from out of town were sometimes surprised at the way we got along in Memphis. Now that I was on one of the city's larger radio stations, I started being visited by record-label owners and promo men who would deliver copies of their latest recordings and make a pitch to get their songs on the air. I met some of the real legendary heavyweights from that side of the business—Leonard Chess of Chess Records, Joe Kolsky of Diamond Records, Jerry Wexler of Atlantic, Morris Levy of Roulette Records, Lester Bihari of RPM Records. These were some real tough guys, some reputed to have mob connections, and I always got the same response from them: they couldn't believe that in Memphis, their high-energy, controversial black rock 'n' roll records were being played for Southern white kids by a little Jewish guy.

One night, Elvis, Dewey, and I went to the Variety Club together—a private club that was the only place in town to serve mixed drinks and stay open past midnight—and I got a real look at some of the kindness and good humor that were such a part of Elvis's nature. In his senior year at Humes, Elvis had worked as an usher at the Loews State movie theater on Main Street in downtown Memphis. In that position he had the chance to watch the movies that played there over and over, and became a real student of film. He watched James Dean and Monty Clift and Marlon Brando and saw how they moved and spoke and got the greatest impact with the littlest gestures. He paid enough attention to pick up an intuitive knowledge of the medium that would later surprise the Hollywood folks when Elvis started making his own movies.

But when Elvis wasn't watching the big screen, he apparently spent a lot of time watching a very pretty girl who worked behind the candy counter—a girl who responded to Elvis's attention by giving him free candy. When another, jealous usher reported the candy giveaways to the theater manager, Elvis and that usher ended up in a fistfight, and Elvis was promptly fired by the manager, a fellow named Arthur Groom.

When Elvis and Dewey and I walked into the Variety Club, who was sitting at the bar but Mr. Groom. He saw us take our seats at a table and came over to say hello. Elvis was already successful enough that he might have felt justified being rude to someone who had once fired him. But he was extremely polite and cordial, still addressing his ex-boss as "Mr. Groom" or "sir." The two shared a couple of laughs, and Groom congratulated Elvis on how well he was doing and joked that if he hadn't fired him, Elvis might have been an assistant manager at the Loews State by now. (For the record, Elvis's first film, *Love Me Tender,* would have its Memphis debut the next year at that very theater he'd been fired from.)

Right around Christmas of 1955, Elvis and Dewey and I were back at the Variety Club. Dewey and I hadn't seen Elvis for a while, but he'd just taken a big step in his career, leaving Memphis's Sun Records for the much larger major-label company RCA. Maybe because it was around the holidays, the three of us were the only ones in there that night, and somewhere around one A.M. Elvis made his way over to the club's beat-up piano.

"GK, Dewey—come on over here," he said. "I want y'all to hear this new song I'm gonna cut."

He played a guitar onstage but piano was his second instrument—he played by ear and could work his way through just about any song he liked. He started playing something that sounded very different from anything we'd heard from him before. It wasn't a high-energy rocker or an up-tempo country tune or a low-down blues. It was something almost spooky, with a stop-and-start rhythm that really pulled you into the song.

He was playing "Heartbreak Hotel."

As he sang through the verses, Dewey and I looked at each other, and we both knew what the other was thinking: This was one hell of a song. As Elvis sang the last line—"Feel so lonely, I could die . . ."—we couldn't contain ourselves. "Shit, Elvis," whooped Dewey, "that's goddamn fantastic. Where'd you get that?"

Elvis explained that it had come from a Florida schoolteacher named Mae Axton, who had done some promotion work for Elvis's new manager,

Colonel Tom Parker. She'd even given him a third of the writer's credit on the song, over his objections, because she hoped he'd earn enough money to bring his parents on a vacation to Florida.

"Damn—that's a smash hit, Elvis," I said.

Elvis smiled shyly and plunked a few more notes on the piano. "I know it," he said. "It's gonna be my first RCA release. I think it's a good way to start."

There couldn't have been a better way to start. In January of 1956, Elvis recorded "Heartbreak Hotel" in Nashville as part of his first RCA recording session. Just weeks later, "Heartbreak Hotel" became his first number-one, million-selling hit record. He wouldn't be playing any more flatbed trucks. He'd shot for Bill Haley and had sailed right past him.

For all his craziness and his extremely entertaining personality, Dewey Phillips had a great ear for music. He took full advantage of the freedom to play whatever he wanted, but he also put together a show that kids like me felt they had to listen to in order to know what was happening on the music scene. Working with Dewey, I learned one of the secrets to his success—he was one of the only jocks to make regular trips to record-distributor warehouses to hear new singles before anybody else. He'd find out what records were just starting to get hot around the country based on their orders and pick up copies from the distributor before any other radio station had them. Time after time, he was the first disc jockey in town to play the new smash from Chuck Berry or Bo Diddley or anybody else.

I followed Dewey's example as I launched my radio career, and got in the habit of going by the same record warehouses to scout new music as it came in. That's the way I got a jump on a lot of the soon-to-be hits I played on the *Rock 'n' Roll Ballroom*, including Elvis's biggest record yet, the double-sided smash single "Don't Be Cruel" backed with "Hound Dog." That record was the talk and the sound of the summer of 1956, and when Elvis headed to Hollywood at the beginning of September to record his second album, I couldn't wait to hear more of his rock 'n' roll magic.

I didn't have to wait as long as I thought I might. One fall day at the RCA record distributor warehouse, I came across his second album—a full couple of weeks before it was supposed to be available to anybody. The album (titled *Elvis,* just like his first) had a great cover photo of Elvis against a golden background, wearing a cool pink-and-gray-striped shirt, strumming his guitar and looking heavenward. I noted right away that the song list included "Paralyzed" by Otis Blackwell, who'd written "Don't Be Cruel," and "Love Me" by Jerry Leiber and Mike Stoller, the young genius rock 'n' roll songwriters who'd come up with "Hound Dog." I was also a little surprised to see that the album included the very first song I'd ever heard Elvis sing—the ode to a faithful dog that he'd performed in Miss Marmann's class back at Humes, "Old Shep."

I went straight to the WMC studio and played the album through in an empty control room so I could enjoy the whole thing all by myself. And by the time I was listening to "Ready Teddy" on side two, it hit me that every time I thought I'd heard the best Elvis could do, he blew me away all over again. As soon as I got to the end of the last track (Webb Pierce's "How Do You Think I Feel"), I picked up the phone and called Elvis at home, knowing he'd just come back to town after finishing his film work on *Love Me Tender.* His mother got him on the line, and I let him know how I felt about the new record. There was silence on his end, then he said, "What record are you talking about, GK?"

"Your second album, Elvis."

"You gotta be kidding. Where'd you get it?"

"I just went down to the distributor and picked it up. I came over here to the station to play it, and it's just plain great."

"Man, GK—I didn't know that thing was out yet, and I don't even have a copy," he said. "Could you bring it over to the house?"

Of course, I said I'd be happy to. And while I was generally hesitant to ask Elvis for any favors, that day I asked him if it was okay for a WMC photographer to come with me when I handed over the album. That was fine by Elvis, and I ended up with some fantastic pictures of us holding the album together, sitting on his big Harley-Davidson motorcycle and standing by his gleaming white Mark II Lincoln Continental.

One afternoon in early December of 1956, Elvis stopped by WMC and offered to give me a ride home in a car I hadn't seen yet—a brand-new Cadillac Eldorado. On that ride, I mentioned to him that WDIA was having its annual Goodwill Revue that night at the Ellis Auditorium, one of two big charity events put on by the station each year to raise money for needy black children and families. The event was well-known for attracting top-notch black talent to play for a large black audience. That year's Goodwill lineup was set to include Ray Charles, former DIA deejay B. B. King, a terrific piano player named Phineas Newborn, a number of gospel groups, and it would be hosted by Rufus Thomas, dressed up as the character Chief Rocking Horse. Elvis got excited about the event right away and suggested that we attend together.

A few hours later, there we were, walking into the backstage area of the Ellis Auditorium. One of the first people we bumped into was Rufus Thomas—who'd actually gotten heat for doing some reverse crossing of color lines by playing Elvis records on WDIA. He came right over with a big smile, grabbed Elvis, and thanked him for coming.

"You gonna sing for us tonight, Elvis?" Rufus asked.

Elvis's biggest concern on the way to the show was that he wanted to be as low-key as possible, and not do anything to distract from the scheduled acts' performances. "This is your night, Rufus," he said. "I don't belong out on that stage."

"Well, if we can't get you to sing," said Rufus, "let me just introduce you and you just take a bow. A lot of people out there sure would love to see you."

"That'd be just fine," said Elvis.

We milled around backstage for a while, meeting that night's performers. We crossed paths with B. B. King and he and Elvis talked for a while—a moment caught by the great photographer Ernie Withers (who would go on to capture so many lasting images of the civil rights movement). Whoever we were talking to, I saw that Elvis always had an ear cocked to the music being played onstage. I'd spent so much time by now enjoying Elvis's music that it was interesting to see him completely transported by the music he was hearing.

When Rufus Thomas got around to introducing Elvis, he practically had to pull him out onstage. As soon as the crowd saw him, the place went crazy. I don't think it crossed Elvis's mind that he was crossing a color line—he didn't think that way. He had simply wanted to be at the Goodwill Revue because he wanted to hear Ray Charles and all the other acts, though I know it must have felt good to him to be accepted so warmly and enthusiastically there. Elvis responded to the crowd by doing one of his little leg shakes, and the place erupted in a roar that sounded like an earthquake, with young black girls charging to the stage just the way white girls did at other appearances.

On the radio, Dewey Phillips had set aside questions of race to play "good music for good people." I'd tried to follow that example in putting great rock 'n' roll music on the air without regard to whether the artist or the audience was black or white. Now Elvis, in the most casual way, could obliterate all the stupid things that were supposed to separate people simply by shaking a leg on the Ellis Auditorium stage.

Yes, there was "raw emotion" there. And, from the sounds of those girls, there was "sexual content," too. Maybe Elvis really was a threat to some of our society's established ideas and attitudes, but maybe that wasn't such a bad thing. Maybe the people who were so afraid of rock 'n' roll music were right: It really did have the power to change the world.

CHAPTER THREE

● ● ● ● ● ● ● ● ● ● ● ●

Dragging Main

As far as I know, I'm the only man who ever slept with Elvis Presley. I can say for sure that he's the only man who's ever slept with me.

I guess I'd better explain.

As the spring of 1957 rolled around, Elvis could no longer be considered just a local sensation—he was a bona fide superstar. He'd just finished his second Hollywood movie, *Loving You*, and his third, tentatively titled *Jailhouse Kid*, was already planned. He was also on his way to holding the number-one spot on the pop charts again with "All Shook Up." In January he'd made his third and final appearance on *The Ed Sullivan Show*, at the end of which Ed made a point of telling the American viewing public that Elvis was "a real decent, fine boy." Even under the gaze of a TV camera—maybe especially under the gaze of that camera—Elvis looked exactly like his music sounded: strong, sexy, cool, and a little crazy. He had the Brando mystique, the James Dean intensity, and he could sing like nobody else. He was the total rock 'n' roll package. There were still some gripes about the effect Elvis was having on the nation's youth, and potshots taken at his musical abilities, but just about everything Elvis did now ended up being more popular and successful than whatever he'd done before.

Things were going great for Elvis, and I thought things were going pretty well for myself, too. I was still one of the most popular afternoon jocks in Memphis, hosting *George Klein's Rock 'n' Roll Ballroom* for WMC.

I loved being the one to play the hottest new rock 'n' roll records for my listeners, from the Platters' "My Prayer" to Fats Domino's "Blueberry Hill" to Elvis's latest singles.

I'd even been a part of what would turn out to be another bit of rock 'n' roll history at the end of '56, when a freshly pressed, unreleased record was brought to me by a couple of producer Sam Phillips's associates—A&R man Jack Clement and Sun session drummer J. M. Van Eaton. The record had been cut a couple days before by a Louisiana piano player who'd come to Sun after being rejected by record labels in Nashville. (Clement told me the piano player and his daddy decided to come through Memphis to sell off some eggs from their farm so that the trip wouldn't be a complete wash.) It was a cover of Ray Price's "Crazy Arms" cut with rockabilly energy, country twang, and definitely some powerful piano work.

I could tell this new piano player was talented, but I didn't really hear the song as a hit. Still, I played it on my show to see what my listeners thought. That's how I became the first disc jockey in the world to put Jerry Lee Lewis on the air. (For the record, listeners did not go crazy for "Crazy Arms," but Jerry Lee would be back soon enough with his breakthrough hit, "Whole Lotta Shakin' Goin' On.")

Life was good: Elvis was selling out concert halls and movie theaters and sitting at the top of the pop charts, I was having a blast on the radio, and rock 'n' roll was on the rise. Then one day I got called into the station manager's office. Bill Grumbles had left WMC to take a job with the RKO company, and I expected there'd be some programming changes under the new manager. But I wasn't quite prepared for what I heard when I got called into that new general manager's office. I was fired, effective immediately.

"What's the matter? What have I done wrong?" I asked.

"You haven't done anything wrong," I was told. "The problem isn't you, George. It's the music."

"But I'm playing the hottest rock 'n' roll records in the country."

"That's the problem," said the general manager. "They're rock 'n' roll records. They're hot today but we don't think the rock 'n' roll thing is going to last. It's a passing fad, just like the mambo fad or the calypso fad, and the station thinks it's just about run its course. We've gotta think about the future, so we're going to have to close down your show. I'm sorry, George."

Just like that, DJ GK was just plain old GK again, and my bright future was suddenly looking like a great big question mark. Feeling like I needed some kind of distraction after a rough day, I headed over to the Chisca Hotel to hang out with Dewey Phillips in the WHBQ studios.

"Damn pea pickers don't know a damn thing, do they?" he howled when I told him about my situation. He'd been having some run-ins with his own management, who felt Dewey's freewheeling style was becoming an awkward fit with the more rigidly formatted shows the station had begun to adopt. We sat and talked some as he played his records, and I did start to feel a little better watching him in action on the air. My mood improved a little more when, toward the end of Dewey's show, Elvis appeared at the door of the control booth. He'd gotten back to town from making *Loving You* and had decided to come spend some time with old friend Daddy-O Dewey. I moved out into the station hallway to say hello and catch up with him.

"How's everything, Elvis?"

"Fine. Just fine, GK." He looked at me with a slightly puzzled expression. "Man, what happened to you?" he asked. "Why weren't you on the air today?"

"Well, Elvis, you're not gonna believe it, but—I was fired."

"Fired?" He actually looked a little hurt and angry—exactly what I was feeling.

"Yeah. WMC is dropping its rock 'n' roll programming, so they fired me." I think I tried to smile a little bit, hoping maybe Elvis could help me laugh all this off. But his hard expression didn't change at all. He looked down at the floor a moment, then back at me.

"You ain't fired anymore, GK."

"What do you mean?"

"You're working for me."

I was dumbstruck for a moment. Then I thought to ask a pretty important question. "Uh, Elvis, what exactly am I gonna do for you?"

He didn't hesitate a bit. "Nothing. You're a traveling companion."

"A traveling companion?"

"That's right. Next week we're going out on a big tour across the country. Then we go to Hollywood to do another movie. Then we go on to Hawaii. You'll come along and you'll be a traveling companion. You don't have to do nothing but be with me."

Just an hour ago I'd been full of worries, wondering exactly what I was going to do with myself. I'd been feeling down because I'd lost my opportunity to be playing rock 'n' roll records. Now, with a few words from Elvis, I was being invited to step away from the records and step right into the actual rocking and rolling. To my mind there was only one way to respond to an invitation like that.

"Wow, Elvis. What do I do to sign on?"

"You're on, man. You're on."

I don't remember what prevented Dewey from going out with us that night—I just remember that Elvis and I left the station together. We drove around town in his white Mark II Continental, and stopped at the Variety Club downtown to have a few cold soft drinks and listen to the jukebox. When it rolled around to closing time at the club, Elvis asked if I wanted to come back to his place to hang out some more.

He and his family were now living on Audubon Drive in East Memphis. They'd been there since May of 1956, when Elvis had earned enough money to move them into the first really nice house they'd ever had. The place was a spacious, Texas-style ranch house in a very nice residential neighborhood, and though it certainly wasn't the biggest house on the block, it happened to be the only one with a swimming pool. Elvis wasn't much of a swimmer, but he'd put the word out that if neighborhood kids wanted to come by and swim, they were welcome. (One of the kids that took up Elvis's offer was a young Fred Smith, who'd grow up to become founder and CEO of Federal Express.)

Even though it was late when we got to Elvis's house, his parents got up to check on us. I'd gotten to know Mrs. Presley a bit through the Humes years, and she seemed especially happy to see me now. With all that was happening to her son so quickly, and with all the smiling strangers he was suddenly doing business with, I think she was relieved to see her son with a Humes High classmate she knew she could trust. As I became more a part of Elvis's life, Mrs. Presley would often tell both of us that she wasn't as worried about Elvis if she knew I was with him (and, though it was years after the fact, she'd often tell me how impressed she'd been with my class president's speech at the Humes graduation ceremony).

That night, after Mr. and Mrs. Presley went to bed, Elvis and I went outside to sit on the patio by the pool, where he talked a lot about the times he'd had in Hollywood: "Everywhere you look there's beautiful girls, GK—one more beautiful than the next. You'll see for yourself, man. It's something." He also showed me one of his newest leisure activities. He'd take a box of the glass cubes used for flash photography and dump them into his pool, then shoot at them with a BB gun. He was a great shot, and when he hit a cube, it would give off this glow in the water that was really a pretty sight (though it made a mess that Mr. Presley would later have to clean out of the pool). At some point we moved inside to listen to records, and eventually we got tired enough to call it a night.

"Elvis, could you give me a ride up to North Memphis?" I asked.

"Aww, hell, GK, that's too far away to get to now. Just stay here with me."

"Fine by me, Elvis. Where do you want me to sleep?" There were three bedrooms in the house: his, his parents', and his Grandma Minnie's. I expected Elvis would point me to a chair or a sofa or a piece of floor to bunk down on.

"You'll sleep in my bed, man. You take that side, I'll take the other. There's plenty of room."

He was right—one of the first luxuries he'd bought for himself at the house was a king-size bed that took up a good portion of his room. So that was how, on a spring night in 1957, I found myself in the unusual position of preparing to get under the covers with the biggest rock 'n' roll star in the world.

As I soon discovered, sleeping alongside Elvis Presley wasn't always a very restful experience. Almost as soon as we laid down on our respective sides of his bed, I became aware of a soft, strange, steady tapping coming from the wall nearest Elvis's bed.

"What's that, Elvis?"

"What's what?"

"What's that knocking sound?"

"Oh, that's just the girls outside. They come around from all over. They figured out where my bedroom is, so now they just sit on the other side of the wall."

I listened closer. Along with the tapping, I could hear whispers, too: "Elvis, we love you." "Elvis, can we come in?"

"What are you going to do?" I asked.

"Nothing. Happens every night. That's why I've got to move out of here."

He was so used to the commotion around him that he didn't seem to have much trouble falling asleep to the tapping and the whispering. I had a harder time dozing off, but eventually I must have, because at some point I woke up with a start and realized there was somebody standing in the bedroom. I bolted up in bed and reached over to wake up Elvis, but his side of the bed was empty. As my eyes adjusted to the dark, I realized that the figure standing in the bedroom shadows was Elvis.

"Elvis? You okay?"

He mumbled something and shuffled around the room a little bit.

Elvis was walking in his sleep.

Earlier in the night, Mrs. Presley had pulled me aside and said that if I was going to stay over, I should be aware that Elvis often walked in his sleep. She'd given me some tips on how to talk gently to him to get him back in bed, so that's what I did now.

"Elvis, why don't you come back to sleep," I said softly.

"Huh?"

"Come back to sleep, Elvis."

He mumbled something else and shuffled away from the bed. I started to get a little more concerned. I stood up, but I didn't get so close as to startle him. He kept talking, like he was lost in thought trying to work something out. And I kept gently asking him to come back to bed. Finally, after a few nervous minutes on my part, he simply walked to the bed, and, without any fuss, climbed in and was out like a light. As for me, I was thrilled to be in Elvis's home, but, my first night there, I didn't sleep too well.

In the morning Elvis didn't say anything about his nightwalking, and I didn't either. It was still early in his career, and early in our friendship, but already I knew that he was a guy with a deep personal pride, and I knew this was the kind of thing that was more likely to embarrass him than be something he'd enjoy kidding around about. He took a lot of knocks from the press and the mainstream public in his early days, and when he let somebody into his world on a personal level, he did it with a great sense of trust. I wasn't going to do anything to make him think that trusting me was a mistake.

A few days later I was back at Audubon Drive in the early evening. In keeping with a real Southern tradition, Elvis and his parents would often sit on their small front porch for some relaxed conversation together after dinner. A lot of times carloads of girls would drive by and call out, "We love you, Elvis," just like the girls who tapped on the walls. This night Elvis and I were in the house while just Mr. and Mrs. Presley sat on the porch. We heard a car screech up to the curb in front of the house and there were some ugly, threatening-sounding shouts before the car squealed away again. Elvis ran out to the porch and could tell from his parents' expressions that they were a little shaken up.

"What'd they say, Mama?"

"Don't worry, Elvis. It's not important," she answered.

"Mama—what'd they say."

She pursed her lips and shrugged a little. "They said, 'Elvis, we're going to get you.' But they were just boys, Elvis."

"Did they cuss at you?"

Mrs. Presley looked away, but his father answered. "They were just a bunch of young rowdies, Elvis. We're okay."

Elvis darted back into the house and quickly returned with a rifle in his hands. He sat down, laid the rifle across his lap, and sat there with a cold, steely expression on his face, just glaring down the road. Needless to say, there wasn't much relaxed conversation after that, but we sat there for two hours waiting for the carload of taunters to return. They never did show up, and to this day I can't really say if Elvis would have taken a shot at them or not.

He told me later that he'd recently received his first death-threat letter. It had an out-of-state postmark but the writer said he was coming to Memphis to kill Elvis. It had been turned over to the FBI, who couldn't trace it back to a specific sender. Nothing ever did come of it, but the threat explained why Elvis was so on edge.

All the attention that Elvis was getting at his home had an impact on the neighborhood, and, despite his offering up his pool to the local kids, his neighbors finally got fed up with all the trampled gardens, blocked driveways, and late-night traffic. Some of them had formed a committee together and came to talk to Mr. Presley. They told him they couldn't be happier that great things were happening for Elvis, but they felt that he'd outgrown their quiet residential street. They'd taken a collection and pooled their money to be able to make an above-market offer to buy the Presleys' house, and they were sure Elvis and the Presleys would be happier moving to a more secluded area. It was hard to argue with the neighbors' points, but if there was one thing Elvis hated, it was the feeling of being pushed around. When he heard about the neighbors' offer, he came up with a counterproposal: He'd buy all their houses and let them move.

It turned out that Vernon Presley didn't ever have to approach the neighbors with Elvis's counteroffer. While Elvis had been in Los Angeles in March of 1957 filming *Loving You,* Mr. and Mrs. Presley had looked at an estate off of Highway 51 South in Whitehaven, close to the

Tennessee-Mississippi border. It was nearly fourteen acres of wooded land around a beautiful brick mansion. The place was empty and needed a lot of work, but the Presleys felt it would make a perfect, private home for the family. Elvis hadn't seen it yet, but the beauty and peace and quiet of the estate was captured in its name: Graceland.

Just days before I headed out of town with Elvis to begin my career as a "travel companion," he and I took an afternoon drive together down Highway 51 South so that he could take a look at the property his mother and father were so excited about. Graceland wasn't much more than a shell of a house when we first saw it, but I can tell you that Elvis fell in love with the place right away. There wasn't any kind of neighborhood at all around it back in those days, and driving up the driveway to the house you had the feeling you were approaching some secluded, forgotten palace. What was really amazing, even on that first visit, was the feeling the grounds gave you. There was a peacefulness and a serenity there that made it more comfortable than any place I'd ever been. I know Elvis felt it, too, because within days he'd worked out a purchase deal and had started hiring designers and contractors to work on the new home.

On the last Friday night before the tour, I was back in Elvis's Lincoln Continental again, and at some point, I thought maybe it would be fun for us to spend this last Memphis weekend doing an old favorite high school pastime. I suggested that we "drag Main."

Now, dragging Main meant you cruised down the most popular strip of Memphis's Main Street, from Beale Street down to the Suzore Theatre, scouting out carloads of girls and trying to get some kind of a party started. You'd drag Main, circle back up Third Street, and head down Main again until you connected with the right car and the right girl. Elvis liked the idea, so we took some time to get dressed right, in sport coats and slacks, and off we headed to drag Main.

Main Street on a Friday night was a pretty hopping spot, but it wasn't so busy that the sight of Elvis Presley in a White Lincoln would go unnoticed for long, and before we'd gone more than a couple of blocks, we had five or six carloads of girls following us. Elvis slowly made it to the end of Main and turned up Third, and a couple of the carloads of girls stayed with us. As we pulled up to a stoplight, he turned to me.

"GK, go back and tell all those girls to come to Audubon Drive. We'll have a little party. But tell 'em not to bring any guys."

"Great, Elvis." I hopped out of the car and ran back to spread the invitation and make sure that everyone was clear on the address and the no-other-guys rule. The girls all screamed and giggled and started touching up their hair and makeup. It looked like it was going to be a great Friday night.

But as I headed back to the Continental, I saw that Elvis wasn't in the driver's seat anymore. He was out of the car and was backed up against the side of it, surrounded by five or six guys who didn't look too friendly. I squirmed through the bunch of them to get to Elvis.

"What's the problem? What's going on here?" I asked one of the guys at the front of the surrounding group, hoping there was still some way to talk through whatever was going on. The big guy didn't take his eyes off Elvis as he answered.

"I'm going to see how tough this movie star is. He's been messing around with my wife and I'm going to whup his ass."

I'd seen guys try to act tough around Elvis, but these guys were serious as hell, and they stood around us like they were standing at attention. That's when I realized that, of all the places we could have stopped in front of, we'd pulled up in front of the USO Club that serviced the thousands of sailors and marines stationed at the Millington Naval Base just north of Memphis. We were now surrounded by a group of angry marines who wanted to teach Elvis Presley a lesson.

"Wait a minute," I said to the big guy. "Elvis just got back from Hollywood. He just made another movie. He's been out of town for over three months—he couldn't have been going out with your wife."

Logic didn't seem to make any difference to this guy.

"Yes he has. He's been going out with my wife and now I'm going to see how tough he really is."

I'd never been much of a fighter, but I braced myself as the guys started slowly closing in on us, and I balled up my fists. Elvis had been very still leaning against the car, but now he snapped into action. He reached into his sport jacket's inside pocket and calmly, smoothly, pulled out a gun, then quickly extended his arm so that the barrel was just an inch away from a spot right between the big guy's eyes.

"Okay, you badass son of a bitch," he growled. "Let's see what you can do now."

The guy's eyes opened wide and the color drained out of his face in a flash. His friends went pale, too. The big guy slowly put his hands up, and now spoke with a very different tone of voice.

"Don't shoot, Mr. Presley. We were just having fun with you. Just goofing around. We didn't mean anything by it."

Elvis wasn't in any mood to accept an apology. "Screw you," he said. He lowered his hand to his waist but kept the gun pointed straight at the big guy. "GK, get in the car." I hopped in as fast as I could. Elvis got to the driver's door and spoke to the marines again. "I'll shoot the first person who moves," he said. Elvis climbed in, and we burned rubber peeling out of there. In my passenger-side mirror I caught a glimpse of the marines, barely moving and still looking stunned. I realized then how hard my heart was beating and how rapid my breathing had become—I'd been just one step away from a military-style, all-out brawl. I looked over at Elvis, who somehow seemed to be taking the whole damn thing in stride, like it was just part of an average night out on the town.

"Where'd that come from?" I shouted.

"What's that, GK?"

"Where in the world did you get that gun?"

He reached into his pocket again, pulled the gun out, and handed it to me. I hesitated to take a hold of it, but he pushed it into my hand. It felt a lot lighter than what I expected.

"That's a Hollywood prop gun, GK. The prop man at Paramount Studios gave it to me."

"Aww, man, Elvis. You mean you just scared the shit out of a bunch of guys with something that only fires blanks?"

"It got the job done, GK," he laughed.

In all the confusion of our standoff with the marines, we'd lost track of the girls we'd found on Main, but not too long after we got back to Elvis's house on Audubon, a couple carloads of them showed up. His family was asleep, but the way the house was laid out we could make quite a bit of noise in the den without waking anybody up. The girls came in, all looking great, and we got a party started.

Now it might seem strange that a late-night, private party with Elvis and a bunch of pretty young girls could be called innocent, but we really did have a lot of good-natured fun that night. There wasn't any liquor and certainly no drugs—just Pepsis and maybe a few cigarettes. Elvis went to the piano in the den and sang some songs—never his own, just old favorites he enjoyed singing, and some of the girls sang along with him. The rest of the time it was just me and Elvis bouncing around and flirting with as many of the girls as we could (obviously I had to flirt a lot harder than he did). There was some teasing and kissing with some of them, but there was no wild orgy. Elvis wasn't interested in that kind of thing, especially not in the house where his parents were sleeping. The girls were thrilled because every one of them thought they had a shot at being Elvis's next girlfriend. I was happy just to get a phone number or two and a couple of kisses. I suppose it was a different time back then, but we had some great rock 'n' roll fun that night without anything getting too heavy.

As our party was winding down at about four in the morning, there was a knock at the door. I went to answer it and was relieved upon opening the door to see a couple of local press guys I knew, rather than another platoon of marines. One of the guys was a reporter, the other a photographer. When I asked what they were doing there, the reporter spoke up.

"Well, GK, this marine has gone down to the police station and has sworn out a warrant. He said Elvis tried to kill him tonight. We were wondering if Elvis would tell us what happened."

Elvis had grown very wary of reporters—he really had been treated unfairly by a lot of them. But this time he came outside and seemed perfectly happy to explain the evening's whole chain of events while the Memphis reporter took notes.

"I didn't really want to hurt anybody," said Elvis. "I was just trying to protect myself."

The reporter insisted he'd tell Elvis's side of the story, and asked if he could get a photo of Elvis and me in the Lincoln. I was a little surprised that Elvis agreed to that, but he did. So we posed for the camera, sitting in the car together, with Elvis even holding up the prop gun he'd used.

That's the picture that was splashed across the next day's paper, with a full write-up of the encounter between Elvis and the marines. The following day the story hit the national wire, and on Monday morning, just two days before we were supposed to head to Chicago to begin the tour, Elvis and I were facing down that big marine once more, this time in the chambers of a Memphis judge.

Colonel Parker was already in Chicago doing advance work, but he called and wanted to put Elvis in touch with some top lawyers who could help get everything straightened out. Elvis told him he didn't need any attorneys—he said he and I would be able to take care of it on our own. Standing in the judge's chambers, I began to think that had been a mistake. The marine had shown up with a Marine Corps lawyer, a Navy lawyer, and a civilian lawyer to help him argue his side. Elvis just had me.

The judge wasn't interested in hearing lawyers speak, though. He asked the marine to tell his side of the story for himself, then he asked Elvis to tell his side of the story. After hearing what the two parties had to say, the judge stared down at the papers on his desk for a while, and when he looked up you could almost see a little smirk on his face. He looked over at the marine.

"Son, how long you been in the marines?"

"Two years, sir."

"And don't they tell you what a real gun looks like in the marines?"

"Yes, sir."

"Well, evidently they didn't do too good a job of it. Case dismissed."

The marine turned just about as pale as he had been with the prop gun pointed at him, and his team of lawyers looked as stunned as his buddies had. Elvis and I tried to maintain straight faces, and we didn't say a word to each other until we got outside the courtroom. Just as we allowed ourselves some smiles and started to talk about what we'd just witnessed, I saw that the big marine was approaching us. I braced again for another confrontation, but this time the guy wasn't looking for a fight.

"Mr. Presley, I'm so sorry this had to happen," he said quietly.

"So am I," said Elvis. "But it's over. No hard feelings."

"No hard feelings, sir. But can I ask you something?"

"Sure."

"Well, sir, I'm from St. Louis and I see you're going to be playing St. Louis soon. Is there any way my wife and I can come to the show? She sure would love to come backstage to meet you."

I don't know if my jaw actually dropped open, but I could not believe what I was hearing. This guy had been ready to pummel Elvis to a pulp because he thought Elvis was making moves on his wife—now he wanted to bring that wife to Elvis's dressing room.

"Okay," said Elvis. "You just come to the security gate at the St. Louis show and ask for this man—George Klein. He'll take care of you."

I'm pretty sure Elvis was thinking some of the same unprintable words I was thinking—but he didn't say any of them. Instead he remained as nice as could be, wishing the marine well as we turned to walk out of the courthouse that this guy had dragged us into.

CHAPTER FOUR

Good Rockin' Tonight

In the early days of fifties rock 'n' roll, "roadie" didn't exist as a word or a profession. When Elvis went out on his road tours—and he was touring like crazy in between his movies—he took a few guys he knew and trusted, guys who could take care of the driving and the luggage and the instruments and run a little defense for him when he needed it. In the earliest days, Red West had been the one-man stage crew for Elvis, Scotty, and Bill. I'd known Red since before our Humes days—I'd played some Pee Wee League baseball with him—and one thing about him had never changed: He was one of the toughest guys in North Memphis, if not all of Tennessee. But he could also surprise you with just how sharp he was and how well he understood music, and he and Elvis were extremely tight as friends.

By 1957, Elvis had become the world's first rock 'n' roll superstar, and he was bringing more guys along with him on the road. He'd found an unusual sort of right-hand man in his cousin, Gene Smith. Elvis and Gene had always been very close—so close that they had their own private language together that was almost impossible for anyone else to make sense of. Gene wasn't what you'd call book smart, but he was funny, easygoing, and was one of those one-of-a-kind characters Elvis always seemed to enjoy. Most important, he was as loyal as could be to Elvis, whom he always called "Cuz."

Elvis had also been traveling with a big fellow named Arthur Hooton, whose mother had worked with Mrs. Presley over at Saint Joseph's hospital in Memphis. Arthur looked like a pretty imposing bodyguard—he stood six foot two and must have weighed three hundred pounds. But he was a friendly, good-natured guy and, compared to somebody like Red West, didn't have much fight in him. In fact, I think Elvis would have thrown a punch before Arthur would, but Arthur had a good head on his shoulders and, devoted as he was to Elvis, was somebody Elvis could always count on. Then there was Cliff Gleaves, a part-time deejay from Jackson, Tennessee, who'd also gotten close enough to Elvis to be a "traveling companion." Among some of the Memphis guys, Cliff stood out as a sharp dresser and even sharper talker—the kind of guy who had a con man's flair for spinning a great adventure tale out of just about anything he did. You were never sure how much truth was in Cliff's jived-up, fast-talking stories, but they were always fun to listen to.

Cliff had stayed in Los Angeles after the filming of *Loving You* to see if he could get an acting career of his own started (though he'd find out pretty quickly that Hollywood doors didn't fly open quite as easily when he wasn't with Elvis). And Red West was off doing a term of enlistment with the marines. So, though it was both kind and generous of Elvis to have offered me a position with him, he really did need somebody to help him out. I was glad, and proud, that I could be that somebody.

Of course, there was one more important figure in Elvis's world that anyone entering it had to deal with: Colonel Tom Parker. Colonel Parker was a shadowy figure—nobody knew exactly what he was a colonel of, and his background included varied jobs on the Southern carnival circuit and promotional and management work with a number of country artists. After being tipped off by one of his talent scouts, Parker had helped book Elvis onto some shows with country star Hank Snow, who was a business partner with the Colonel at the time. When Snow informed Parker that crowds were still screaming over Elvis's opening act when Snow came onstage to headline, Parker had a sense that something big was happening. In Elvis's earliest days, he was managed by guitarist Scotty Moore, then signed on with a Memphis deejay named Bob Neal. Throughout 1955, as Elvis got hotter and hotter, Colonel Parker became increasingly involved with promoting Elvis's appearances, aiming to win him over as a client.

Mrs. Presley never did like the Colonel, but she and Mr. Presley did like Hank Snow, and after some personal visits from Snow, the Presleys were convinced that signing on with Parker and Snow was a good career move for their son. Except that, once papers were drawn up, they were in the Colonel's name only. Hank Snow told me years later that he heard about the signing while on the road, and when he met up with the Colonel again he offered a congratulatory, "Hey—we got that Presley kid." The Colonel's response was: "What do you mean 'we,' Hank?" Snow had been squeezed out, and that was the end of his partnership with Colonel Parker.

The Colonel was the ultimate old-school showman—a great promoter, negotiator, and conniver. He had no artistic talent whatsoever and couldn't spot a hit act or a hit song himself—but he knew what would sell tickets and records and he knew how to call attention to the things he wanted to sell. Much the same way that Elvis blazed trails as an artist, the Colonel blazed trails in managing the world's first rock 'n' roll superstar. A lot of what he did in those days was brilliant: When Elvis said he wanted to be in movies, the Colonel started handing out questionnaires to fans at Elvis's shows, with questions like "Do you want to see Elvis in motion pictures?" and "How many times would you go to see an Elvis movie?" He bundled up hundreds of those and sent them to Hollywood film producer Hal Wallis (*Casablanca*). The idea helped get Elvis a Hollywood screen test, and Wallis went on to produce many of Elvis's films.

Although Colonel Parker was undeniably a master when it came to getting Elvis money and attention, he was also ruthless about the pursuit of both. He was a big man who, despite his financial success, dressed almost like a hobo, and he was as brash a person as I'd ever met—he seemed to be yelling at you even if he was just saying good morning. And whether or not he was a real colonel didn't seem to matter: Whatever room he walked into, he was in charge. It was obvious he didn't think much of the guys who traveled with Elvis, and he made a point of having as little to do with that group as possible. He eyed me a little less suspiciously—I think he was aware that I was on the ball enough to have a college degree and a radio career. But for me, really stepping into the Elvis world for the first time, the Colonel was more a force of nature to be aware of than a person I was going to get to know.

When I told my mother that I was about to go out on the road with Elvis, she quickly gave me her blessing. She'd always been supportive of my radio career, though I'm not sure that she understood the appeal of the rock 'n' roll records I loved so much (or why some other mothers got so upset over some of those records). I'm not sure she really understood all the fuss over Elvis either, but she knew that, with him, a world of opportunities just might open up for me.

My career as a rock 'n' roll traveling companion began in Chicago, the first city on Elvis's spring tour. Gene Smith, Arthur Hooton, and I traveled with Elvis while the band—Scotty, Bill, drummer D. J. Fontana, and backup vocal group the Jordanaires—traveled separately. I did have a little more to do than just hang out with Elvis—I was trusted with carrying the new gold-leaf suit that Colonel Parker had commissioned from the famous Hollywood "cowboy tailor," Nudie Cohen. The trick was that it was put into a regular-looking suit bag, so that it didn't attract any special attention when I carried it from train to car to hotel to theater; for all anyone knew, the bag had my clothes in it rather than five thousand dollars' worth of gold. Even so, I was a nervous wreck carrying that thing around and was glad every time I could turn it back over to Elvis (though a couple of times, when I got separated from Elvis before a show, the only way I could get through the backstage security was to unzip that bag a bit and show a flash of his gold suit).

On the way to our show at Chicago's International Amphitheater, I got my first taste of how crazy life on the road could be. The Colonel had arranged for Elvis and me to be driven to the theater by two Chicago Police Department detectives in an unmarked police car. At one intersection, the driver stopped the car about a foot into the pedestrian walkway. A wino-looking guy crossing the street was angered by this, so he slapped the hood of the car and hollered, "Back up your damn car!"

In a flash, the detective in the passenger seat was out of the car with his gun drawn on the wino. "Get the hell out of here, you motherf——er, or I'll blow your goddamn brains out," he growled. The wino whimpered some apologies and stumbled away. I looked over at Elvis, and he just looked back at me. The cop calmly got back in the car, turned to us in the backseat, and said, "Elvis, if you hadn't been with me, I would have shot him. But we don't have time to blow him away and get to the show on time." We never knew how much of a joke that was supposed to be, but we got the impression that Chicago was a pretty tough town.

Even so, Elvis sure did win them over. I'd seen a lot of rock 'n' roll action in Memphis, but nothing prepared me for the rush of excitement that hit when he walked onstage in that gold suit that night. The whole building seemed to shake, and even though the house lights were down, the room stayed lit up from all the flashbulbs popping out in the crowd. Those flashes sparkling like strobe lights on Elvis's gold suit was truly a fantastic sight, and I didn't see how the energy in the room could get any higher. I also didn't see how Elvis could handle being at the center of it all—even on the side of the stage, I felt so nervous and excited I almost got sick.

The energy level did in fact jump even higher as soon as the music began. The band was in peak form, playing like they owned the place. I'd seen Elvis perform before, but watching him from the wings I felt like I was really seeing him for the first time. He was absolutely wild onstage but somehow always in control, too—every move and gesture he made was perfectly timed with the music and only served to make his vocal performance that much more powerful. I'd seen him work a hometown crowd, but this was something else entirely—something truly awesome.

Things were so wild onstage and the screaming of the crowd was so loud that, frankly, I didn't see how the band could hear themselves enough to hold together—they were playing through very small amplifiers and didn't have the benefit of any stage monitors. Years later I asked D. J.

Fontana about that, and he said, "We were probably the first band ever conducted by an ass. If we couldn't hear anything, we just watched Elvis's butt and played along to that."

Elvis's backside was dressed in gold that night, and the gold pants didn't hold up too well when subjected to an Elvis performance. During some of his more dramatic stage moves, bits and pieces of the gold leaf flaked off. After the show, Colonel Parker complained to Elvis with a typical concern for the bottom line: "Elvis, every time you go down on your knees, it's costing us fifty bucks." He suggested that Elvis take it easy on the pants and not move around as much next time, but that was like asking a hurricane to sit still. After just a couple concerts of money-losing stage moves, Elvis gave up on the gold pants altogether and just wore the gold jacket with black slacks.

After the Chicago show, Elvis, Gene, Arthur, and I were running down a ramp in Union Station to catch a late train to St. Louis, when we became aware of a pack of guys chasing after us. That put us all on edge because Elvis had taken plenty of shots from jealous guys—I'd been in a car with him once when a guy walked up to the driver's-side window, asked for Elvis's autograph, then took a swing at him. (The punch missed Elvis but clipped the girl he was taking out on a date that night.) We tried to move a little faster toward the train until we heard a voice call out: "Elvis! Humes High class of '53! Albert Teague, Ed Leek, and Bobby Bland!"

We stopped dead in our tracks—these were old classmates. The guys caught up with us and in the few moments we had before we needed to board the train, they told us that they'd all moved to Chicago after school. They'd heard Elvis was in town, had gone to the show, then decided to try to catch us the way they did. Ed Leek let Elvis know that he still had a very valuable item that Elvis had given him at some point—an acetate of "My Happiness," the very first song Elvis had recorded at Memphis Recording Service—one he had actually paid to record. Elvis had let Ed bring it home to play for his grandma and had never asked for it back.

"Hold on to that, Ed," Elvis said. "Keep it safe for me."

With that we hopped on the train, pulled out of town, and never did see those guys again (though Ed Leek did hold on to and protect the acetate—a bit of history that Sam Phillips once called "the Mona Lisa of recordings").

I got another taste of craziness in St. Louis, where we stayed in a hotel suite that had three adjoining rooms—one for Arthur and me, one for Gene and Elvis, and a sitting room in between. The afternoon of the show there, Gene and I were stepping into the lobby elevator to go up to the suite when we were joined by a very forward female reporter and a photographer.

"What room is Elvis in?" the woman asked.

"I dunno," shrugged Gene.

"Aren't you his cousin?" She'd done her homework.

"Yup," said Gene.

"Well, what room is he in?"

"I dunno."

"Here's fifty dollars for you."

"Elvis is in room 730," said Gene.

But Gene was a little slyer than he sounded. He'd taken the money and given them my room number. So, a few minutes later, there was a pounding on my door. There was the reporter and the photographer again.

"Where's Elvis?" she asked as she pushed her way into the room. The photographer began clicking away.

"Not here—get out of my room," I shouted.

The reporter poked around and the photographer took pictures of my laundry until they realized they weren't going to meet Elvis. Then they scurried off, cussing us out for costing them fifty bucks.

At the Kiel Auditorium that night, we were getting ready for the show when a security guy came backstage looking for George Klein. I identified myself and he said there was someone at the gate looking for me. I couldn't think of anyone I knew in St. Louis, but I followed the guard to the gate—and there was that big marine who'd charged Elvis with assault after our "dragging Main" incident in Memphis. He had a grin on his face and an arm around his wife.

"Hello, sir," he said. "Do you remember me?"

"Uh—yeah. I do."

"Well, is there any chance Mr. Presley might get us into the show?"

"Why don't you let me go check with Elvis and the Colonel about that," I told him, and headed backstage again. When I told Elvis who was standing out there asking for free tickets, he just about exploded.

"*What!*" he shouted loud enough to make me jump. "Screw that SOB."

"Well, what do you want me to tell him, Elvis?"

"Don't go back there and tell him anything. Let him just stand there with the wife he's so worried about."

Elvis by nature was a nice guy, and he worked hard to stay a nice guy even while under a lot of pressure. But he had an edge to him, too, and when he got angry that tiger in him was a fighter you didn't want to mess with.

My main job on tour was supposed to be providing Elvis with companionship and conversation, but I found out quickly there really wasn't much time for either. Since Elvis had experienced some dicey plane landings on earlier tours, Mrs. Presley did not want her son to fly from place to place, and when Mrs. Presley spoke, that was the law as far as Elvis was concerned. So, at a time before you could rent a tour bus, we traveled in trains and limousines and Cadillacs. We'd roll into town, get to a hotel, get to a theater, hit the stage, party at the hotel, leave town, and do it all over again. Sometimes we'd tape newspaper over the limo windows to keep the backseat dark enough for Elvis to stretch out and get some sleep. There was hardly a moment of downtime, and I got used to recognizing cities by the back entrances to hotels and the alleyways behind the auditoriums.

The band members didn't mind flying, so that was one of the reasons we traveled separately. But even when we got to a town, they'd stay in a different hotel than us. This seemed a little weird to me, because there was real friendship between Elvis and his musicians. At first I thought it was one of Colonel Parker's ideas, but both Scotty and D.J. told me that they were the ones who asked for separate accommodations. For one thing, that kept them away from the Colonel. But it also meant that wherever the band stayed, they were the big stars in that hotel, whereas whenever they were around Elvis they were just backup players. I remember telling Scotty that he was missing out on some wild situations at Elvis's hotel.

"Believe me, GK," he replied. "We've got our own situations. It's probably best if we keep them separate."

As the tour moved on, cities, trains, limos, hotels, shows, and parties flew by. In Fort Wayne, Indiana, Elvis performed in a hockey arena—something so foreign to us that security guards had to explain what the high boards around the floor were for. In Detroit, Elvis handled the press in a new way: Against what I thought was the good traveling-companion advice I gave him, he had a fling with a pretty young UPI reporter. (That reporter's name was Gael Greene, and she went on to become a renowned restaurant critic.) In Buffalo, New York, we were treated to our first "bomb scare"—another new term to us—but got through the show without anything blowing up. In Toronto, Elvis and I got some funny looks from a Mountie when we asked who the lady was in the big picture hanging in Maple Leaf Gardens.

"That's the queen of England, sir," he replied.

Well—we'd never seen a picture of her before.

I should mention one more responsibility I had on the road with Elvis. He said that I was the best talker of the group—a title that really wasn't too hard to hold next to Gene Smith and Arthur Hooton. But as best talker, Elvis wanted me to go into the audiences at intermission, scout out the best-looking girls I could find, and invite them back to our hotel for a party.

This was a part of the job I could really put my heart into, and night after night the scene unfolded the same way: I'd walk right up to a group of beautiful girls and say, "How you doing?" They'd look at me like I was crazy. I'd say, "I'm with Elvis Presley, and we're having a party at the hotel after the show. If you meet me in the lobby, I'll take you up to the party." They still thought I was crazy. Back then, we didn't have the kind of big laminated backstage passes you wear around your neck; we just had a little red or gold ribbon that said ELVIS PRESLEY SHOW that you'd pin to your shirt or jacket. I'd show the girls my ribbon and say, "Wait a minute—look at this. I'm with Elvis Presley."

The usual response was: "Anybody could get one of those. Get lost."

That's when I'd turn to my secret weapon. I'd take out my wallet and pull out a couple of pictures of me and Elvis together.

"All right, well, look at this."

And the beautiful girls would say, "Hey—that's you. With Elvis!"

"Right. Now as I was saying—get to the hotel after the show and I'll meet you in the lobby."

And every night, those beautiful girls would be waiting for me right there in the hotel lobby. I'd take them up to Elvis's room for a party—the kind of party that quite often did get a little wild and a little heavier than Pepsis and sing-alongs.

Even in between cities, we were thinking of girls. I remember on one train ride, our sleeping compartment was next to the compartment of a very striking woman. The compartments on this train were separated by removable walls, and there was about a half inch of space between the floor and the wall. Good old Cousin Gene came up with what he thought was a pretty clever idea: He took a butter knife, polished it up, angled it against that little half-inch gap, and claimed he got a full show when the woman dressed and undressed. So, of course, we all ended up down on the floor of that little sleeping compartment. To be honest, I couldn't see anything. But I tried to, and so did Elvis.

"What do you see, cuz?" Gene asked when Elvis was down there taking his look.

"I see a butter knife," said Elvis.

The last show of that tour was in Philadelphia, where Elvis became a target of sorts. At the show, Elvis was just getting ready to go into "Don't Be Cruel" when a guy in a trench coat in the front of the crowd threw an egg at the stage. The egg missed Elvis but hit Scotty Moore's guitar strings, making a very strange sound through his amplifier. The egg thrower turned and tried to run away, but he didn't get very far; the little girls in the crowd started hitting him with purses and fists and anything else they could swing. The next day we heard that the egg thrower was a college kid and that his college wanted to suspend him, and the police wanted to press charges against him. Both authorities asked Elvis how he wanted to proceed.

"It's just a damn college prank," he said to us. "The kid wanted to be the guy that threw an egg at Elvis Presley. I ain't pressing any charges."

He also instructed the Colonel to tell the college he did not want the kid suspended. It amazed me again that with everything coming at him—eggs included—Elvis worked hard to remain decent and fair most of the time.

Still, he had a sharp temper lurking under the surface. When we were back in Memphis after the tour, with some time off before Elvis headed back to Hollywood, he had a visit from Yvonne Lime, a starlet he had dated during the making of *Loving You*. Elvis wanted to show her around Memphis and wanted her to take a look at Graceland, which was in the process of being renovated for the Presleys. One day Elvis decided to take Yvonne out for a typical Southern activity—snake hunting—and he took Arthur Hooton and me along, too. We drove about fifteen miles south of Graceland across the state line to a lake in Mississippi. It was a beautiful spring day and we were having a really nice time. Elvis had a shotgun and was doing all the hunting, which left Arthur and me free to spend time with Yvonne. We all kept losing sight of each other as we walked through the wilds around the lake, and at one point Arthur came up behind Yvonne and gave her a playful little hug. She was startled and let out a little scream, then broke into laughter. But Arthur hadn't seen Elvis approaching behind him.

All of a sudden, Elvis had his gun up to Arthur's head, and he said, "You do that again and I'll blow your f——ing head off."

I'd never heard him talk like that—not to somebody he really knew. Arthur was a sweet-natured guy who loved Elvis to death and hadn't meant a thing with that hug. He certainly wasn't making any serious move on Elvis's girl.

"Elvis . . ." I started, hoping to calm things down.

"Shut up," he growled.

I just stood there shuffling my feet, Yvonne didn't know what to say, and Arthur started apologizing so much he was almost in tears. Elvis finally backed away and put the gun down, but his mood never lifted. The rest of that day was not pleasant and it felt like a long ride back to Memphis.

That was the first time I saw how dark Elvis's moods could become. I guess it hit me hard because I'd spent so much time watching him do amazing things and seeing him handle so many crazy situations so beautifully—when he did something small that proved he really was just a regular human being, it was actually kind of shocking. There was no excuse for scaring Arthur that way, but I realized that while the rest of us saw Elvis as a truly extraordinary person, he didn't necessarily see himself that way. He loved the fame and fortune that were coming to him, but somewhere inside he was still the guy who'd been picked on by more popular kids at Humes High.

I was over at Audubon Drive a few months later on an April night, just before we were to leave for California, where Elvis would begin work on his next film, still tentatively called *Jailhouse Kid*. Elvis had a visit that night from Freddy Bienstock, the liaison for the Hill and Range music-publishing company that generally supplied Elvis with the songs he recorded. Freddy had a stack of acetate demo recordings of songs that might be featured in the new film. I later learned that producers would mark Elvis scripts where songs might be included, and the scripts were then sent to a number of songwriters who would try to come up with something that fit the scenes and worked for Elvis. Freddy had demos of several different versions of what would be the movie's most energetic rock 'n' roll tune, "Jailhouse Rock."

I sat with Elvis as he played the demos on his record player, and while he nodded along to the first couple, nothing really grabbed him. Then he played a demo of a version that had been written by Mike Stoller and Jerry Leiber, two of the hottest young songwriters out there. Even as a demo, the song knocked us out.

"Damn, Elvis," I said. "Little Richard would give his right arm for something like that."

"Yeah, but he ain't getting it," said Elvis. "That's the one I'm cutting."

Up until this point, there really hadn't been much time for "companionship" while Elvis was on tour. But once Elvis, Gene, Arthur, and I boarded the train out of Memphis's Central Station for the three-day trip to the West Coast, it was a very different situation. This time, Elvis had me stay with him in his train compartment instead of Gene. He had a specific task for me in mind: He wanted to work with me on his *Jailhouse Kid* script.

I think it's important to mention just how hard Elvis worked at what he did, including being a film actor. He was a big enough star that he certainly could have gotten away with being lazy or difficult, and I think that's what Hollywood expected of him at first. But starting with *Love Me Tender,* Elvis made sure he knew his script backward and forward and was always on the set on time and ready to work.

So, as the trip began, I would read the lines of every other character in the movie, and Elvis would practice his lines. (When I saw that there was a role for a disc jockey in the film, I thought I might be up for it, but that part eventually went to actor Dean Jones.) This became the first stretch of quality one-on-one time I'd had with Elvis in a while, and as we got the script work done, sitting across from each other in the tight quarters of that sleeping compartment, Elvis began to relax and talk with me in a more personal way than he ever had before. So much had happened to him in just a couple of years that I think he appreciated the chance to speak freely about anything and everything to someone he could trust.

"You know why I dye my hair, GK?" he asked, setting the script aside.

"Why's that, Elvis?"

"The blond-headed guys in Hollywood don't last long," he said. "The guys with dark hair and dark looks—Clark Gable, Tony Curtis, Brando—they get a better career."

He told me that during the screen test for *Loving You*, the Paramount makeup department had wanted to darken his hair to play off his blue eyes. He told them to go as dark as they could, and he liked the results so much that he didn't just go with the look on screen—he started dyeing his hair all the time.

The second night of the trip, I was reading the script with Elvis and getting into one of the climactic scenes between Elvis's character, Vince Everett, and Vince's prison-buddy-turned-rival Hunk Houghton, played in the movie by Mickey Shaughnessy. I'd read one of Hunk's more intense lines and was waiting for Elvis's response. But he just peered out the train window at the lights flashing by us and gently put the script down.

"I wonder what they think now, GK," he said quietly.

"Who, Elvis?"

"All the guys who put me down and told me I wouldn't amount to anything. All the people who said I didn't have a shot at making something of myself."

"You've been through an awful lot to get where you are, Elvis."

He looked at me hard with a kind of twisted smile. "Eddie Bond, man. Eddie Bond."

"What happened with Eddie Bond?"

Bond was a Memphis country disc jockey who moonlighted with a country band. In 1954 his band had been looking for a singer, and Elvis had auditioned for him.

"He told me, 'You ain't got it,'" said Elvis. "Just about broke my heart."

Elvis went on to talk about playing with Scotty and Bill at the Grand Ole Opry—a gig he'd wanted so badly that Sam Phillips had helped set up the appearance. They'd played "Blue Moon of Kentucky" to polite applause, and afterward the Opry's longtime talent manager, Jim Denny, told Elvis that he just didn't think Elvis was the right kind of act for the legendary venue.

"Same damn thing," said Elvis. "Told me to keep driving a truck. We thought we were on our way, and that about crushed me."

He told me about a dispiriting audition for Arthur Godfrey's television show—a program that was a real career maker back in 1955. He and the band had been snickered at there, and hadn't even met Godfrey. Elvis was told not to expect a phone call; a letter would be sent out if he made the cut. Elvis said he spent a month getting angry and depressed every time the mail arrived without a word from the show.

We talked and talked and talked some more. Elvis had Gene and Arthur bring us some dinner, and we kept talking. I told him about the ups and downs of my radio career, I told him Dewey Phillips stories, and I told him more personal things about myself than I think I'd ever shared with anybody. He told me more and more about what he'd been through—and it certainly wasn't all negative. I learned that after one of his Ed Sullivan appearances, he answered a knock on his dressing-room door to discover a voluptuous European starlet who proceeded to kiss him in places he'd never been kissed before.

"I don't know if what she did has a name," he said. "But I didn't fight it."

When we got back to a more serious discussion about careers, he told me he was particularly proud that he'd stood up for the sound he'd developed with Sam Phillips when he made the jump from Sun to RCA.

"Sam gave me the best advice I ever got," said Elvis. "He said, 'Whatever you do—wherever you go—don't let them change your style.' He said that when I went to Nashville, I had to look out for the country guys because they resented what I was doing and weren't gonna know what to do with me. Sam said, 'Don't let them put you in a country bag. I'm not going to be there and the Colonel isn't gonna know what I'm talking about. You've got to stand up for yourself.' He was right."

Elvis went on to explain that at his first Nashville session, the group worked with Chet Atkins, the legendary country guitarist who was also a record producer. When the group started warming up and running through their first tune, Atkins approached Scotty Moore and started giving him some friendly pointers on guitar playing. Scotty was flattered, because here was Mr. Guitar giving him a private lesson. And Atkins's tips were probably good ones. But Elvis remembered what Sam had told him.

"GK, I thought to myself, 'Oh, shit—here we go into that bag.' And it took all the guts in the world to do it, but I did it."

"Did what, Elvis?"

"I went over and said, 'Mr. Atkins, we appreciate your guidance, but we've got our own style and I wish you wouldn't tell my guitar player how to play.'"

"What happened?"

"Well, I knew Mr. Atkins was a little ticked, because I could see the hair on the back of his neck stand up," laughed Elvis. "But I had to do it. I had to speak up. It wasn't my nature, but I had to do it. My career was on the line."

"Have you seen Chet Atkins again?"

"Yeah, but we don't talk much," said Elvis. "We just kind of nod at each other."

Elvis and I kept talking through the night. I remember him telling me that he hated strings on rock 'n' roll records, and wasn't happy that Marty Robbins had recorded "That's All Right, Mama" after Elvis showed him how to play it backstage at the Grand Ole Opry. He talked about his love of gospel music, and we exchanged memories about times at the Memphis Fairgrounds.

Somewhere along the tracks, as that train hurtled toward Hollywood, I crossed into a new territory with Elvis. I'd thought of him as a rising star who I just happened to be friends with. Now it felt flipped around: The closest friend I'd ever had just happened to be Elvis Presley.

CHAPTER FIVE

Penthouse Rock

I'd thought that life on the road with Elvis was pretty sweet, but living the Hollywood life with Elvis was even sweeter.

We stayed at the luxurious Beverly Wilshire hotel, which to me looked like every Hollywood dream I'd ever had come true. Elvis was in the presidential suite—a beautiful layout of rooms that was so big I think you could have fit a few of our North Memphis homes inside it. There was a long hallway that led to the bedrooms Elvis and Gene Smith took, while Arthur Hooton and I settled into the smaller, though equally magnificent, penthouse rooms. (When Elvis slept in, Arthur and I would have breakfast on the rooftop terrace and feel like kings of the world.) No sooner had we checked in than the group was rejoined by smooth talker Cliff Gleaves, who took the third bedroom in the presidential suite and got us even more excited about where we were with his almost nonstop hepcat cheerleading ("Hollywood! Elvis! M-G-M! Let the good times roll, baby!"). The band took a look at the Beverly Wilshire but quickly decided to check in over at the Knickerbocker Hotel in the middle of Hollywood. The Colonel was with us, in a room a few floors below.

Elvis's first order of work was to record his new film's soundtrack. Songwriters Jerry Leiber and Mike Stoller—who had a string of hits such as "Kansas City," "Searchin'," and the Elvis smash "Hound Dog"—were developing the movie material for Elvis, and, in a departure from the way

Elvis sessions were usually run, the writers would be present in the room as Elvis recorded their songs. At first, the pair didn't seem to be particularly thrilled about working with Elvis. But when they got a sense of how hard he was willing to work and how much he knew about favorite artists they had in common—such as Ray Charles and Ruth Brown—Leiber, Stoller, and Elvis began to work as a powerhouse team.

The first thing to be worked on was the theme song Leiber and Stoller had come up with, "Jailhouse Rock." The movie to be made was still being called *Jailhouse Kid*, to distinguish it from some of the quickie rock 'n' roll films that were being cranked out at the time: *Rock, Pretty Baby; Don't Knock the Rock; Rock, Rock, Rock.* But when Elvis ripped into what Leiber and Stoller had written for him, it was clear to everybody at the session, and quickly clear to everybody at MGM, that this song was one of Elvis's finest performances and destined to be his next number-one hit. (It was.) So, after one day's work, *Jailhouse Kid* was out and *Jailhouse Rock* was in. I got goosebumps watching the way Elvis threw himself into the song, and I felt that a rock 'n' roll song just couldn't be packed with more energy and excitement than what Elvis put into that one.

However, on the second day of recording, things did not go as smoothly. MGM wanted to save a little time and money by having Elvis record on a movie-lot soundstage rather than at a recording studio, and though Elvis agreed to this arrangement, he wasn't entirely comfortable with it. The soundstage was a huge room, and Elvis was never at ease recording in that kind of space. He was an advocate of Sam Phillips's belief that rock 'n' roll was meant to be recorded in small spaces, where intimate performances were easier to deliver, and where the compact sound of close walls added something indefinable to the beat and the feel. Elvis had nailed "Jailhouse Rock" the first day, but the second morning, he felt he needed to warm up to get into a recording mood. So he did what he always did to warm up— he sat at the piano and sang gospel tunes. At ten A.M., he had the Jordanaires gathered around him singing spirituals, and at noon they were still singing spirituals. When the break for lunch was called, not a bit of soundtrack recording had been done.

When we returned to the soundstage, Elvis went straight to the piano and started singing another gospel tune. But this time Gordon Stoker and Hugh Jarrett and the rest of the Jordanaires didn't join him—they just kind of shuffled their feet and seemed to be taking pains to stay as far away from the piano as they could. This puzzled Elvis, who called out to them to come over and sing. They responded by just shuffling their feet some more.

"Come here, Gordon, what's wrong with you?" asked Elvis, a little sharply. "Don't you want to sing spirituals with me?"

Gordon came over and said, "Can I be honest, Elvis?"

"Yeah."

"The studio people told us not to sing gospel with you. They want you to get on with the session."

"*What?*" hollered Elvis, looking like he was ready to take a swing at somebody. He glared around the big room, took a deep breath, then turned back to his backup singer. "Gordon, who signs your check—me or MGM?"

"You do, Elvis."

"Well, get the Jordanaires over here and let's sing some more gospel."

The singers joined Elvis around the soundstage piano, and they did sing gospel—for another four hours. When the five P.M. quitting time rolled around, not a single *Jailhouse Rock* song had been cut.

After the session, Arthur and Gene and Cliff and I all piled into a limousine with Elvis for the ride back to the Beverly Wilshire, and while we made small talk about the beautiful Hollywood women we'd already spotted, Elvis didn't say one word.

Back in the presidential suite, Elvis headed straight to one of the dens, a room done up in high style with smoked-glass windows, museum-quality paintings in beautiful frames, and a huge framed mirror that took up almost a whole wall. It also had a little bumper pool table in it. Elvis picked up a pool cue and starting shooting the balls around the pool table, still without saying anything to us. Then he set up the balls to do a trick shot that we'd seen him do before: He could make one ball jump over another and drop into a corner pocket. He lined up the shot but hit the cue ball much harder than he needed to—it caromed off the table, hit a little smoked-glass end table, and shattered it.

A collective *Oh, shit* came out of the group watching, but Elvis didn't even smile. He just positioned another ball on the table and this time took deliberate aim at a painting on the wall. He hit the ball even harder and made it take off like a rocket. Sure enough, it hit the painting dead center and completely shattered its glass frame. We were still all kind of hoping that he was kidding around, so I said, "Elvis, I never liked that painting over there on the other wall—see if you can hit that one."

Almost before I finished speaking, he'd fired off another ball and shattered that painting's glass. One of the other guys pointed out a small mirror that looked liked an antique.

Bull's-eye. It was shattered.

We ran out into the hallway to avoid the flying glass and peeped back in to call out target suggestions. But Elvis wasn't waiting for suggestions. He just moved around the table firing off shots and shattering just about everything in that room that was breakable, including the wall-sized mirror. As much as we wanted what was happening to feel like boys-will-be-boys fun, it was obvious that Elvis was in a dark, dark mood. When he ran out of balls to shoot, he turned the pool cue around in his hands and began to swing it like a golf club at the bumpers on the pool table. They shot off like missiles and broke the large windows across the room. When the bumpers were all knocked off, Elvis threw the pool cue down, grabbed the edge of the pool table, heaved it over, and kicked it until the table itself was cracked. Then he barreled past us, muttering that he wanted his dinner sent to his room.

We were all aware that Elvis had a temper, but this kind of thing was way out of character. He'd been the one who'd made us promise to him that we weren't ever going to trash the places we stayed in: Elvis and rock 'n' roll in general were already looked down upon by a lot of folks, and he didn't want us to do anything to add to the negative image.

I did what I thought was the responsible thing to do: I called the Colonel. I let him know that Elvis was okay, but that something had occurred that needed his attention. He came up to our rooms quickly, and I saw a look of great concern on his face. I took him to the damaged den and tried to explain as best I could what we'd witnessed.

"All right," he said to the assembled group. "I don't want anybody to talk about what happened up here tonight. I want you to get all the sheets and bedding off all of your beds and hang them over the mirrors and the windows and the pool table and everything else that's been destroyed. Cover it all, then stay out of this room."

"What are you going to do, Colonel?" I asked.

"I'm going to go downstairs and tell the management that you guys had a wild party and trashed the room and that we'll be more than happy to pay for everything."

He turned and left, never speaking to Elvis.

I'm not sure if Elvis came out of his room again until a day later when the next recording session was rescheduled. We had our nine A.M. pickup and Elvis still didn't say a word on the ride to the studio. He walked onto the soundstage, sat down at the piano, and began singing gospel tunes. I believe I saw the faces of some of the studio representatives go white, but after just a few songs Elvis was ready. He put in a full, energized day of work that basically got the rest of the *Jailhouse* soundtrack recorded.

Looking back on the whole incident, it reminds me of how fiercely Elvis cared about his music in those years. He was very willing to do what was asked of him up to a point, but when anyone or anything interfered with his process as a musician, that furious tiger in him was unleashed.

Elvis was becoming one of the biggest stars the world had ever seen, but it's important to keep in mind that in 1957, Elvis was still only twenty-two years old. What's amazing to me is how rare the explosions of temper were, and how beautifully he handled the demands of fame and his work schedule most of the time. Gene, Arthur, Cliff, and I tried to offer support to him as best we could, but we were just kids, too, and it was hard for us not to be a little dizzy in the Hollywood world we were living in.

Elvis was never very interested in becoming a part of the Hollywood social scene or the celebrity party circuit, but the weekend before production began on *Jailhouse Rock*, he decided to take us out for a couple nights on the town. When we took a look at who was performing in the Los Angeles nightclubs, there was no question where we'd be heading. Dean Martin had always been one of Elvis's favorite singers—one of the few singers he'd ever cite as a personal influence on his own style. Dean was doing a show at a Hollywood Club called the Moulin Rouge, a phenomenal showplace with a full-scale floor show where the Emmy-award dinners were sometimes held. We were off to the Moulin Rouge.

We saw a great Dino performance, and after the show Elvis asked me if I wanted to meet Dean. Cliff and Gene stayed at our table, while Elvis and I headed backstage. Dean and Elvis had met before when Elvis was in L.A., and Dean seemed very happy to see him again. They made some showbiz-style small talk, and then, right in front of Dean, Elvis turned to me and said, "You know, GK, Dean Martin gave me the best advice I ever got from anybody in Hollywood." Dean kind of laughed, but Elvis was very serious, and he continued.

"Dean told me, 'You and I are singers, not actors, and if we try to act we're gonna be dead in the water. It's gonna come off phony.' Dean said that what I had to do was be as natural as possible in front of the camera and not try to do any real acting until I really learned how to act. Man, that got me through two movies."

"That's great advice," I said. Dean laughed again and I think he actually blushed a little. But it also seemed to me that he really appreciated the heartfelt gratitude Elvis was expressing. And I've always felt that if you listen to Elvis's recording of "Suspicion," you can hear just how strong an influence Dean had on Elvis's phrasing. Both of them could make a brilliant performance sound so easy and so natural.

I remember one other night at the Moulin Rouge when we caught a performance by Billy Ward and the Dominoes, who were still knocking out a great version of "Sixty-Minute Man." Billy acknowledged the visiting star out in his audience by introducing "Elvis 'the Mighty Pelvis'

Presley." Elvis had a great sense of humor, but I knew he had never been happy about being tagged with the "Pelvis" nickname. This night, though, he leaned over to me with a smile and said, "You know, the way Billy Ward puts the 'Mighty' in there, I kind of like it."

A few days later, it was time for Elvis to report to the MGM lot, where he was given the biggest, nicest dressing room available—one that had been Clark Gable's. I'd been thrilled to break into radio, to see the real nuts-and-bolts business behind the voices and music I heard on my radio dial. Getting the chance to be inside Hollywood—in the company of Elvis Presley, no less—was even more thrilling, and I treated every moment on the MGM set like it was showbiz grad school. I was fascinated by the way sets were built, the way scenes were lit, where microphones were placed to record dialogue, how the actors were guided through their performances by the director. A lot of times the other guys were off playing cards or flirting with pretty extras, but I watched the production around Elvis like a hawk.

Anybody who's been on a film set knows, however, that there are some long stretches of downtime, and when things weren't particularly interesting on the *Jailhouse Rock* set, I got in the habit of wandering around the MGM lot to see what else was going on. Sometimes I wandered with Elvis and the other guys: In fact, one of our first days on the lot, we were all thrown off the set of *The Brothers Karamazov*. We were there so that Elvis could say hello to Yul Brynner, with whom he'd struck up an improbable friendship when they'd both worked on the Paramount lot. We didn't see Yul, but we began to whisper about the fact that the *Karamazov* director was Richard Brooks, who'd also directed one of our favorite films, *Blackboard Jungle*. We must've whispered a little too loudly, because after a moment Brooks hollered into the shadows where we were standing, "I don't know who you sons of bitches are, but this is a closed set and I want you the hell off of it." (When Brooks later heard who he'd booted out, he sent Elvis a warm invitation back to the set, and we did in fact hang out a bit with Mr. Brynner.) Another day, Cliff Gleaves and I commandeered an empty rehearsal room and Cliff, who had a fair amount of musical talent, began playing a piano there. It took a moment before we realized we had been joined by a dapper older gentleman.

"I just wrote this song," Cliff called out to the visitor in his typically breezy way. "What do you think?"

"Very nice," the visitor answered. "Needs work, but very nice."

It was only later we figured out that Cliff had been critiqued by Cole Porter, who was on the lot to work on the musical *Les Girls*.

I got a real thrill from seeing certain movie stars up close—I remember running out of Elvis's dressing room as fast as I could to get a good look at bombshell actress Kim Novak. Other times, it was the Hollywood folks who came up to me, in hopes of getting closer to Elvis. One of the nicest of these was a young actor named Vince Edwards, who was getting small movie parts and would eventually become famous starring as the TV doctor Ben Casey. Vince got along with Elvis and the group so well that he began hanging out at the Beverly Wilshire with us. So did Rafael Campos, the young Latino character actor who'd delivered some of Elvis's favorite lines in *Blackboard Jungle*.

Vince also introduced us to a fellow who became one of the most memorable and entertaining of the characters around Elvis—Billy Murphy. Murphy was an older bit player who had a long string of credits in war movies and westerns, including a notable role in one of Elvis's favorite John Wayne films, *The Sands of Iwo Jima*. Murphy was a true Hollywood character, often seen strutting up and down Hollywood Boulevard, looking like a grizzled gunfighter all dressed in black. When he spoke you always got the sense that he was letting you in on some dark mystery. I heard from someone that Billy had been a local football star, so I asked him one day, "Billy, did you make all-American when you played at USC?"

"Yes, mister," he answered. "But somebody else got credit for it."

No further explanation was forthcoming. That was Billy Murphy. And the more he began hanging out with us, the more we Elvis guys picked up on his habit of calling everyone "Mister."

One very big Hollywood celebrity actually turned up at our door over at the Beverly Wilshire. I answered a knock one night to discover the large figure of actor Robert Mitchum in our hallway, a bottle of whiskey in one hand and a script in the other.

"I'm Bob," he said. "What's your name?"

I introduced myself, showed him in, and went to tell Elvis who was in our sitting room. I knew this was one star Elvis would enjoy meeting: More than once he'd told us that Mitchum had the best walk of any movie star. Elvis and Mitchum did seem to hit it off when they met, before long exchanging stories of their hardscrabble backgrounds— Mitchum said he'd first come to Hollywood by hopping freight trains across the country and taking his meals at the hobo villages along the rails. When Elvis talked about some of the fights he'd gotten into early in his career with roughnecks who'd come at him after shows, Mitchum answered with a story of how he'd once fought off an obnoxious fan in a restaurant by bending a fork around his fist and punching the guy in the chin.

Elvis was more relaxed with Bob than with most of the celebrities I'd seen him deal with, and eventually Mitchum explained that he'd brought the script for a film called *Thunder Road* because he thought it was something he and Elvis could do together. Mitchum himself had come up with the story, and right there in the Beverly Wilshire he and Elvis began reading the pages out loud. Elvis got excited about the writing and said he wanted to do the film. At the end of the night, he asked Mitchum to give a call to Colonel Parker to work out details.

We saw Mitchum again a few days later at his house. Mitchum understood that Elvis was uncomfortable at big Hollywood parties, so he set up a small dinner party for a dozen or so guests. Elvis brought Arthur and me, and it really was a lovely evening. But Elvis's involvement in *Thunder Road* never made it past the Colonel's involvement. The Colonel claimed that Elvis had too many obligations to fulfill and too many film contracts already pending to take on Mitchum's project, but I think the real problem was that he was unhappy that someone had gotten straight to Elvis without going through him. Mitchum went on to make *Thunder Road* without

Elvis, and even had a minor hit record singing the movie's theme song himself. Unfortunately it wouldn't be the last time that Elvis's enthusiasm for a creative project would be undercut.

As production began on *Jailhouse Rock,* there was one piece of work that Elvis was dreading: the dance sequence that accompanied the title song. As athletically as Elvis could move on stage, he was nervous about trying to execute some real Hollywood dance moves. The choreographer on the film, Alex Romero, was given a day to teach Elvis the steps, and I was with Elvis on that rehearsal day, in one of those classic dance-studio rooms with dance barres and mirrors along the walls.

Romero got right to work. He put on an acetate recording of "Jailhouse Rock" and went through the dance sequence, moving in a smooth, powerful style. When he finished, he looked to Elvis—who looked like his worst fears about dancing had come true.

"Alex," he said, "I can't do that. It's just not me. I'm a rock 'n' roll guy—I can't move like Gene Kelly."

"Will you try it?" asked Alex.

"Sure, I can try, but I don't think it'll be worth a damn."

Alex cued up the record again and led Elvis through the steps. And Elvis was right: It wasn't worth a damn. He just couldn't make Alex's moves seem natural for him. It looked like all of Romero's work was going to have to be scrapped, leaving a hole where the dance sequence should be. Then the choreographer had a flash of inspiration.

"Elvis—do you have some of your records over in your dressing room?"

"Yeah."

Romero sent me to get the records, which included Elvis's latest number one, "All Shook Up." While I was on that errand, the choreographer called the MGM sound department and had a speaker system and a microphone on a stand sent over to the dance studio. When the gear was set up, Romero turned back to us.

"Okay, Elvis, here's what I want you to do. George is going to play the music, and you get up like you're onstage. Use the microphone, and show me what you do in concert."

I played "Don't Be Cruel" and "All Shook Up" and Elvis went through all the best moves he'd been using onstage while he was on tour—windmilling his arms, working his hips and shaking his legs, snapping into dramatic poses in time with the music, and cutting loose with some knee slides on the floor.

"I've got it," said Romero, as the music came to an end. "Meet me back here tomorrow."

Elvis and I went back to that dance studio the next day, and I know he was still nervous about what to expect. But when Romero cued up "Jailhouse Rock" again and went through a new dance sequence, what we saw was a stroke of brilliance. Romero had taken all of Elvis's natural stage moves and turned them into a routine that fit what needed to be done in the scene. Now when the choreographer stopped dancing, Elvis looked ready for action.

"That's me, man," he said. "I can do that all day long."

The record got cued up again, Elvis had a go at it, and this time he looked even better at it than Romero. He and Romero worked the rest of the day on the flow of the sequence, with Elvis adding new moves when they felt right to him and fine-tuning what would go on to be considered one of the best dance sequences ever in a rock 'n' roll movie.

I wasn't able to be there when Elvis actually shot the dance sequence because I was in a Beverly Hills hospital receiving one of the most unusual and personal gifts Elvis ever gave me: a nose job. One of his makeup artists at MGM had told him about a top plastic surgeon in town, Dr. Maury Parks, and one day while he was still in his makeup chair he called me in and asked if I'd ever considered having my nose fixed. I had a prominent hooked nose at the time that wasn't made any prettier by a break that had never healed properly. I told Elvis that I'd thought about it, especially since I had hoped my radio work might someday lead to television work. But I knew that kind of surgery was something I couldn't possibly afford.

"Would you do it if I paid for it?" Elvis asked.

"Are you serious, Elvis?"

"Yeah. I'll pay for it. Let's get that thing trimmed down."

So that day I was in a limo headed to the office of Dr. Parks. And a day or two later, while Elvis was dancing at MGM, I was bandaged up in the hospital with a brand-new nose. I was just a few hours out of surgery when the phone rang. It was Elvis, checking up on me.

"GK, how's it going over there?"

"Fine, Elvis. Dr. Parks said everything went well. How are you doing?"

"Well, GK—I'm in the hospital, too."

"The hospital—what happened?"

"I got a dental cap in my lung," he said. "No big thing. You sure they're treating you right over there?"

While going through those athletic "Jailhouse Rock" dance moves, Elvis had inhaled one of the cosmetic caps he'd been wearing on his teeth for the film. At that time the studios had their own doctors and dentists, and the MGM dentist believed that Elvis had swallowed the cap and that it would, somewhat uncomfortably, work its way out. But Elvis knew something felt wrong, and when he told the Colonel how much it hurt and that he had doubts about the diagnosis, the Colonel did the right thing and put concern for Elvis's health above any concerns about holding up production. Elvis was rushed to the hospital, X-rayed, and had the lost cap suctioned out of his lung. I knew Elvis was starting to feel better when he asked me a final question on our hospital-to-hospital call.

"GK—how good-looking are the nurses over there?"

A big fellow named Lamar Fike—with whom Cliff and I had gotten friendly when I worked at WMC—drove straight to Los Angeles when he heard about Elvis being in the hospital. Lamar turned up out of the blue at the presidential suite, and, with Elvis's okay, moved right in.

A few days later, Elvis and I were both back on the *Jailhouse Rock* set, and Elvis was showing me around so that the nose he'd bought me could be admired. When he needed to report to the makeup department, he took me along to show off the nose to MGM's head makeup man, William Tuttle. Elvis had to wear a couple of different wigs in the course of the *Jailhouse* story as his character's hair grew out from a prison crew cut to a more familiar Elvis look. A studio barber was working to fit Elvis's head with the mesh that would be beneath the crew cut wig when the barber suddenly turned ashen and began to tremble.

"What's wrong?" I asked the guy.

"Mr. Presley," he said in a voice that was choked with distress, "I just cut a chunk of your hair off."

I could see Elvis bite his lip. "How bad is it?" he asked.

Before the barber could answer, Tuttle started chewing the guy out. Elvis sometimes jokingly called the makeup man "Wild" Bill Tuttle because he had such a calm and refined demeanor, but now Tuttle really was going wild. I knew how concerned Elvis always was with his hair, and if Elvis had acted the least bit upset, that barber would have been fired on the spot. But instead, Elvis stayed as calm as he could.

"Look, Mr. Tuttle. It was an honest mistake. This guy's just trying to do a good job. Just cover it up the best you can."

A few camera shots had to be changed over the next few days to favor the uncut side of Elvis's head, but things worked out okay, and the barber kept his job. Again, in a situation where a lot of stars might have had a temper tantrum and demanded a firing, Elvis was the star who stuck up for the little guy.

On one of our last days in Los Angeles, with filming completed, Elvis and I took a drive through Beverly Hills. (He's the only star I've ever known who really liked to be at the wheel of his own limo.) We were talking about what we might do back in Memphis, when we passed a little old lady in a beat-up beach chair who was selling maps to the stars' homes. We'd seen her almost every day on the way to the studio, but this time Elvis pulled the car over and said, "You know, she looks a little like my mother."

He got out of the car, walked over to her, talked with her for a bit, and then bought every one of her maps. That's one of the little moments I love to remember, because it reminds me of the generosity and compassion that were such a part of Elvis's spirit. Memphis friends, a studio barber, a little old lady in a beach chair: Elvis was willing to share some of that spirit with all of us.

At the end of June, Elvis and the rest of us boarded a train to head back to Memphis. The group now also included Gene Smith's brother Junior, who'd come out for a week's vacation at the end of the movie shoot. Junior was an ornery guy who was fighting off some demons—he'd served in the Korean War, had come home with what they used to call shell shock, and was now a heavy drinker and a chain-smoker who had trouble holding down a job. When he was drunk he was mean and belligerent, but when sober he was a pretty sharp and funny guy, and I'll always remember one of the great lines he delivered up in our hotel suite. When we were all just sitting around one night, Junior announced to Elvis, "Cuz, I ain't no queer, but you're a good-looking son of a bitch." This was especially funny to us because gossip rags of the day such as *Confidential* magazine were constantly going back and forth between claiming that we were a group of sex maniacs taking advantage of young girls and claiming that we were a group of rowdy Southern homosexuals.

Back in Memphis, it was a little strange to try to settle back into the rhythms of regular life after so many remarkable days and nights with Elvis. And it certainly felt a little strange to be back in my mom's little house across from Humes High after having lived in the Beverly Wilshire penthouse. But in some ways, I still remained Elvis's travel companion, even in Memphis. He and his family had just moved into the renovated Graceland, and rather than wanting to get away from the guys he'd been traveling with, Elvis wanted us to enjoy his new home with him. I'd thought the place was impressive before it was fixed up. Now, with the wrought-iron guitar gates at the entrance to the long driveway and the interior fully redecorated, the place really did feel like the home of a star. But I'd put the accent on "home," because despite some of the luxurious decor and appointments, the place already felt comfortable and welcoming.

Elvis had Graceland's basement rooms set up like the ultimate rock 'n' roll clubhouse. To the right of the stairs was a beautiful game room with a pool table. To the left was a large den—what became known as the TV room—an intimately lit space with low couches, jukebox, and a bar. (Elvis kept it stocked with ice cream and cold soda.) The week we got home from *Jailhouse Rock*, we had planned to get some fireworks and have a big party outdoors at Graceland on the Fourth of July, but we ended up partying in that basement just about all night long on the third. I got back to my house near dawn and hit the bed, expecting to sleep until noon at least. But around nine A.M. there was a knock on my door. My mother wasn't home, so I shook myself out of my sleep and went to answer it. There was Elvis.

"Have you heard?" was all he asked.

"No, Elvis. What's wrong?"

"Judy Tyler and her husband got killed in a car accident."

Judy had been Elvis's female costar in *Jailhouse Rock*, and he had developed a really sweet friendship with her. Judy, who'd been familiar to us as Princess Summerfall Winterspring from *The Howdy Doody Show*, was newly married as the film production began, so there'd been no romantic spark between her and Elvis, but the two shared a similar sense of humor and became very close very quickly.

"Get dressed, GK," said Elvis. "Come on out with us."

He had Arthur Hooton in his car, and as soon as I could jump into some clothes, the three of us started driving all through North Memphis, back through downtown, out on the rural roads—anywhere to just keep moving. Elvis was really upset and distraught, and he kept talking about how good a person Judy was. He drove and talked for hours, reminiscing about almost every moment he'd shared with her, and lamenting the fact that *Jailhouse Rock*—a movie she wouldn't ever get to see—could have been a breakthrough film for her. I'd seen the dark side of Elvis's temper, but I hadn't seen this depth of sadness in him before, and it made me want to do what I could to help him get through it. There really wasn't much to do, though, so Arthur and I just stayed with him all day as we drove without a destination.

A couple days later, on a Saturday afternoon, a group of us were in the Graceland basement watching television with Elvis. There was really only one thing to watch on a Saturday afternoon, and that was *Dance Party*, a local *American Bandstand*–type show that ran on WHBQ's TV station, hosted by a hot disc jockey friend of mine named Wink Martindale. Aside from the music on *Dance Party*, one of the attractions was the good-looking female cohosts that Wink would always have working with him, and for a while I'd been telling Elvis about how pretty the latest cohost was, a young girl named Anita Wood from Jackson, Tennessee. I'd met her through Wink, and I knew that in addition to her blonde hair and great figure she had intelligence, a fine sense of humor, and a warm, bubbly personality.

"Is that the girl you've been telling me about?" asked Elvis, pointing to the TV.

"Yeah, Elvis. That's Anita. I think you'd really like her."

"Set it up," he said.

Anita was already pretty serious about her own career, but the opportunity to go out with Elvis must have sounded exciting to her, and it didn't take too much doing to set up a date. As usual, Elvis took a couple of us guys with him as he drove his big black Cadillac limousine over to pick up Anita at the boardinghouse where she lived. Along the way we started being followed by a couple of cars of teenage girls, so when we got to Anita's place, Elvis stayed in the car and sent me out to get Anita. I went to the door and it was answered by a Memphis lady named Miss Patty, who ran the boardinghouse. Even though it wasn't my date, I wanted to make a good impression on Elvis's behalf.

"Good evening, ma'am. I'm George Klein, here to pick up Anita for her evening with Elvis."

"That's very nice, George," said Miss Patty. "But if Elvis were a real gentleman he'd come up here and pick her up himself."

"Well, Miss Patty, if you look down the street you'll see that some kids have been following us. If Elvis gets out of the car and comes up here, we're going to be stuck for an hour while he signs autographs."

Miss Patty peered out at the limo and the cars behind it, then looked back at me, furrowing her brow just a bit.

"If he was a gentleman, he'd come to the door."

I knew she had a point, and I also started to sense that if she was going to let one of her charges out on the town with Elvis, she wanted her own moment to look him over.

"Pardon me, ma'am."

I went back to the car and explained the situation to Elvis. He just laughed and hopped right out and up to the door. I made the introductions between Elvis and Miss Patty, then introduced Elvis to Anita. He was perfectly polite and thoroughly charming to Miss Patty, and I think by the time we left a few minutes later, she was convinced that Elvis was in fact a real gentleman. The kids behind us didn't hold us up too long, and soon we were all out on Elvis and Anita's first date, which consisted of a drive around Memphis and a stop for hamburgers. It was easy for Elvis to spend time with just about any pretty girl he desired, but you could tell when there was a little extra spark for him, and it was there right away with Anita.

Elvis had been involved with some steady girlfriends before—in fact, one of the traveling-companion jobs Elvis asked me to carry out was to act as a sort of go-between, letting some of the local girls down easy as his career took off. Now Elvis was a red-hot star, and it was hard to imagine him as a one-woman man. But Anita was strong and smart and beautiful, and Elvis quickly made her an important part of his life. She became the steadiest and most serious relationship he had had up to that point.

Between the time Elvis spent with Anita, his parents, his extended family, and the gang of Cliff, Lamar, and myself, it wasn't easy to have a moment alone with him. But I felt that's what I needed, because I wanted to let him know about something that had been heavy on my mind for a while. I had slowly come to the realization that as wonderful, incredible, and life-changing as it was to be invited into the dream come true of Elvis's life, there were some dreams of my own that I just hadn't been able to toss away. One afternoon, things were quiet around Graceland and Elvis was up in his bedroom by himself, so I took the opportunity to speak with him.

"Elvis, you're about the best friend I've ever had, and I can't thank you enough for everything you've done for me."

"You don't have to thank me," he said. But he could tell I had more to say. "What's wrong, GK?"

"Elvis, I don't know how to say this except just to say it—I really miss radio."

"Yeah, I can tell that, GK. It's what you're good at." He looked at me hard, waiting for me to go on.

"Well, Elvis—if you ever needed me for anything—anything at all— you know I'd be right here for you. But if you don't mind, I'd like to stop traveling with you and try to get back into radio. I did have a little career going, and I just don't want to say goodbye to that completely."

He nodded slowly, then spoke.

"I don't blame you at all, GK. You ought to be doing what you love doing. I respect that. But remember this—you've got an open invitation to come back with me anytime. You want to come out to Hollywood for one of the movies or go back out on a tour, we'll make a place for you."

"That'd be great, Elvis. Thank you."

"And one more thing—you'll still come over here whenever I'm home."

"I can do that for sure, Elvis."

We moved on to some small talk, and I realized that I'd never felt more encouraged or supported by anyone. Elvis had welcomed me along into a world of rock 'n' roll parties, beautiful women, waiting limousines, Hollywood movies, and the VIP treatment in a Beverly Hills penthouse, but he wasn't the least bit upset that I was asking to step away from all that to go back to an uncertain future as a disc jockey. He wasn't slighted or insulted—he just seemed concerned that I'd remain in his circle of friends. He didn't need to worry about that; I'd stick around.

My timing seemed perfect for a return to radio. My mentor Bill Grumbles was back at WHBQ, and when I got in touch with him, right away he said he felt bad about the way I'd been treated at WMC—the station that fired me because they didn't see a future in rock 'n' roll. Mr. Grumbles had an offer for me: He thought that if I took WHBQ's afternoon radio slot leading into Dewey Phillips's nighttime show, it'd be a dynamite combination. In terms of a working situation, that sounded great to me, though the truth was that on a social level, Dewey and I weren't such a dynamite combination anymore.

Elvis and I had had a bit of a falling-out with Dewey after he came to L.A. for a visit during the making of *Jailhouse Rock*. Rather than easing into the new environment Elvis was working in, Dewey cranked up his Memphis "Daddy-O" persona and managed to rub a lot of people the wrong way. Among those people was Yul Brynner: When Elvis introduced Dewey to his actor friend, Dewey's salutation was, "My, you're a short little mother, aren't you?"—obviously embarrassing Elvis a great deal. Dewey ended his Hollywood trip by taking Elvis's personal acetate copy of his next single, "Teddy Bear," and playing it on the radio before it had been officially released by RCA. Some of this Elvis shrugged off as Dewey being Dewey, but he was less forgiving when he received a distressed call from his mother just before we got home from filming *Jailhouse Rock*. Dewey, apparently full of drink, had somehow gotten through the Graceland gates in the wee hours of the morning and had pounded on the front door. He put a terrible fright into Mr. and Mrs. Presley, who had to talk him down and turn him away.

Within a week after my conversation with Mr. Grumbles, I sat in one afternoon at WHBQ so the rest of station management could hear me at work. It was fantastic to be back behind the microphone, and all my experiences with Elvis gave me that much more rock 'n' roll confidence. As I pattered through my intros to "Whole Lotta Shakin' Goin' On" by Jerry Lee Lewis, "Youngblood" by the Coasters (another great song written by Leiber and Stoller), and "Bye Bye Love" by a new act called the Everly Brothers, I felt once more that I was right where I wanted to be.

Unfortunately, the feeling didn't last long. The next day Mr. Grumbles called me again and asked if I could meet with him along with the station's general manager and sales manager. They all told me they liked my work, but that Dewey Phillips had told the station he would quit if they hired me. The station had decided to stick with Dewey.

I felt absolutely horrible. I left the meeting and ran things through again and again, trying to figure out why Dewey would undercut me that way. Was it just because we weren't as close as we had been? Did he see the fact that I had become closer to Elvis as some kind of threat? I didn't know, but the more I thought about it, the angrier I got. That week, when I bumped into an old college friend who was now working as a reporter for the local paper, I let the anger get the better of me and told the reporter that while I couldn't give him anything on Elvis, I did have something pretty hot about Dewey. I proceeded to tell him about Dewey's drunken incident at the front door of Graceland. This was a scoop, as Elvis and his family had kept it out of the papers, not wanting any readers to get the idea that it was easy to get through the Graceland gates.

I was in the Graceland kitchen the next day when Elvis picked up that morning's newspaper. He read for a minute or two before something caught his attention.

"Damn. Did you see this, GK?"

I looked at the paper and saw a story about Dewey bothering Mr. and Mrs. Presley. I quickly scanned the piece and saw that I hadn't been named or quoted.

"Who could have told that reporter about that?" Elvis asked.

"I don't know, Elvis."

He didn't react much to it, and we sat there a while longer before he went upstairs to change his clothes. I sat by myself for what seemed like an awfully long time, feeling worse and worse as the seconds ticked by. I didn't particularly care if I never spoke to Dewey again, but I'd just been untruthful to Elvis and that really bothered me. I headed upstairs and found him combing his hair.

"Elvis, I can't lie to you."

"What are you talking about, GK?"

"I didn't come clean with you just now. It was me who told that reporter about Dewey." I went on to explain the whole situation to him—how I'd had a chance at the WHBQ job and how Dewey had shot it down. "I was just feeling so hurt, Elvis. I did it for revenge. It was stupid to talk to the reporter and stupid to lie to you, and I'm sorry. I'm sorry for you, and I'm sorry for your parents."

I learned a lesson that day that I'd see borne out many times over the years: If you created any kind of trouble or problem that involved Elvis, the best thing to do was to go to him and tell him about it straight-up. If he heard it from you first, it wasn't a problem. If he heard about it some other way, it could be a big problem and he might never speak to you again. Going to him that day and confessing was something that carried through my entire association with Elvis because he knew—and would say to me and to others—that I was one of the guys who would never lie to him.

Still, having his family dragged into the papers wasn't the kind of thing he just shrugged off. He didn't look my way as he continued to comb his hair. Finally, he said, "It's all right, George. Don't worry about it. Mama likes you—always has. And if Dewey catches hell for scaring my parents half to death, that's fine by me."

Hours later, as a group of us was getting ready to go out to a private midnight movie screening, Elvis made it clear that our friendship was still solid.

"So, GK, you don't have another radio job lined up?" he asked.

"No, Elvis, not yet."

"We got a Northwest tour coming up. I think you better come along."

I could do that. If WHBQ wasn't ready to let me do some rockin' and rollin' in Memphis, I'd hit the road and do some more rockin' and rollin' with the King.

CHAPTER SIX

Pan Pacific

How many Elvis fans does it take to derail a train?

I can't tell you exactly, but we came awfully close to finding out on the Northwest tour at the end of the summer of 1957. Elvis had gone from being a singing star to becoming an absolute national sensation, and it wasn't just the young girls who wanted to get close to him—he could create a commotion just about everywhere he went. As our Memphis train headed into some remote stretches of the American West, hundreds of people would show up at tiny depots to watch us speed by, and when the train made its stops in small towns, it seemed the entire population was there to try to get a look at Elvis. At a couple of stops, when they didn't get the glimpse they were after, the crowd decided to try to shake Elvis out, and actually began pushing on the train hard enough to rock it on its tracks. I wanted to assume that there was no way a crowd could tip a whole train over, but the panicked look on the faces of some of the conductors made me think otherwise.

The nights were quieter, and Lamar, Cliff, and I discovered the beauty of the train's dome car—the glass-topped lounge that allowed for some amazing views of the star-filled Western sky. Elvis generally stayed in his cabin to avoid creating a scene, but one late night as we wound our way through the Rocky Mountains, the dome car was empty and he came out to join us. We were enjoying ourselves when a young teenage girl entered the car. She came down the aisle and stopped next to Elvis, her eyes wide with disbelief.

"Johnny Cash!" she said in an excited whisper.

We started laughing, but Elvis quickly hushed us and started talking to the girl. She told him how much she loved his—Johnny Cash's—records and how she'd been to one of his—Cash's—shows. Finally, she asked, "Johnny, would you sing me one of your songs?"

Elvis would never sing one of his own songs in that type of situation, but for this little Johnny Cash fan he dropped his voice to its lowest notes and started singing a few lines of "Hey Porter," a song Cash had cut at Sun that seemed especially appropriate for a midnight train ride. The girl was thrilled, and even ended up with an autograph from Elvis, which read: "Best Wishes, Johnny Cash."

The commotion we experienced on the train was only magnified at concerts. In Vancouver, I was sent to scout out the football field where Elvis was going to perform for twenty-five thousand fans, and what I discovered unnerved me. A stage had been set up at one end of the field, with a series of iron spikes set in front of it as a small security barrier. But there were no seats on the field: Tickets had been sold to fill only the open bleachers around the field. The Royal Mounties were going to be providing security, and I asked one what was going to stop fans from rushing out of the stands. He told me it had been well publicized that anyone who stepped on the field would be fined a hundred dollars. I told him to get ready to write a whole lot of tickets.

As the evening began, people did take their seats and stayed off the field. The concert began with Elvis, in his gold suit, taking a kind of preshow warm-up lap as he sat on the back of a Cadillac convertible and was driven around the field's track to wave hello to everybody. Right away you could feel a rumble of excitement that was rising to a barely containable level. When the car got Elvis to the stage, he ran up, ready to start with his big opener, "Heartbreak Hotel." And he did something he liked to do—he really milked that first word: "Wellll . . ."

Boom. There were suddenly twenty-five thousand Canadians charging the stage, not slowed in the least by the threat of a hundred-dollar ticket. The first ones to get close to the stage bounded right over the security spikes, even ripping some of them out of the ground. It was scary enough that even Colonel Parker looked taken aback, and he had us run out and get Elvis off the stage and into a curtained-off, makeshift backstage area. The Colonel told Elvis that if he played with the audience and got them worked up any more than they were, we'd be lucky to get out of there alive.

"Calm them down," said the Colonel. "Tell them to get in their seats and you'll give them a good show."

Elvis went out and did manage to calm the crowd down. It took about twenty minutes before everyone was off the field and back in their seats again. Finally the band took its place and Elvis started the show again.

"Since my baby left me . . ." he sang, giving his leg one of its famous shakes.

Boom. The same scene all over again. This time even more of the security spikes were ripped out and more people got right up to the stage, which wasn't all that substantial to begin with. We whisked Elvis backstage again, and then I saw something I'd never seen before. Colonel Parker himself hustled out onstage and grabbed Elvis's microphone.

"Ladies and gentlemen," he bellowed. "This is a security situation. You cannot charge the stage—you're putting Elvis and yourselves at risk of injury. You must take your seats."

All those Canadians just stood on the field staring at him, not making a move toward the seats. After a quick meeting with the Royal Mounties, the Colonel addressed the crowd again and told them that they could stay on the field if they didn't rush the stage. Elvis went out again and did a quick thirty-minute set, then ran off as quick as he could, sprinting around the limo that had brought us there to jump into a police car behind it.

As he sped off, Bill Black, D. J. Fontana, Scotty Moore, and I jumped into the limo. Scotty was at the wheel, but before he could pull away there were fans swarming all over the car, thinking that Elvis was somewhere behind the tinted windows. They started rocking the car and just about pulling it apart—somebody tore the license plate off, another got the antenna. It really was terrifying, and poor Scotty wasn't sure what to do. I hollered for him to lay on the horn and step on the gas, and we managed to start moving forward without rolling over anybody. I remember looking out the back window and seeing a full rock 'n' roll riot breaking out: The fans had actually knocked over and demolished the entire stage, grabbing up broken bits of wood and music gear for souvenirs. I also remember noting one delicate detail: The sheets of paper on which the band had written their set lists were gracefully wafting through the air, floating just above the chaos.

After a few more equally crazy concerts, we were back in Los Angeles, where Elvis was going to record a Christmas album for RCA at Radio Recorders studio. Elvis had a good time bringing his style to some holiday classics, and he was particularly happy when he and the band worked up a version of "White Christmas" patterned after one by Clyde McPhatter and the Drifters. (It sounded great to me, though it would be denounced by its writer, Irving Berlin.) Elvis was working closely again with Leiber and Stoller, whom he'd come to think of as his good-luck charms in the studio. At one of the session breaks, Elvis asked the writers if they could come up with a real pretty ballad for him. This wasn't their specialty, but they said they'd try, and left the studio. Elvis continued recording, and at the end of the day we went back to our Los Angeles home, the wonderful Beverly Wilshire hotel.

Late that night I answered a knock at the door of the presidential suite to find Leiber and Stoller standing there with an acetate. In less than a day they'd written a song for Elvis and cut a demo of it with a popular session singer named Young Jessie. Elvis wanted to hear it right away, so we all headed to the den that had a record player in it. Elvis put the record on, and as soon as the song began he looked as happy as a kid on Christmas morning. I felt it, too. The song, "Don't," was a little masterpiece.

"Oh, shit," I said. "That's great."

"Oh, shit, is right," said Elvis. "I'm cutting this tomorrow."

He did, and his performance of the song made it even more of a masterpiece. Unfortunately, the Colonel turned up in the studio while the song was being recorded, and when he found out that the writers had committed the unpardonable sin of bringing a song straight to Elvis instead of going through Hill and Range publishing, he hit the roof and chewed out the writers like they were misbehaving brats rather than what they were: artists who'd just created Elvis's next number-one hit.

His lack of appreciation for their talents was made increasingly clear the following day. When Elvis mentioned to the writers that he really liked Charles Brown's sexy holiday song "Merry Christmas Baby," Leiber and Stoller disappeared into a little room in the back of the studio for no more than twenty minutes and came back with "Santa Claus Is Back in Town" for Elvis. Elvis loved it, but the Colonel's comment to the writers was, "What took you so long?"

Unfortunately, the writers weren't the only talents around Elvis that the Colonel failed to appreciate. When Elvis first began recording and performing, he and Scotty Moore and Bill Black had come up with a handshake agreement that would give each of the musicians a percentage of everything Elvis earned. But when the Colonel signed Elvis, Scotty and Bill became salaried players, and not very highly salaried players at that. As a small bonus, Elvis had said that Scotty, Bill, and D.J. could use some of his session time at Radio Recorders in order to cut some of their own instrumentals, which they intended to release as the EP *Continentals.*

After Elvis finished his Christmas album work, Scotty and Bill began to move their equipment around for their own session. That's when Tom Diskin, the Colonel's not-much-liked "lieutenant," appeared and told them that there had been a change of plans: They weren't going to get any session time after all. I'd been standing around looking forward to hearing what the guys had put together, and it was awful to see the change that came over them. Bill Black was furious, slamming his bass into its case and kicking around music stands. Scotty—always such a calm, steady presence—was as angry as I'd ever seen him, and it was painful to watch him trying to hold it in and remain professional. D.J. just muttered to himself, making sure Diskin heard a few of the words intended for him.

I eased out of there and found Elvis in his limo and we headed back to the hotel. I wasn't sure if Elvis was aware of what Diskin had done, but he didn't look too happy either. We weren't back at the hotel an hour when a letter was delivered to the suite. The letter was respectful in tone, almost apologetic. But its meaning was clear: Bill and Scotty were resigning.

Elvis was hurt, but I think he knew the guys had very good reason to be quitting. He wanted to be fair to them but I don't think he knew how to deal with something that fell in between friendship and business. And I think I realized for the first time that for all the Colonel's loud confidence, he could be absolutely wrong about something. Here the Colonel had a chance to manage two acts for the price of one, and to have a great built-in opening act for every Elvis concert. Keeping Bill and Scotty happy would have made sense in terms of the bottom line, but, more important, it would have kept Elvis working with musicians he loved and trusted—guys who'd been there from the first take of "That's All Right, Mama." In my humble opinion, the Colonel blew it.

A few weeks later, Elvis was scheduled to do a charity concert in his hometown, Tupelo, Mississippi—his second big show there. A couple of other players were hired for the show: guitarist Hank "Sugarfoot" Garland and bassist Chuck Wiggington, and D.J. agreed to stay on. Garland already had a reputation as a top session guy in Nashville, and there was no denying that he was talented. But after the show I said to Elvis, "These guys are great, but something was a little off. It just didn't have the same energy."

"I know, GK," he said. "The feel wasn't there. Scotty and Bill aren't the greatest technical players in the world, but man, they've got that feel."

The whole trip to Tupelo was slightly bittersweet. Of course Elvis was celebrated there as a hometown hero, but for him the town did not hold many pleasant memories. It was a place where his family had been dirt poor and had struggled mightily to get by. I'd been with him on the road when some Tupelo guys he'd known came up to his hotel room. They told some stories and had some laughs, but after they left Elvis said, "They kept saying, 'Remember Tupelo? Remember Tupelo?' Man, I don't want to remember Tupelo—those were hard times."

Before we headed back to Memphis, we spent an evening at the very nice home of Ikey Savery, one of Tupelo's most prominent citizens. At one point, Elvis leaned over to me and said, "Five years ago this guy wouldn't have let me cut his grass. Now he's serving me dinner. Kind of strange . . ."

I felt Elvis needed some fun and some distraction, so I suggested we go to the Monday-night wrestling matches at Ellis Auditorium. A guy from our neighborhood who had gone to Humes was the stage manager on those nights, and he brought us in the back door and sat us in a VIP section on the stage side of the wrestling ring. Elvis really enjoyed watching the lady wrestlers take each other on, and we saw quite a few good female matches that night. Elvis was particularly impressed by an attractive wrestler named Penny Banner, and was happily surprised when, after her match, she came over to where we were sitting to tell Elvis what a big fan of his she was.

"Well, I like the way you wrestle, honey," was his response.

Anita Wood was about as serious a girlfriend as Elvis wanted at the time—she'd come on the road with him, she'd stayed at the Beverly Wilshire with him as the Christmas album was being finished, and she was with him for the trip to Tupelo. Elvis always spoke fondly of her and wanted her with him constantly. She was always a part of group outings and parties at Graceland. But Anita was also busy pursuing her own show-business career, and while I think she knew that Elvis was devoted to her when he was with her, she must have also known Elvis Presley was not going to be a typical steady boyfriend.

So, Elvis being Elvis, he wasn't going to let the opportunity to get closer to a lady wrestler slip away. Penny Banner ended up coming back to Graceland with us, and this wasn't one of those communal, let's-go-get-hamburgers dates. Elvis and Penny went straight upstairs to work on their own wrestling moves, and I was left alone.

The lady wrestler may have put Elvis in the mood to have some more fun, because a few days later I was at home in North Memphis when I got a call from Lamar.

"Pack," he said.

"What do you mean, 'pack'?" I asked.

"We're going to Las Vegas."

That was the way Elvis liked to do things, and within a few hours Elvis, Cliff, Gene, Lamar, and I were on a train out of Memphis, heading for a ten-day vacation in Vegas. The train took us through Kansas City, where we had a ten-hour layover and checked into the city's famed Mulebach Hotel. When we got up to our rooms we saw that the management had sent up gift baskets of food and some very fine bottles of whiskey. Elvis didn't drink, and I didn't drink, and Lamar didn't drink much, but Cliff and Gene liked to get at the hard stuff, and sometimes that led to them getting into trouble. So one of the first things Elvis did was open those bottles of fine whiskey and pour them down the bathroom sink. I swear, Gene and Cliff were almost crying, "Elvis, please don't do that." But he shut them up with a firm response: "Nobody's getting drunk tonight."

When it was time to catch our next train, we followed the plan the Colonel had set up for us—we had cabs that would take us to the back entrance of the station, where we'd contact the stationmaster and be escorted to the train. We got to the station fine, but as we walked in we were greeted with a startling sight: five thousand screaming girls waiting for us. It happened that there was a sorority convention in town, and all day a local deejay had been talking about which train Elvis might be on. By the time we showed up, the place was absolutely packed with sorority sisters who all wanted to get their hands on Elvis. They charged at us, and we did the only thing we could—we started running.

We flew out a side door and around a few corners and all of a sudden we were actually running across the tracks of the train yard. We zipped around a few of the parked freight cars, and the rest of us were a little surprised when Elvis darted right under a boxcar. We joined him under there and huddled together, listening for the sounds of our pursuers. I remember thinking at the time how bizarre it was that the same guy who'd taken me to a Beverly Hills penthouse now had me crouching behind the greasy wheels of a Kansas City freight train. I finally went back inside, working my way through the multitude of skirts and sweaters to find the station-master. He seemed both surprised and impressed when I told him the biggest star in the world was hiding under a train in his yard, and he proceeded to lead Elvis and the group on a secret route to our train, which we boarded just in time for departure.

We checked into the Sahara Hotel, and as our first full day in Vegas began, Elvis called the group together to have breakfast with him. I'd packed some flashy clothes for our nights out, though I'd also assumed there'd be some time spent relaxing. But I guess I showed up for that first breakfast looking a little too relaxed in my boxer shorts and a T-shirt. Elvis took one look at me and wouldn't let me sit down at the breakfast table.

"GK—go back and put some damn clothes on," he snapped. Even on vacation he didn't want us looking too informal. I went and got fully dressed, then came back to eat my cold pancakes.

I made up for that wardrobe mistake a little later as we got ready to go out on the Strip. In my deepest, smoothest radio voice, I announced to the group, "Ladies and gentlemen, here I am, George Klein, live from Las Vegas, the entertainment capital of the world, with Mr. Elvis Presley, the number-one entertainer in the world!" Elvis always liked hearing Cliff or me do these kind of hokey, overdramatic announcements, and for some reason this one really cracked him up. He had me do it over and over again, giving it more of a buildup each time.

What I remember most from that Vegas trip are a few encounters Elvis had with the local females. One night he picked up a stunning young woman at a casino, and he let us know that he was going to take her home in the car that the Sahara had provided us. We expected to see him back by the end of the night, but as four, five, then six A.M. rolled around we began to get worried. Finally around seven he came in with a strange little grin on his face.

"Elvis, where the shit you been?" was the way I greeted him.

"Y'all won't believe what happened."

He went on to explain that he'd taken the girl home and had left his car running as he walked her in. One thing led to another in her home, and by the time Elvis came back out the car was dead. He started walking toward the Strip and decided to hitchhike, and the first car that passed him was a young girl on her way to school. She hit the brakes, backed up to him, rolled down the window, and said, "Sir, my mom and dad told me to never pick up any hitchhikers. But you look so much like Elvis Presley, I'll give you a ride."

Another night we caught an act on the Strip named Tempest Storm, the famous, old-style stripper who was well-known for her flaming red hair and for an enormous pair of what she called "moneymakers." We went to see her show and toward the end the maitre d' came over and passed the message along that Miss Storm would like to meet Elvis in her dressing room after the show. We were not invited. Elvis ended up spending the night at Miss Storm's apartment and had a heck of a time. But when Elvis met her in the dressing room (which was, he told us, full of completely naked showgirls), he'd had a picture taken with Tempest, and that was an unforgivable sin as far as Colonel Parker was concerned. The picture hit the wire services and was picked up by dozens of papers. Elvis said the Colonel was furious that Elvis was adding to rock 'n' roll's negative image by "dating a stripper."

"I told him I didn't date her," Elvis explained. "I just spent the night with her."

After our Las Vegas trip, we met up with the band in San Francisco to begin a string of West Coast concerts. Things had been patched up enough with Bill and Scotty at this point that they agreed to a gig-by-gig contract. With D. J. Fontana and the Jordanaires, the lineup still sounded as sharp as it ever had. But it was hard not to feel that some of the magic and the chemistry of those players working together had been squandered by the Colonel's concern for the bottom line.

The thing I remember most about the San Francisco show is what I learned about Elvis's early days in Memphis. We were all backstage at the venue when a call came out that somebody was at the stage door asking for George Klein. I went out to see who it could be and was just about dumbstruck to see Rabbi Alfred Fruchter, the rabbi from the North Memphis temple I had attended as a kid. We exchanged hugs and handshakes and he explained that he'd been transferred to a temple in San Francisco and just wanted to come by to say hello. I couldn't quite figure out how he'd known I'd be with Elvis, but I enjoyed seeing him anyway. He asked if he could say hello to Elvis, and I said I'd go check. When I started to explain to Elvis who was out there, his eyes lit up. "I know Rabbi Fruchter," he said. "I used to live with him. Get him back here."

During Elvis's senior year at Humes, the Presley family moved several times, and at one point lived in the bottom floor of a boardinghouse, where their upstairs neighbors were Rabbi Fruchter and his wife. Elvis explained to me that he used to work as the rabbi's "shabbos goy," turning on and off the lights and doing odd jobs for the couple on Saturday sabbath, when Orthodox Jews were forbidden to engage in certain kinds of work. The rabbi had also allowed the Presleys to use his telephone, saving them the expense of getting their own. He and the rabbi had a great time backstage, and Elvis insisted that Rabbi Fruchter accompany him to a preshow press conference. Let me tell you, there were a lot of surprised faces among those reporters when Elvis announced, "Ladies and gentlemen, I'd like you to meet my rabbi."

After San Francisco, we came down the coast to Los Angeles and checked back into the Beverly Wilshire so that Elvis could do two performances at the Pan Pacific Auditorium. Right away our group was joined at the hotel by Vince Edwards, the young actor we'd met at the Beverly Wilshire who would later play Ben Casey, crazy old Billy Murphy, and Nick Adams, another young actor whom Elvis had met while making *Love Me Tender* and who'd been in *Rebel Without a Cause*. Nick was really Elvis's first Hollywood friend and had been out to Memphis to visit Elvis and the Presleys. He was a great storyteller and a real fun guy to be around, and one of the nicest things he'd done for Elvis was to introduce him to Natalie Wood, which led to those two becoming an item for a short while.

Despite how crazy Elvis had seen his audiences become, he still loved the response he got when he moved wildly across a stage, and at the first Pan Pacific show he was wild. The Colonel thought to set a large plastic replica of RCA's mascot, Nipper the Dog, onstage, and at this show Elvis had a lot of fun singing to that pooch and rolling around on the floor with him. To me it looked like Elvis was trying to put on as energetic a show as possible to impress a showbiz-heavy L.A. crowd. What he did certainly wasn't any wilder than what we'd seen from black artists like James Brown and Jackie Wilson, or from performers at WDIA's Goodwill Revue. But there were some folks in the Los Angeles audience who couldn't handle it, I guess. He got a lot of bad reviews in the paper the next day talking about how "vulgar" he'd been and claiming that what he did onstage was unfit to be seen by youth.

Elvis was looking forward to giving just as exciting a performance the second night, but word came down that the Los Angeles Police Department was actually going to film the concert, and if Elvis did anything "vulgar" onstage, they'd use the film as evidence to prosecute him.

Having a squad of cops critiquing his dance moves could have made that performance a humiliating night for Elvis, but he played it beautifully. By the time the show started, the story of the police warnings had been all over the radio. So when Elvis came onstage, shuffling a little like a guy on a chain gang, and with his hands held out together like they were cuffed, the kids in the crowd knew what he was doing and went just as crazy as if he'd been shaking all over. He got to the microphone, held up a hand, and just wiggled one finger. The crowd went even crazier. And as eager as the cops may have been to bust Elvis, even they knew it was a stretch to say that a man standing still save for one wiggling finger was being vulgar. Elvis managed to give the crowd a great show, though he stayed off the floor and didn't go anywhere near Nipper.

The party at the Beverly Wilshire after that second show was a great one, with all kinds of celebrities mingling about. There was Ricky Nelson, the young TV star who'd recently kicked off a second career as a pop singer, and there was Venetia Stevenson, a starlet Elvis had once dated who'd been proclaimed "the world's most photogenic girl" by a movie magazine. Vince Edwards turned up with a friend he wanted to introduce to Elvis, Sammy Davis Jr. He and Elvis got along right away, and, as much as Elvis was the star of that party, Sammy wasn't in our suite ten minutes before he was performing a private show for all of us. I don't remember the whole act, but I do recall that he and Nick Adams had everyone busted up with dueling Brando imitations.

Billy Murphy was there in a typical all-black outfit doing a good job of both entertaining and spooking people. When Cliff Gleaves recounted some problems he was having with a particular girl, Billy said, "The shark has got bad brakes."

"What are you talking about, Billy?" I asked.

Billy explained that the "shark" was his old car, and that its brakes weren't too good, and if a certain lady took a ride with Murph up in the hills, anything could happen.

There was a hushed silence, then Cliff made it clear that such a tactic wouldn't be necessary.

"Well, if you need it, mister," said Billy, "the shark has bad brakes."

Elvis wasn't happy with every guest who came by the Beverly Wilshire that week, though. He was looking forward to a visit from Faron Young, a country and now film star whom Elvis considered to be one of the cooler of the country guys he'd toured with early on. But Elvis was none too pleased when Young showed up accompanied by another, older guy. I didn't catch the other guy's name, but we all sat around the suite and talked pleasantly for a while before Elvis said he had other business to get to. He and I walked Faron and his friend down the long hallway to the door, and I heard the friend say to Elvis, "Do me a favor and mention me to Colonel Parker—maybe we could do some work together."

Elvis said he would, goodbyes were said, then the two left. As Elvis shut the door, he turned to me.

"God damn that SOB. That f——in' bastard."

"Elvis, what's wrong with you?"

"Don't you know who that was with Faron?"

"No."

"That's Jim Denny. The motherf——er that kicked me off the Grand Ole Opry."

He went on and on, just cussing away. In front of Faron, Elvis had been perfectly nice to Denny, who was now working as a talent manager and music publisher. But once they were gone, I heard him work himself into a foul-mouthed tirade unlike any I'd ever heard come out of him. Elvis would forgive, but he never forgot.

Halloween fell a few days after the Pan Pacific shows, and our group was thrilled to have been invited to a party thrown by Sy Devore, the top Hollywood designer known as the "tailor to the stars." Except that the invitation was really for Elvis, and he didn't want to go. The more excitedly we talked about the party, the less interested he was in it, and when somebody made the mistake of saying, "Everyone's going to be there," that about clinched it: He didn't want anything to do with the Halloween party. But he didn't count on an early-evening visit from Billy Murphy, who turned up with a handmade Halloween present for Elvis: a beautifully put-together, gold Mardi Gras–style mask. Elvis took one look at Murphy's mask and said, "All right, we're going to the party."

That sent us into a mad scramble to get ready to go out before he changed his mind again. Within minutes we had piled into a limo and were on our way to Devore's home. When I pointed out that maybe the rest of us ought to have something to wear, he screeched the car over to the curb at the first drugstore we spotted and handed me fifty dollars. I ran in and scooped up the only costume items they had left on Halloween night—Lone Ranger masks for me, Cliff, Gene, Lamar, and Billy Murphy.

The party was pretty amazing, even by Hollywood standards. I remember getting excited that a very cute little clown seemed to be flirting with me, until Cliff pointed out that the little clown was Debbie Reynolds, and that right at that moment she was sitting on the lap of her husband, Eddie Fisher. Joan Collins, a red-hot young beauty at the time, was turning heads and almost snapping necks with a remarkable costume that consisted of nothing but playing cards—the four aces—in strategic places.

I walked into one of the party rooms and saw a costume that topped them all: Nat King Cole was dressed as Elvis, with a black leather jacket, pasted-on sideburns, and a guitar around his neck. Elvis and I had always loved Cole's music, and I went right up to him and introduced myself. He was extremely nice, and when he heard I was with Elvis, he said he really wanted to meet him. I went to find Elvis, and at first it was hard to get him away from the pretty girls he was talking to. But as soon as I told him who Nat King Cole was dressed as, he had me lead him there. I'll never forget the sight of Mardi Gras Elvis standing there talking to Nat King Cole Presley.

In the first week of November '57, we left Los Angeles and headed to our most exotic destination yet: Hawaii. When we first heard that the Colonel had booked some concerts in Honolulu, we wanted to maximize our time in the tropical paradise and asked Elvis if he might consider flying over to the island. But he stayed true to the promise he'd made his mother and insisted that if we wanted to go to Hawaii, it would be on a ship.

On our day of departure, as Lamar, Gene, Cliff, and I got ready to check out of the Beverly Wilshire and head to the docks, we were surprised to run into Billy Murphy, holding one battered suitcase tied together with a piece of rope. It soon became clear that Elvis had mentioned the Hawaii trip to Billy, and that Billy had assumed he'd be a part of that trip. We explained to Billy that there was no ticket for him and no accommodations. He simply shrugged and said, "The King invited me." And, sure enough, when I told Elvis that Billy Murphy thought he was coming to Hawaii with us, Elvis just shrugged and said, "Tell Tom Diskin to get him a ticket." Diskin, acting as the Colonel's delegated penny-pincher, was very reluctant to make any last-minute arrangements for Murphy. But I asked Diskin if he wanted to be the one to tell Elvis that one of his friends wasn't allowed to travel with him. By the time we all got to the dock to board the U.S.S. *Matsonia*, Billy Murphy was ticketed along with the rest of us.

In the end, it was fun to have him along, and his best line of the trip came one night at dinner, when he interrupted one of Cliff's jive-talking stories to stand up at the table and say: "Mr. Gleaves, you're colorful and you're interesting, but you're ninety percent bullshit and ten percent lies." Then he just walked away. Cliff had never been summed up so well.

The Colonel traveled on the ship with us, and when we arrived in Hawaii he had local authorities lined up to meet us at the dock. We much preferred the welcome we got from the bunch of beautiful Hawaiian girls whose responsibility it was to give new arrivals a kiss on the cheek and a floral lei. I think it was supposed to be one each per customer—that's what the rest of us got. But by the time we made it to our limo Elvis had so many leis on you could barely see his face, and what you could see was covered in lipstick.

We stayed at the truly spectacular Kaiser Hawaiian Village Hotel, and of course Elvis was booked into the fanciest suite there. On the road, Cliff and I were always curious about who else stayed in these VIP suites besides us, and the clerk at the Hawaiian Village front desk told us that Elvis's room had recently been used as a honeymoon suite by Mike Todd and Elizabeth Taylor. Cliff and I rushed up to the room, jumped onto the bed, and started rolling around together.

"What the hell are you guys doing?" asked Elvis.

"Don't you see?" said Cliff. "Now we can say we've been in the same bed as Elizabeth Taylor."

There was some work to do around the couple of concerts Elvis had scheduled, but I spent a lot of time with Cliff just enjoying the locale as much as possible. We delighted in calling room service to order up fresh coconuts and pineapple, and in the mornings, before Elvis was up, we'd go down to the beach together. The first morning there we brought a little radio along with our beach blankets, and we laid out under the Hawaiian sun, listening to the lazy surf, feeling the warm breezes, and keeping an eye out for revealing bikinis. When we clicked the radio on, we heard Roy Orbison singing "Ooby Dooby."

"Do you believe this?" asked Cliff. "We're all the way in Hawaii, listening to something that was cut in Memphis."

I was already relaxed enough that "No shit" was about all I could come up with for an answer.

"And the thing is," Cliff continued, "we came over to Hawaii in a first-class cabin on a luxury liner, we're staying with Elvis Presley in the swankiest hotel on the island, we're lying on a perfect beach—and I ain't got a damn dime in my pocket."

I had to admit—it was not a bad lifestyle.

There was a radio station on the top floor of the Hawaiian Village, and the pair of jocks who did the afternoon show there—Tom Moffat and Ron Jacobs—were guys I knew a little bit from my radio work. They called me in my room one morning, reintroduced themselves, and said that while they knew they couldn't get Elvis on the air, they wanted to know if I would do an interview with them. I was in a great mood to begin with, and the chance to get behind a radio station mike sounded too good to resist. I decided I wouldn't bother telling the Colonel about it, since he'd only find some way to talk me out of it. Instead, I asked Elvis if it was okay. He said to go ahead and do it and simply wanted to know when it would be happening.

Moffat and Jacobs were big Elvis fans and asked me all kinds of typical questions: how I'd met him, what it was like to travel with him, what songs he was playing on tour. Then we started talking about his recordings, and I realized I had the opportunity to say something I'd thought about for a long time. I began to explain that while Elvis was recognized as a great singer, he didn't get recognition for being one of the greatest rock 'n' roll producers. But he knew exactly how to bring a song to life in the studio, often drawing on everything he'd learned from working with Sam Phillips. Though Elvis didn't have the training to tell a band what specific notes to play, he had an unbelievable ear and was very skilled at communicating to musicians the structure and the feel of what he wanted, while always leaving room for great players to improvise.

"I love to hear him sing as much as anybody," I told the jocks, "but I really love to watch him run a session. When you hear an Elvis Presley record, it really is an Elvis Presley production—but nobody talks about that."

Moffat and Jacobs were impressed by this, and after we talked awhile longer, they thanked me for my time. I headed back down to the suite to get ready to go out with the guys. I think I was looking in the closet trying to decide what shirt to put on when all of a sudden I was in a tight grip. Elvis was next to me, with his arm around my shoulders.

"GK, I heard the interview," he said. He had a stone-faced expression, so it was hard to guess what he was thinking.

"How'd I do?"

"You did great. But I really want to thank you for something." Elvis didn't offer up a lot of thank-yous.

"What's that, Elvis?"

"You're the first guy to give me some credit for being more than a voice. To give me some credit for what happens in the studio. That was real nice to hear."

"Elvis, it's the truth."

"Yeah, but only we know it."

A little while later I was confronted by a red-faced Tom Diskin, who was upset that I'd granted an "unauthorized" interview to the press.

"You should have cleared it with the Colonel," he sputtered.

"I cleared it with Elvis," I shouted back. "And he liked it. End of story."

If I'd learned anything on the road with Elvis so far, it was that there was only one guy whose welfare and happiness I was going to worry about. And that guy wasn't the Colonel.

● ● ●   ● ● ●   ● ● ●   ● ● ●

CHAPTER SEVEN

G.I. Blues

"Greetings," the letter began. It was the last pleasant word on the page. Elvis was being drafted.

I'd turned up at Graceland just before Christmas, and when Elvis came downstairs he didn't say a word—just handed me the piece of paper he was holding. Rumors had been out around Memphis that Elvis might receive a draft notice, but nobody had given them much thought. There was no war on, and it seemed to all of us that Elvis was worth a lot more to his country paying the sizable income tax on his sizable earnings than he would be in uniform. We'd known the draft was a possibility, but it still felt like an awful shock to see the words in official U.S. army black and white.

"Aww, no, Elvis," I said. "They can't draft you."

"They just did, GK."

"What are you going to do?"

"I don't know, GK. I just don't know."

Elvis was devastated. Everything had been going so well for him—*Jailhouse Rock* had been a huge hit movie, the title track was a number-one single, and his Christmas album had hit the top of the album charts. But I think he had a very well-founded fear that all his success could easily disappear if he had to put his music on hold for two years while in the service. As young as rock 'n' roll still was, we'd already seen artists go from being hotter than hot to stone cold, and Hollywood history was full of stars who'd burned brightly for a moment and then flamed out. As far as Elvis knew, when that draft notice arrived in December of 1957, his life as an entertainer was over. I don't think he was really afraid of any of the physical dangers he might confront in the army, but he was deeply worried that his two years of service would mark the end of his career. He was worried that at twenty-two, his future had just been taken away.

I couldn't help but feel a little guilty about what was happening to Elvis. When we'd returned to Memphis after our Hawaiian trip, I'd told him again of my desire to get back into radio, and again he had been completely understanding. This time, though, an opportunity came my way that Dewey Phillips couldn't shoot down. Sam Phillips had become a real rock 'n' roll entrepreneur: In addition to running Sun Records and managing Sun artists, Sam had gotten into radio, first launching Memphis-based WHER, the first ever "All-Girl Radio Station," and then WHEY, a small but powerful station located near the naval base north of Memphis in Millington, Tennessee. Sam had become someone I considered both a local hero and a good friend, and when he offered me a job at WHEY, I took it and went right to work on an afternoon two-to-six shift. I'd stepped away from Elvis to get my own career back on track, and now he had the real concern that he was about to lose everything he'd worked for.

Before that draft notice turned up, our time back in Memphis after the Hawaii trip had been full of the same good times we'd been used to. Even though I was a regular at Graceland, it always had that same magical feeling it'd had for me my first time there. Elvis and the Presleys were still getting the place just the way they wanted it, but no matter what was going on, you walked into that house and it was so easy to relax and shut out the outside world—and that's exactly what Elvis and the rest of us did with those great parties in the Graceland basement. I still had the traveling-companion responsibility of lining up beautiful girls to come up through the Graceland gates for our get-togethers, and I'd use all my radio and nightclub connections to find them.

The point of what I've come to call our "rockin' fifties parties" wasn't to get drunk or to notch up one-night stands, though—it was to truly enjoy the moment of being together in that remarkable place. There was a real sweetness to those Graceland nights. There was never hard liquor around, and Elvis didn't even want beer in the house—he'd seen too many beer drunks as a kid and thought it was a low-class beverage. There were nights when the wildest thing that happened was having Elvis lead us through a round of Name That Tune. (He loved the fact that I—his disc jockey friend—was terrible at this game, and I remember being completely stumped as he gave me note after note of the melody to Johnny Mathis's "Chances Are.") Because the feel of those Graceland parties wasn't rock 'n' roll abandon but an easygoing camaraderie we could all enjoy, it was crucial that anybody who was invited understood how to act and how to approach Elvis without making him uncomfortable or putting him on the defensive.

I remember hearing a girl I'd invited to one of those parties say something about Elvis's hair—I thought she'd said he dyed his hair so black it looked purple, and, knowing how sensitive Elvis was about the look of his hair, I kind of snapped at her harshly, "What did you say?"

"Cool it, GK," Elvis said with a smile. "Calm down, man."

"Well, what'd she say?"

"She said my hair would look good whether it was purple or polka-dotted."

Around that holiday season of 1957, I finally introduced Elvis to a couple of other people very close to me. Since family was so important to Elvis, I thought it only made sense that he meet mine, so one afternoon I brought my mom and my sister Dorothy up to Graceland. I have to admit I was a little nervous about how my family might react to Elvis, so I went over some of the basic ground rules I always laid out for people making their first visit to Graceland. I told them to keep things positive—I'd seen people try to act cool around Elvis by having a negative, critical attitude, and he never responded well to that. The other thing was that you didn't have to assume you couldn't say anything nice to him because you thought he'd probably heard it all before. He didn't want to hear anything phony, but he was only human and always enjoyed hearing compliments.

It turned out that I didn't have much to worry about. My mom and Mrs. Presley hit it off famously right away, and my sister won over Elvis when she walked up to him without hesitation and said, "You're not only great-looking, but you've got the most beautiful blue eyes I've ever seen." Mom was a hit with Elvis, too. Just before we left Graceland, she turned to him and said, "I think you're so much better looking than Clark Gable." He really liked that.

Still, that Christmas season wasn't an easy one for Elvis. The draft notice raised concerns about what the future might hold, although his immediate future was taken care of when Colonel Parker got Elvis a ninety-day deferment so that he would have time to complete his next film, *King Creole*. But that was only three months, and the clock was ticking. I soon learned from an acquaintance who'd become a higher-up in the air force that there might be another option for Elvis. He wanted to keep things very hush-hush, but asked me to pass along to Elvis a deal that the guy said had been cleared at the highest levels: If Elvis enlisted in the air force, he'd work strictly as a public-relations officer, primarily touring air force bases to keep morale high and to call attention to that branch of the armed forces. He'd wear custom uniforms, be given excellent lodging, and be treated as a military VIP.

"That sounds pretty cool," I said to the recruitment officer. "But there's one little problem—Elvis doesn't like to fly."

The guy paused just for a beat, then said, "We can work around that."

I don't know how the air force would have worked around having a public-relations VIP who didn't want to board a plane, but it soon became a moot point. Colonel Parker told Elvis he'd be savaged in the press if he got any kind of preferential treatment from the military. We respectfully declined the air force's offer.

In the meantime, I had the pleasure of going to work for Sam Phillips at WHEY. I'd enjoyed spending time with him ever since I'd met him through Dewey, and I always considered him a great source of advice and guidance. Sam was sharp about every aspect of the record business, primarily because he'd worked every job in the record business. When he started Memphis Recording Service and Sun Records, he'd staked everything he had on his passion for rhythm and blues music and had really operated as a one-man label. He engineered, he produced, he promoted; he took the acetates out to the Plastic Products plant in North Memphis to watch his records get pressed. History will always see him as the man who gave Elvis his first big break, but Sam worked so hard with great artists before Elvis: B. B. King, Howlin' Wolf, Rufus Thomas, and Ike Turner, to name a few. It's hard to overstate just what kind of courage and dedication it took for a white businessman in early-fifties Memphis to commit himself to that music.

The other special thing about Sam was that if he knew you loved music the way he did, he treated you as an equal: He treated me with the same respect and warmth whether I was Dewey's gofer, the hottest jock in town, or a guest in his home.

When I wasn't doing my shifts at WHEY up in Millington, I spent as much time as I could at Graceland so that I could have some quality time with Elvis before he headed back to Los Angeles to begin *King Creole*. I could tell his work and military obligations were both weighing heavily on him, and one Sunday we decided to work off some of the tension with a low-key afternoon of badminton. The game doesn't exactly sound like a rock 'n' roll kind of pastime now, but back then it was considered a leisure activity of the Hollywood stars, and Elvis had bought a badminton set to put up in the little yard in back of Graceland's den. It was a nice cool day just before Elvis's twenty-third birthday—January 8—and we set up some folding chairs so that Mr. and Mrs. Presley could watch Elvis, Cliff, Lamar, and me hit the birdie back and forth over the net.

The game started as fun, but quickly got a little too intense. Cliff had made some typical Cliff comments about how he'd been a college bad-minton champion, and every time Lamar smashed the birdie past him, Lamar would really rib Cliff about it.

We took a break and settled into some chairs near Mr. and Mrs. Pres-ley. As Lamar sat down, he made some final crack at Cliff's expense, and Cliff just absolutely snapped. He attacked Lamar with his badminton racket and hit him hard enough to break the racket and knock Lamar over in his chair. Mrs. Presley was screaming, she was so upset by the whole spectacle. Mr. Presley and Elvis hauled Cliff off of Lamar, and Elvis barked at both of them to get inside the house and up to their room—at that time they were both staying in Graceland's extra upstairs bedroom.

Elvis ended up asking them to move out, giving them money to cover a few days at a motel. As Cliff and Lamar dejectedly got their things together, they tried to return the shirts, sweaters, jackets, and ties they'd borrowed from Elvis, but he told them to keep it all. ("They didn't have anything to pack," he said later. "It all belonged to me.") The two were gone from Graceland for a while, but after Mrs. Presley made it clear she didn't hold anything against them, it wasn't too long before both were for-given and back up at the house again.

Just before Elvis left for California, he asked again if I would come with him. I told him how much I appreciated the consideration, but things were starting to feel really good at WHEY, and I didn't want to ask Sam Phillips for time off so soon after he'd hired me. Elvis understood, and was grateful that I'd hooked him up with a strong replacement: I'd felt that if I was going to leave Elvis's side to head back to radio, I needed to come up with some-body who might replace me as a satisfactory traveling companion, and I'd thought of my friend Alan Fortas. Arthur Hooton had moved on to a job with the city—he never stopped loving Elvis, but he really didn't ever take to a showbiz lifestyle. Cousin Gene was still in the picture, but I think Elvis was beginning to see that his interest in being a part of the rock 'n' roll world was limited. Cliff and Lamar, well—they were Cliff and Lamar.

Alan Fortas was a childhood friend of mine through our times spent at Memphis's Jewish Community Center. He'd been an all-city football player and was a huge Elvis fan. I'd brought him by Graceland a few times, and Elvis liked him right away, even giving him a special nickname, "Hog Ears." When Elvis headed off to make *King Creole*, Alan was his newest traveling companion.

Behind the mike at WHEY, I found I was as comfortable on-air as ever, and I was happy to learn that a lot of my listeners still remembered me as DJ-uh-GK from *The Rock 'n' Roll Ballroom* show. In addition to my afternoon rock 'n' roll shifts, I also began hosting record hops around town. I'd set up a turntable and speaker gear at a high school or church social hall or community center and basically do what I did during the *Ballroom* days: put on a live, high-energy deejay show. It was an exciting time for rock 'n' roll, and great new records just kept coming one after the other, from fun up-tempo stuff like Jerry Lee Lewis's "Great Balls of Fire" and Danny and the Juniors' "At the Hop" to the smooth romance of Sam Cooke's "You Send Me" and the Platters' "Twilight Time."

I got almost daily phone reports from Alan Fortas in Los Angeles, and one day he passed along an invitation from Elvis to come to New Orleans for a couple weeks of location shooting. New Orleans was close enough that I could make the trip over a long weekend, so I immediately worked out a travel plan. When I did get down there, it was hard to figure out where the production was centered, and the first familiar face I saw belonged to Tom Diskin. When I asked him how to find Elvis, he said Elvis was busy working and suggested that I take in a movie before checking in at the Roosevelt Hotel. I won't repeat exactly how I responded to that, but I think Diskin got the message that I hadn't come all the way down to New Orleans to go to the movies. I tracked Elvis down on set and, even in the middle of his workday, he was happy to see me.

On *King Creole*, Elvis had a top-rate script to work with—one that had originally been written with James Dean in mind. He was working with renowned director Michael Curtiz (*Casablanca, The Jazz Singer*) and had a strong supporting cast that included Walter Matthau, Carolyn Jones, and Vic Morrow. He worked as hard as ever, and ended up with one of his best film performances. But what he didn't have was the close working relationship with songwriters Leiber and Stoller that he'd had on *Jailhouse Rock*.

The writers had been humiliated by Colonel Parker during that film, but they had enjoyed working with Elvis enough that they were looking for a project that would serve them all well. When they pitched the idea of Elvis starring in a film version of the Nelson Algren novel *Walk on the Wild Side*, which they'd write songs for, the Colonel told them that if they ever tried to interfere in Elvis's affairs again, he'd see to it that they never worked again in Hollywood or New York. Leiber and Stoller were furious and frustrated, and while they'd already committed to writing some songs that Elvis would sing in *King Creole*, the chance for any close collaboration was snuffed out. Here were two of the finest rock 'n' roll songwriters ever, but the Colonel never seemed to understand that the songwriting was the fuel that powered Elvis's best performances. Again, the Colonel blew it.

On *King Creole*, I know Elvis worked particularly hard to prove that he had some serious abilities as an actor, and one of the reasons for that was that he had his impending army service on his mind. One night he said to me, "If rock 'n' roll is over when I get out of the army, I can still have a movie career."

Even with the more serious mood on the set, we still had some laughs. Cliff Gleaves spotted an extra wearing a very sharp blazer, and found out that the guy's father owned a men's clothing shop. Over the course of a day's shoot, Cliff convinced the guy that his dad's store couldn't get any better promotion than to give Elvis and his guys some free blazers to wear when we traveled. We were measured that night and had our blazers the next day. Of course as soon as the Colonel caught wind of it, he was furious that Cliff had engineered an endorsement deal and started coming down hard on him. But Cliff said, "Colonel, if we bought the blazers, we'd be giving away the endorsement for free." That stopped the Colonel in his tracks, and he couldn't hide the fact that he was actually impressed. We kept the handsome blazers and even had one fitted for the Colonel. From that day on, the Colonel began to say of Cliff, "That boy reminds me of myself."

I also remember Elvis and me getting back to the Roosevelt Hotel after a day of shooting and heading into a waiting elevator. Elvis nodded to the elevator operator and said, "Tenth floor."

The elevator operator shook his head and said, "Sir, I can't stop on the tenth floor."

"Why not?" I asked.

"Man," said the operator, "Elvis Presley is staying on the tenth floor."

Without missing a beat, Elvis said, "That's okay. Let us off on the ninth floor and we'll walk up." That's exactly what we did.

Elvis returned to Hollywood to finish the film, then came back to Memphis with just about a week to spare before he was to head off to basic training. We spent most of those evenings over at the Rainbow Roller-drome, a popular Memphis skating rink. Elvis had gotten in the habit of renting out the whole rink after hours, and he loved getting all his guys out there to play some very physical games of Last Man Standing, or to link arms to create long, fast-moving "whips." As a teenager, I'd hurt my back pretty badly doing menial labor for a summer job, and even aside from the bad back, I wasn't into playing quite as hard and rough as Elvis or Red West. I put skates on once in a while, but when those whips started coming together, I stayed safe in the seats around the rink's railing.

The night before Elvis was to head off to Fort Hood, Texas, to begin army basic training, he took Anita Wood out for a final date (along with Alan Fortas and myself). Despite his passing interests in other women, Elvis and Anita still seemed to be a strong couple, and rumors about an Elvis-Anita wedding had been circulating since they'd first been seen together.

Elvis was driving his own Cadillac limo, and he took us over to a drive-in theater to see a film called *Sing Boy Sing*, starring pop star Tommy

Sands. This was the feature version of a TV movie called *The Singing Idol,* which had been created as a kind of takeoff on Elvis's life story. Elvis had been approached to play the part, but, as he was already under contract with MGM, he and Colonel Parker suggested Sands, whom the Colonel had recently signed to RCA. Sands became an Elvis stand-in for both projects, and a song he sang in the TV version, "Teenage Crush," actually became a hit on the *Billboard* charts. Cliff, Lamar, Gene, Arthur Hooton, and I were part of the story, too—though we were rolled into one composite character named CK ("Cliff" plus "GK," I suppose), who was portrayed by our old friend Nick Adams.

We headed back to Graceland after the movie and talked late into the night about how the story lined up with real events in Elvis's life. We didn't make too much of a big deal of our goodbyes that night, but I don't think anyone could shake the feeling that the good times we'd known were done for now, and the times ahead were uncertain at best.

Elvis did look good in an army uniform. I got to see it on him when he came back to Memphis in June on a two-week furlough before his advanced training began. Elvis squeezed in a Nashville recording session during that break, but he also filled a lot of the time with favorite activities such as trips to the Rainbow.

From our Humes days on, he had also always loved the rides over at the Memphis Fairgrounds: a merry-go-round, dodgem cars, and the formidable Pippin roller coaster in addition to the usual carnival games. At Memphis State College, I'd become friendly with a fellow named Wimpy Adams who went on to become the manager of the Fairgrounds. With that inside connection, Elvis was able to rent out the whole Fairgrounds the same way we rented the roller rink. In that period after basic training, when Elvis must have been thinking that he didn't know if he'd ever have the opportunity again, he rented out the Fairgrounds for several nights, and it really did give him a great chance to step away from his worries. He loved delivering a crushing hit to an unsuspecting driver over at the dodgem car course, and more than once he'd climb out of his Pippin car when it slowed on an incline and climb down the roller-coaster supports, making everyone who saw his car come back around the track without him panic that he'd been thrown out somewhere along the line.

As Elvis headed back to Fort Hood for his advanced training, I added a new sideline to my radio career: I became a Sun Records recording artist. A couple of producer/songwriters named Dickie Goodman and Bill Buchanan had had a smash hit with a record called "The Flying Saucer," which was probably the first-ever pop record to make use of what we now call sampling. "The Flying Saucer" was a "break-in" record, meaning that instead of being an actual song, it was a story in the form of a narrated news report, with a fake newsman's questions about a Martian invasion answered by snippets of hit records from Fats Domino, Little Richard, and Elvis ("Mr. Presley, what would you do if the flying saucer landed?" *Just take a walk down Lonely Street . . .*). Listeners loved the record, but record labels felt differently—they were trying to track Goodman and Buchanan down to haul them into court for copyright infringement. The record was eventually ruled to be an example of fair-use parody, but the idea was out there that if you put together a "break-in" record with music you already had the rights to, you could score an easy hit.

I'd been spending a lot of time over at Sun after my Millington shifts, and one day I walked in to find staff producer Jack Clement very excited about something he'd just written. A scandal had just erupted around Jerry Lee Lewis, because, while he was on tour in England, it had been discovered that his new bride was actually his thirteen-year-old cousin. (Elvis had the great line, "They say I'm corrupting America's youth, but Jerry Lee's marrying 'em.") Jack Clement had written a "Flying Saucer"–style parody called "The Return of Jerry Lee" that played out as an interview with Jerry Lee, using snippets of his Sun records as responses. Jack wanted to put the record together on the spot, with me taking the part of the interviewer, "Edward R. Edward."

I was with a friend that day, Louis Harris, a real nice Memphis guy who'd also spent some time traveling with Elvis. (Louis deserves recognition here for one other honor: He taught me how to drive in the first car I owned, a big old '58 Chevrolet Impala.) Louis read a couple of opening lines, then I went to work laying in the questions that Jerry Lee's records would respond to ("Jerry, what did the Queen of England say about you?" *Goodness gracious, great balls of fire* . . .). We got it all done quickly and only expected it to be an in-house joke for Sam Phillips, but when Sam heard it, he liked it so much he wanted to put it out right away. We cut it on a Friday, and on Monday "The Return of Jerry Lee" was released by Sun Records' newest act, George & Louis. I have to admit that when I heard it played a few times on local radio, I began to think about what I might wear for my debut Ed Sullivan appearance. But the record fizzled out pretty quickly, and Mr. Sullivan never came calling.

At Fort Hood, Elvis had taken advantage of the regular rules that allowed soldiers to live off base with family, and had rented a house so that his parents could come out to stay with him. Throughout that summer, though, Mrs. Presley was feeling ill and run-down, and in August she had to be rushed back to Memphis and admitted to the hospital. When her condition turned critical, Elvis asked for leave to go to her, but for unknown reasons the army was very slow to grant permission. Elvis later told me that after waiting patiently for hours, he stormed into a commanding officer's office and announced that he was going AWOL and was going to hold a press conference in Memphis to say that the army would not allow him to visit his gravely ill mother. That got his leave granted and processed in about fifteen minutes.

Making a rare break from his mother's wishes, Elvis flew to Memphis, and Mr. Presley and I picked him up at the airport and got him over to the hospital. Alan Fortas, Elvis's young cousin Billy Smith, and I kept Elvis company all night in the hospital waiting room as Mrs. Presley's condition was monitored. She wasn't getting any better, but she wasn't getting any worse, so sometime after midnight Elvis went back to Graceland to rest and Alan Fortas gave me a ride back to my place. I'd just started to drift off to sleep when Alan called me with the awful news: Mrs. Presley had passed away. She was gone at the age of forty-six.

Friends and family first got together at Mr. Presley's brother Vester's house to avoid dealing with the fans gathered outside of Graceland. I was already in a state of grief—I'd loved Mrs. Presley like a second mother. But the sight of Elvis in his grief just ripped me apart. This friend of mine who had always been so strong for the rest of us was now crying so hard he could barely stand. And every time it seemed he'd calmed down a bit, he'd burst into sobs all over again. He was so distraught and so broken up—I'd just never seen a grown man in that much pain.

Elvis wanted to go back to Graceland, so we all went back with him. There wasn't anything any of us could really say that would help him, but we all wanted to be around to support him. Over the terrible week that followed, Mrs. Presley's funeral was planned. Elvis was like a lost soul, and several times I found him sitting in his mother's room, holding an article of her clothing and just weeping over it. Other times he and Vernon would simply hold each other and cry. Many of the friends that Elvis had made in Hollywood sent condolences and beautiful floral pieces, and Nick Adams actually turned up at the house. He never told Elvis, but he let me know that he'd taken himself out of the running for a big film part because he wanted to be there for his friend. By the time of the funeral, Elvis looked so weak that I worried he might collapse during the service.

After Mrs. Presley was laid to rest, during one of the quieter moments in the house, I found myself alone with Elvis, and he said, "You know, GK, all this Graceland stuff, the movies, the records, it's all been for my mom. It was all for her, and now she can't enjoy it."

That had me so choked up that I couldn't answer him.

Much has been made of Elvis's relationship with his mother, but what I saw was that they were so similar in nature that in addition to sharing the love of a mother and son, they also had a dearly cherished friendship. She cared for him so much, and, truly, she was the anchor in his crazy life. He always counted on her for her support, her encouragement, her keen judge of character, and her unconditional love. I've come to believe that if Mrs. Presley had lived a full life, Elvis would be with us today.

I know Elvis must have been dazed and deeply depressed when he returned to Fort Hood to complete his training, and I know his spirits weren't lifted any when the army gave him his service assignment: He'd be spending the next two years with the Third Armored Division in Germany. Right away he started making arrangements to rent a house off the base in Germany for his father, his Grandma Minnie, and any other friends who were willing to come over. Red and Cliff and Lamar quickly agreed to make the trip. Elvis asked me if I wanted to come over too, but I had to admit to him that in 1958, just thirteen years after the end of World War II, Germany did not seem all that comfortable a place for an Orthodox Jew. Elvis understood, and asked me to be his eyes and ears in Memphis while he was away.

I had just finished a shift at WHEY when I got a very rare personal phone call from Colonel Parker. He informed me that Elvis was going to board a troop train in Texas that would take him to New York, where he'd then ship out to Germany. This particular train would make a regularly scheduled stop in Memphis, and the Colonel wanted to make that stop a media event. He wanted me to alert all the media contacts I could think of, without letting on that the whole thing was being orchestrated by the Colonel.

"I want the biggest crowd you can imagine out there to welcome Elvis back and see him off, George," said the Colonel. "Let's give those army people fits and show them how big a star they got."

I made calls and, the next day, an hour before Elvis's train rolled in, there was a huge crowd of fans gathered in that train yard. I was there with Alan Fortas and Louis Harris, the friend I'd done the "Return of Jerry Lee" recording with. Falling into my old travel-companion habits, I zoomed in on a nearby pretty brunette named Jane Wilbanks and asked if she'd like to meet Elvis with us.

I'll never forget the moment when that train came rolling in. As it slowed, we saw all the faces of these soldiers roll by, then, all of a sudden, there was Elvis. His face lit up like a Christmas tree—he was just so happy to see us. We ran alongside his car as the train came to a halt, and when he put his hands up on the glass of his window, we put our hands up and pressed back. When the train stopped, Elvis made his way to the platform at the end of the train and we greeted him properly.

"You guys are a sight for sore eyes," he said. "I'm glad you're here."

The train was only stopping for a short while, and Elvis wasn't allowed to get off of it, so it was a strange time of mixed emotions. We were all so happy to see each other, yet we were about to be pulled apart again. I wanted to be cool and strong for Elvis's sake, but it was no use. As that train slowly began to chug out of the yard, tears were rolling down my face. I didn't know when I was going to see my best friend again.

Actually, it didn't take long to hear from Elvis. He'd been overseas less than a week when I got the first of many phone calls from him. He gave me the mailing address for the base he was at and asked if every couple of weeks I would send him a box of the latest records to keep him up to date. He asked me to keep an eye on Anita Wood while he was gone. And finally, Elvis being Elvis, he asked about little dark-haired Jane Wilbanks. He wanted her phone number, and he wanted me to pass along his address so that they could start up a correspondence. Since there was an ocean between Elvis and Jane, I knew this couldn't be just another "fling," and the fact that Elvis wanted to communicate with her was the first indication to me that maybe things weren't as serious with Anita as I'd thought. (Elvis and Jane did stay in touch quite a bit, and, oddly enough, it turned out that her uncle was an army chaplain also stationed in Germany. When she went over to visit her uncle, she did get to spend time with Elvis and his family.)

I was serious about the responsibility of keeping Elvis up to date with what was happening in rock 'n' roll, and I regularly put together deejay samples of the week's top twenty-five hit records to send over to him. I also sent him a few nonhits: Alan Fortas would come up to the WHEY studio and make tapes of us singing some of Elvis's favorites. I think the first one we sent over was us doing the Coasters' "Searchin'," and as soon as Elvis got it, he called me up himself to pass judgment: "Just like I told you around the piano at Graceland, GK—you can't sing a lick."

I talked with Elvis maybe once a month while he was in Germany and kept up on his life over there. I learned that as hard as he was trying to be treated like every other soldier, he objected to the custom of having to holler his yes-sir's and no-sir's to his officers: He felt like he was damaging his voice and his livelihood. He was granted permission not to holler.

I kept playing rock 'n' roll up in Millington, but suddenly there wasn't that much good rockin' to be had. As the fifties came to a close, Elvis was overseas, Jerry Lee hadn't bounced back from his scandal, Chuck Berry was in prison on Mann Act violations, Little Richard had found religion, and Buddy Holly, Ritchie Valens, and the Big Bopper had all perished in the same plane crash. Without the real rockers making records, a lot of radio stations turned to the packaged pop of teen idols like Fabian, Frankie Avalon, and Bobby Rydell.

I tried to keep things interesting by focusing as much as possible on some of the great rhythm and blues acts that were out there such as Big Joe Turner, Jimmy Reed, and LaVern Baker. I'd try to catch those acts when they came through town on their package tours, and I got in the habit of lugging along a reel-to-reel tape player and asking the artists to read a station break for me, something along the lines of, "Hi, this is so-and-so, and whenever I'm in Memphis I listen to George Klein on WHEY." One night I went to see Big Joe Turner, met up with him backstage, and asked him if he'd read a break for me.

"No, no," said Big Joe, sounding a little on edge. "I don't do that."

I explained that all he had to do was read the one line of copy and put his name in, but he was adamant.

"I appreciate your playing my records, George, but I don't do those things."

Something about the way he responded seemed a little off to me, and I guessed that maybe the problem was not that I was asking for a station break but that I was asking him to read. I knew how hard my immigrant mother had worked to learn to read and write, and how sensitive she was about that. And I knew that a lot of black artists of Big Joe's generation just hadn't ever been given much opportunity for any schooling. By asking him to read I was putting him on the spot.

"Well, how about this, Big Joe," I said. "I know you probably wouldn't like what I've written here—why don't you just ad-lib something for me and say whatever you want to say and we'll use that."

"I can do that," he said. "What do you want me to say?"

I got a great station break from him, and managed to spare him any embarrassment.

While Elvis was away, I got one more of those rare personal calls from Colonel Parker. This time, he didn't need my help—he just wanted my company.

"George, the Cotton Carnival is in town. Why don't we meet up and walk the midway?" he asked.

The Cotton Carnival was like Memphis's answer to Mardi Gras, featuring the crowning of a king and queen in addition to all kinds of open-air entertainment. I accepted the Colonel's offer and met him to walk the carnival's midway lineup of games and attractions. The Colonel lived in Madison, Tennessee, outside of Nashville, and I'd wondered at first why he'd be so interested in attending the Memphis carnival, but walking with him I got the sense that he felt like something of a returning hero, back in his most comfortable element. Every other stand we passed he hollered out, "Hey, Joe!" "Hey, Charlie!" and some old carny would look up and shout back "Hey, Colonel—great work with that Elvis kid."

It was a strange situation, to be spending something closer to personal time with a man whom I generally regarded as an authority figure, and after a while I felt free to inquire a little about his history with Elvis.

"Colonel, is it true that you're the one who got Elvis on the Louisiana Hayride?" I asked.

"I did better than that, George," he bellowed.

"How's that, Colonel?"

"I'm the one that got him off the Louisiana Hayride."

Early on the morning of March 7, 1960, Memphis was blanketed with an unseasonably heavy snowstorm. I was standing outside, but I wasn't the least bit concerned with the cold. I was fully focused on the train pulling into the Central Station platform. After two years away, Elvis was coming home.

In addition to sending over the hit records for the last two years, I'd sent Elvis a cosmetic product I thought he might find useful. He'd complained about the gray weather and lack of sun in Germany, and was worried that he was developing an unhealthy, pale appearance. I didn't think he had much to worry about in the appearance department, but I sent him a product that had been touted on the radio station: Man Tan. It was one of the first products of its kind: a lotion that induced an artificial tan. Sure enough, when Elvis stepped off that train in Memphis, not only did he look sharp in his army uniform, he also had a perfect golden glow to his skin.

When I could get up to him, I said, "Elvis, you look great."

"Thanks to your packages," he said, and gave me a wink.

He worked his way down the train platform, saying hello to the crowd of fans, which included Gary Pepper, a wheelchair-bound young guy who'd become one of Elvis's first fan-club presidents. Elvis was mobbed for a while, but didn't seem to mind it at all.

The next time I had a chance to speak to him, I said words I'd been waiting two years to speak.

"Elvis, Graceland is going to rock tonight."

He smiled back at me. "You got that right, GK."

●●● ●●● ●●● ●●●

CHAPTER EIGHT

Can't Help Falling in Love

The whip was cracking out there on the polished floor of the Rainbow Rollerdrome skating rink, and bodies were flying. The hard-hitting action might not have been part of the holiday festivities for most groups, but this was just one of the unique ways Elvis and his friends celebrated the Christmas season of 1962. The group now included a few new faces: Red West had started bringing his cousin Sonny along to our get-togethers, and another of Elvis's cousins, twenty-year-old Billy Smith, had become a very hardworking and devoted member of Elvis's team. Ray "Chief" Sitton, a three-hundred-pound Memphis boy, was another of those likable characters Elvis enjoyed having around. (Chief thought he'd gotten a special, personalized nickname from Elvis, not realizing that, at the time, Elvis was in the habit of calling everyone Chief.) Also with us were a couple of buddies Elvis had met during his army time, Charlie Hodge and Joe Esposito, who had quickly become a part of the inner circle.

As much as Elvis enjoyed dominating the action out in the rink, this night he spent a good deal of time sitting in the seats over by me. It wasn't me he was interested in staying close to, though. He wanted to be near a very special guest he'd brought to the rink for the first time—a young lady named Priscilla Beaulieu.

I'd first heard about a girl named Priscilla during Elvis's phone calls from Germany in the fall of 1959. Given all the Graceland parties, road adventures, and Hollywood times I'd shared with Elvis, we'd talked about a lot of girls, and he'd always spoken affectionately of Anita Wood. But when I heard him talk about Priscilla, it was the first time I ever heard him sound like a guy who was head over heels in love. I don't remember there being a big breakup scene with Anita, but once Elvis met Priscilla, that was the beginning of the end of whatever plans for the future Elvis and Anita had discussed.

For three years now, Elvis had been telling me that Priscilla was the most beautiful girl he'd ever seen, and when I first met her at Graceland before we all headed out to the rink that night, I could finally see what Elvis had been talking about: Priscilla was drop-dead gorgeous. She was young; she'd only been fourteen when she and Elvis met in Germany, and now she was seventeen. But she had a calm and a poise to her that made her seem much older. She was quiet and understandably a little awed by the world she was stepping into. But Elvis was so gentle and thoughtful toward her, as I got to see throughout our night at the Rainbow, that it was pretty obvious his feelings for her were stronger than anything he'd felt before.

At some point in the evening, when there was a little lull in the roller-skating wars in front of us, Elvis turned around in his seat and leaned back toward me.

"GK, you and I are with the two prettiest girls here."

I agreed with him wholeheartedly. Elvis had found Priscilla in Germany, and I'd found my own special romantic interest right at home in Memphis. I'd been out at a fair one day when I ran into a girl I knew, who promptly introduced me to her cousin, a girl named Barbara Little. Barbara was a striking dark-haired beauty who looked to me like Memphis's answer to Elizabeth Taylor. I was smitten right away, got Barbara's phone number from her cousin as soon as I could, and within a week or so was taking her out on dates. After the third or fourth, I knew that my feelings for her were different and deeper than anything I'd felt before. She was great-looking, she was easy to be with, and, to top it off, she loved rock 'n' roll. It seemed to me that Elvis and I had found a couple of great ladies.

When Elvis came back home after his army service, in the spring of 1960, things went back to being much the same: There were parties at Graceland and nights at the Fairgrounds, and right away Elvis went back to juggling a schedule of film production (*G.I. Blues*) and recording dates. But even as we were happy to return to the kind of Elvis-centered life and the get-togethers we'd been missing so much, there was an undeniably different feel in the air. Graceland was as peaceful and welcoming as ever, but for a while after Elvis came back, you couldn't help but feel the absence of Mrs. Presley. Elvis himself was changed, too. He was a twenty-five-year-old veteran now and was a little more intense, with a slightly tougher edge that I thought must have been partly the product of military training. You could see it in the way he stood and walked and carried himself.

His image changed, too. He had served his country without complaining, and that earned him a level of respect and acceptance he hadn't had before. Frank Sinatra—who had been an outspoken denouncer of rock 'n' roll—even invited Elvis to make his first big return appearance in March of 1960 on Sinatra's variety show. (Elvis signaled that he wasn't the same old fifties rocker by wearing a tux.) Elvis had one of his biggest number-one hits ever in the summer of 1960, not with a rock 'n' roll tune but with "It's Now or Never," which convinced a lot of people that he had a lot more talent than they'd ever given him credit for. I know Elvis hated giving up Graceland for army barracks for two years, but by doing so he gained an even greater appeal than he'd had before.

The new army buddies that Elvis brought to Graceland were easy to get along with and great additions to the group. Charlie Hodge was a small, energetic, fun-loving guy who'd had a career performing with the Foggy River Boys singing group. Joe Esposito was just an all-around solid guy, as sharp as he was friendly. I worried a little at first that a Chicago boy like Joe might have some trouble adapting to life in the South, but he fit right in from the start. Joe quickly began handling a lot of the business details of Elvis's career such as scheduling and keeping track of expenses, and everybody—RCA, Hollywood, Vernon Presley, even the Colonel—was thrilled that Elvis now had a real point man and go-to guy for all those matters. With Joe helping to run things, Elvis's world became a lot more organized, and the guys around Elvis started taking on more defined work roles and handling specific duties.

There was a natural flow to the circle of people around Elvis. As guys like Gene Smith or Arthur Hooton had reached the limits of what they could do for him, they moved on and guys like Alan Fortas and Joe and Charlie stepped in (though Gene, being family, was still around quite a bit). Red West maintained his longtime friendship with Elvis and managed to balance his own career with doing work for Elvis. Lamar Fike was still a part of things, though Cliff Gleaves was not—he and Elvis had been through another falling-out. I considered myself lucky to have a friendship with Elvis that seemed as solid as ever, even though I was no longer on his payroll. Actually, I think the fact that I wasn't working for Elvis let both of us appreciate our friendship even more; although there was generally a casual atmosphere between Elvis and the guys working for him, at some point all those guys had to consider Elvis as their employer, not just their buddy. I never had any problem putting friendship above everything else where Elvis was concerned.

With Elvis being the powerful presence at the center of our circle, it really was pretty easy for everybody to get along, and there was a real camaraderie that grew from all of our desire to do our best for Elvis. However, there were a couple of moments when the new guys clashed with the old guys in unexpected ways. I remember one particular night when we were all at the Fairgrounds, playing one of Elvis's favorite games, the Walking Charlie. The Walking Charlie was a sort of mannequin hooked up to a mechanical wheel system that made the mannequin come toward you as you tried to knock off his hat with a baseball. Since we were running the games for ourselves that night, we had to pick up the balls after they were thrown, and Red West was doing some picking up when

Joe Esposito took aim at a Walking Charlie. He missed Charlie's hat but hit Red right in the eye—hard enough that Red had to make a late-night trip to the hospital. It took quite a while for Red's black eye to heal, and it was quite a while before Red wanted anything to do with Joe again.

Just before Elvis came back to the States, I had made the move from Sam Phillips's WHEY up in Millington to WHHM, a hot station that put me back in the middle of the Memphis scene. Once Elvis was home, I felt I had the best of both worlds: I could be as much a part of his life as I was and still have my own career. There were some nights when a balance between work hours and Elvis hours wasn't so easy, though. Sometimes we'd get back to Graceland from the Rainbow or the Fairgrounds in the wee hours of the morning, and Elvis would want to sit at the piano in the music room and sing. Well, he could stay up all night because he could sleep all day, but on my work schedule, the late hours sometimes caught up with me. I remember one night when he was singing for a few of us and I was having trouble keeping my eyes open. I tried to fight off a big yawn but I couldn't—and somewhere in mid-yawn I realized that the music had stopped.

"Am I keeping you awake, GK?"

"No, no, Elvis," I stammered. "Go ahead."

"You're getting a free damn concert from Elvis Presley," he said with mock anger. "Sit up and pay attention."

There were other moments when I felt closer to him than ever—like when he and I would drive out to his mother's grave at Forest Hill cemetery not far from Graceland. He never spoke much on those visits, but it was clear to me how much sadness was still there and how much he still missed her. I was simply glad to be able to give him whatever support I could during those times.

Elvis came home from the army with a keen interest in a physical discipline that sounded very exotic to us in 1960: karate. He'd studied with some masters over in Germany, and had really taken to karate's mix of intense concentration and explosive power. After he got back, he put on karate demonstrations at Graceland, and all of us who got to watch him in action were just blown away. Watching him break boards with a quick hand chop or throw a controlled kick that could knock the cigarettes out of someone's shirt pocket without hurting them—it was almost like watching magic tricks.

I was with Elvis on a summer day in 1960 when he received an honor that would always mean a great deal to him: his first-degree karate black belt certification. Elvis had gotten in contact with a fellow army man, a sergeant major in the 101st Airborne Division named Hank Slomanski. A career soldier, Slomanski had been stationed in both Japan and Korea and became one of the first Americans to be considered a martial arts master. I imagine Slomanski was a little skeptical about taking Elvis on as a student, and if anything he probably put him through more rigorous training than any other student. The day I met him, Slomanski was putting on an exhibition at a Memphis school and Elvis had been invited to attend to take some publicity pictures. After the event, Slomanski put Elvis through his final test and awarded him his first black belt. I know that in later years, Elvis received some black belt certifications that were more honorary in nature, but there was nothing honorary about that first one. Slomanski put Elvis through a test that pushed him to the limit, and Elvis proved himself worthy.

While Elvis enjoyed the new thrill of karate, he didn't give up on some of his old favorite activities, either. He still loved putting together touch football games and would rent out the lighted, well-maintained field at Whitehaven High School for games. He also loved to water-ski on McKellar Lake south of downtown Memphis, and had a sixteen-foot powerboat (named *Karate*) that he, Alan, and I took out a lot. Alan and Joe and I ended up buying that boat when Elvis, deciding he needed something bigger and more stylish, purchased a twenty-one-foot Coronado with a 325-horsepower engine.

Beyond his newfound karate interest, I did notice a few very specific changes in Elvis's behavior when he came back from the army. For one thing, I noticed that when he picked up any cup that had a handle on it, he would drink from right where the handle was, rather than holding the handle out to the side. After I saw this a couple of times, I asked him about it.

"Oh, that's just an army habit, GK," he explained. "I was never sure how well things got cleaned over there, but I figured if you drank from where the handle was, probably nobody else's mouth had been there."

Some other army habits were a little more troubling. Elvis told us that when he'd had to do the long, grueling midnight-to-dawn guard shifts in Germany, he'd been introduced to "bennies"—benzedrine tablets that soldiers would take to stay alert through the night. One night, when he was back in Memphis, he and Red West and I were driving around, and Elvis started saying he wanted to drive over to Alan Fortas's house. I didn't pick up on why Elvis wanted to go to Alan's house so badly, but Red did. Somehow, Alan had been able to get a hold of a supply of benzedrine.

"I don't think we need to go over there," said Red.

"Come on," Elvis laughed. "It's what we used all the time in the army. They're just bennies. All they do is keep you awake."

There was a slightly awkward silence for a moment. Then Red spoke in a surprisingly forceful voice. "Elvis, you know that's how Hank Williams died. He started messing with those damned pills."

Red wasn't telling Elvis what to do—nobody ever really did. But Red was making sure his concerns were heard. And they were. The mood in the car changed. Elvis didn't laugh anymore, but he didn't argue the point. In fact, he didn't say another word. He just slowed the car down and turned around, and we drove back to Graceland in silence.

I was working over at WHHM at this time, where I got to see quite a bit of a new coworker: Anita Wood. She'd kicked off her career cohosting Wink Martindale's *Dance Party* TV show, but she also had great talent as a disc jockey, and when I was working a split shift of mornings and afternoons at WHHM, she had the midday show. Anita and I had always gotten along well, but things had been made a little awkward between us because Elvis had asked me to "keep an eye on her" while he was away. I took this to mean that he didn't want her dating anybody else, though I knew he certainly wasn't going to hold himself to the same rule. When Elvis returned, Anita was still a part of the scene at Graceland and still a big part of Elvis's life, but the feelings for the new love in his life—Priscilla—couldn't stay a secret. By the time Priscilla came to Memphis at the end of 1962, Elvis and Anita had parted for good, though they did remain friendly in later years.

Elvis soon returned to a hectic pace of moviemaking, and in his first year back starred in *G.I. Blues, Flaming Star,* and *Wild in the Country.* Colonel Parker had decided to phase Elvis out of live concert tours in order to maintain his film-production and soundtrack-recording schedules, but he and Elvis gave Memphis fans a treat with a final headlining appearance at a big charity show at Ellis Auditorium on February 25, 1961. Elvis performed with his longtime backup players Scotty Moore, D. J. Fontana, and the Jordanaires. (I don't think there was any lingering animosity between Elvis and bassist Bill Black, but once they parted ways in the fifties, they never played together again.) Elvis also wanted a new, more powerful sound onstage, so he borrowed an idea he'd seen James Brown use: He put together a band that featured two drummers, adding Nashville session man Buddy Harman to his lineup.

In the spring of 1961, Elvis headed off to L.A. and then the islands to film *Blue Hawaii.* I focused on my radio career and looked for some other ways to make money. In the early days of rock 'n' roll, one of the easiest ways for a disc jockey to get income on the side was to accept payola—cash and gifts from promoters and labels in exchange for playing their records. For a while this had been legal as long as deejays declared what they accepted as income. Things changed when pioneering rock 'n' roll deejay Alan Freed got caught up in a payola scandal and was charged with accepting bribes to play specific records. Freed's career was ruined, Congress cracked down on the shadowy exchanges of money in the radio world, and by the early sixties payola was officially a criminal activity.

Even as a beginning jock, I'd never been interested in accepting any-thing that felt like payola. That didn't come from any principled stand—I could have used the cash as much as anybody. But I liked the fact that when I was on the air I picked the music I played, and I never wanted to owe anybody any favors when it came to playing records. Still, I was always looking for side jobs and opportunities, and in the early sixties I continued to host record hops at schools and community centers around Memphis. At one of those I noticed some kids doing a crazy new dance that I hadn't seen anywhere else before. They'd kind of groove along snapping their fin-gers, but at certain points in a song they'd all go through the motion of shooting a basketball, or hitting a baseball or throwing a football. I asked the kids what it was called and they told me it was the UT—a kind of dance-floor celebration of the University of Tennessee's athletic teams. I knew a dance record could sweep the country and become a huge hit real quick—we'd already seen that happen with Ray Bryant's "Madison Time" and Chubby Checker's "The Twist." I didn't see any reason why the UT couldn't be the next big thing. But, like the other dance crazes before it, the dance needed its own song.

Sam Phillips liked the idea and set up a recording session in his new Memphis studio at 639 Madison Avenue. I brought in the kids I'd met who knew the dance, and I teamed with Sun producer/engineer Charlie Underwood to come up with a song that would work with their moves. I started coming up with rhymes ("shoot the ball, y'all") while Charlie worked out a groove with an ace bunch of session players—Charlie Rich on piano, Billy Lee Riley on bass, and J. M. Van Eaton on drums. We got a great little song cut that worked well for the kids to dance to, "UT Party Time."

Once the song was done, we took things a step further. The term "music video" wasn't around yet, but some singers had put out little movies of themselves singing a hit song. I figured nobody could learn the dance just from hearing the song, but if we made a little movie of the kids dancing the UT and sent copies to the top nine or ten *Dance Party*–style shows around the country, the whole thing had a good chance of taking off. Sam didn't have much of a budget for that kind of thing and had never shot a movie for anybody else at Sun, but he decided to take the chance. We filmed the kids doing the dance, sent it out, and I made a point of calling the hosts and giving the UT my best pitch. We got a good initial response, but just as "UT Party Time" was starting to make a little noise, we got outcrazed. In June of 1961, Chubby Checker released "Let's Twist Again," a monster hit that was at the top of the charts all summer long. Once kids were twisting again, there was just no way they were going to be interested in pretending to shoot hoops to "UT Party Time." So, like "The Return of Jerry Lee," my second and final Sun record was, to put it mildly, not a smash hit.

I did have success hustling some side money in other ways, though. I began moonlighting as the announcer at drag races, even though I didn't know much about cars (I'm not sure I even had my driver's license when I started doing the announcing). I got pretty good at talking to the racers and picking up just enough insider terms about engines. While I might have quickly run out of things to say during a long stock car race, the drag races were over in about ten seconds, so people ended up thinking I knew what I was talking about. By the time Elvis was back from army service, I was the voice of a beautiful brand-new Lakeland International Raceway outside of Memphis.

Elvis had always loved going to the movies, and as soon as he was able to, he'd set up private screenings for us in the movie theaters around Memphis. Vernon Presley had become friendly with a Mr. Shafer, who was the city manager for the Malco chain's Memphis theaters in addition to having access to the Mid-South Film Exchange. Through Mr. Shafer, Elvis was able to rent out the Memphian Theater just about whenever he wanted to, paying the overtime wages to keep a projectionist and a candy-counter attendant on hand, and picking whatever titles sounded good to him from what was available at the exchange.

We began spending a lot of nights at the Memphian. It was always a treat to see a first-run movie before it was out anywhere else, but there was a catch. Elvis was the biggest film buff of all of us, and if he liked a movie, he wanted to see it over and over again. I remember a few nights at the Memphian when I wasn't sure I could make it through one more screening of *The Guns of Navarone* or *To Kill a Mockingbird.*

Everybody had their favorite spots in the theater. Elvis would always sit center-row about twelve rows back from the screen, and my seat was on the aisle about fifteen rows back from Elvis and ten rows from the exit. That meant that I could hear anything Elvis said, and he could hear me. But if he went for a second or third feature in a night and I was worried about getting up for work, I could sneak away without calling attention to myself.

Through our nights at the Memphian, I also developed a side job. When I asked Mr. Shafer who made all the tapes of announcements I heard at drive-in theaters, he basically shrugged and asked me if I wanted to do it. He got a contract drawn up for me, and for about five years I was the voice of Memphis drive-ins, letting people know that hot french fries were available at the refreshment stand or that the second feature would be starting in five minutes. Recorded music was sometimes played at the drive-ins before or between movies, and I started having fun adding my voice to the music tapes, dedicating songs to "the girl in the blue Chevrolet over there," so that people got the impression I was actually watching over the drive-in lot. A friend told me that he was at the drive-in one night when one of my tapes dedicated a love song to "that cute couple in the red Buick." Suddenly, a red Buick sped out of the lot. We suspected that I'd inadvertently called attention to some Buick owner who was at the movies with somebody else's girlfriend.

Soon the group around Elvis started being referred to as the Memphis Mafia—a title we didn't come up with but didn't really object to either. Slowly, the Memphis Mafia expanded. I brought in a new guy named Marty Lacker, who I'd known back at Humes and had crossed paths with at the Memphis Jewish Community Center. Marty got involved with taking care of some of the day-to-day concerns at Graceland, and Elvis appreciated having someone else he could trust looking after his business. By the end of 1962, a couple of other very sharp guys who'd hung out at Graceland, Richard Davis and Jimmy Kingsley, had been deemed cool and capable enough by Elvis to become regular members of the Mafia. A young, strong, solid guy named Jerry Schilling was also around quite a bit. He wasn't yet old enough to go to work for Elvis, but he was a regular face around Graceland and one of Elvis's favorite guys to play football with.

Brother Dave Gardner wasn't ever a member of Elvis's inner circle, but for a while he was a familiar face at Graceland and somebody Elvis really enjoyed spending time with. Brother Dave was out of Jackson, Tennessee, and he was one of the first "out there" stand-up comics we'd ever seen— sort of the South's answer to Lenny Bruce ("Let them that don't want none have memories of never gittin' any" was one of his great lines). Elvis had first seen Brother Dave at Gus Stevens's nightclub in Biloxi, Mississippi, in July 1956, when Elvis was on vacation with his girlfriend at the time, June Juanico. Elvis always did enjoy a twisted sense of humor, and Brother Dave was about as twisted as they came. He was the first guy I knew who smoked marijuana, and the first to talk about something called LSD (I declined invitations from Brother Dave to try either of those). And Elvis wasn't the only big celebrity who enjoyed Brother Dave's work. One night in 1962, during a period when Elvis was away shooting a movie, I went to see Brother Dave perform in Memphis and found myself seated at a table with Bob Hope and his wife. After Dave delivered what I considered a wild and funny set, I asked Mr. Hope what he thought of the comic.

"We're trying to put a man on the moon," he said. "Here's a guy who's already gone and come back."

There was a true camaraderie among the guys around Elvis, old-timers and new faces alike. But the guy you really wanted to spend time with was always, of course, Elvis, and I felt lucky every time I got to spend more personal moments with him. I remember one particular Memphian night when a few carloads of guys had taken off from Graceland to head for the theater, and Elvis and Alan Fortas and I were the only ones left in the house. When the phone rang at about eleven P.M., I picked it up and was surprised to hear the voice of Sam Phillips.

"George," he said, "Jerry Lee and I are in the neighborhood just messing around, and we were wondering if you could ask Elvis if it's all right to come up and visit a while."

I asked Elvis, and it was fine by him. Within a few minutes, Sam and Jerry Lee Lewis were sitting on the big white couch in the Graceland living room talking away with Elvis, Alan, and me. Jerry Lee had fought hard to get his career back together after the scandal he'd been through and had begun making some great records at Sun with Sam Phillips again (his cover of Ray Charles's "What'd I Say" in 1961 was his first big postscandal hit). Elvis and Jerry Lee started trading old road stories, and the more they talked about things that had happened as they performed particular songs, the more I could sense what was about to happen. They each got to the point where they couldn't just explain what they were talking about—they wanted to play it. So all of a sudden Elvis and Jerry Lee were sitting together at the music room's grand piano, laughing their way through a four-handed jam session. Elvis was on the left end of the keyboard playing bass lines while Jerry played the chords up top, and after a couple of stories they just focused in on the piano and did more playing than talking. Jerry would start singing an Elvis song, with Elvis playing along, and then Elvis would sing a Jerry Lee song with Jerry Lee just playing. The few times there was any kind of lull in the music, Sam would call out something that would get them fired up to play again. I remember one of Elvis's favorite songs at the time was a hit that Clyde McPhatter and the Drifters had in the fifties, "Come What May," and after he showed Jerry Lee how the song went they must have played that together ten times.

Alan and I stood around the piano like smiling statues: We were hearing one of the best concerts of our lives and didn't want to say a word that might stop the music. Sam stood with us beaming like a proud papa—he'd "discovered" both of these great talents, and here they were showing off their greatness in the most casual and wonderful of ways.

Finally, about an hour after they'd started, Elvis said, "Sam, Jerry—I got some people waiting for me over at the movie theater. You want to come out with us?"

Sam and Jerry declined, but as we said goodbye we all agreed that it'd been great for them to come by. Minutes later we were climbing into Elvis's Cadillac limo to head toward the Memphian. Just before Elvis got in the car, he turned to me and said, "You know, GK, that guy's a genius on the piano."

"I know it, Elvis," I said excitedly. "He really is a great player. He don't play like anybody else. And when you see him up close like that, you can see that he's not just pounding—he's really a great player."

Elvis got in behind the wheel, and Alan and I piled into the car.

"Man, that Jerry Lee is something else," said Alan.

"Can he play the damn piano or what?" I asked.

We started going back and forth on just how great a jam session we'd witnessed, with particular attention to how fine a player Jerry Lee was. We went on and on, not quite picking up on the fact that Elvis wasn't saying anything.

"Damn, that was historic," said Alan. "Jerry Lee singing Elvis Presley. I wish we'd recorded that."

"That Killer is a helluva player," I said. "A helluva player."

We just kept talking about how great Jerry Lee was until, finally, Elvis spoke up.

"Look, you sons of bitches," he said. "If you all like Jerry Lee so much, why don't you go work for him."

Alan and I sat in stunned silence for a moment or two. Then we quickly began backpedaling to make up for our mistake.

"Jerry Lee sounded good playing with *you*, Elvis," said Alan. "He don't ever sound that good on his own records."

"He's a visual performer," I said, "but he's nowhere near as musical as you are, Elvis." Our attempts at belated flattery were a little too obvious.

"Aw, shut the hell up," said Elvis. "I know what you're doing."

The car stayed quiet for another mile or two.

Then Alan said, very softly, "That Jerry Lee sure is something, though."

"Goddamn you guys," hollered Elvis, but this time he couldn't help but bust out laughing.

New Year's Eve, 1962. The year had shown Elvis to be as big a superstar as he'd ever been, with more successful movies (*Follow That Dream, Kid Gala-had, Girls, Girls, Girls*) and more hit singles at the top of the pop charts ("Can't Help Falling in Love," "Good Luck Charm," "Return to Sender"). But more important, he was together with Priscilla—the girl he'd fallen for in Germany, who had now finally come to Memphis to be with him as she finished her schooling. The year's end called for a special celebration, and Elvis had asked Alan Fortas and me to set up a killer private party. We both knew Billy Hill, who ran a hot little nightspot just north of Grace-land called the Manhattan Club, and he was thrilled when we approached him with the idea of having Elvis Presley's New Year's party in his club. The club's smoking house band was fronted by a terrific soul man named Willie Mitchell, who also worked with the great vocal group the Four Kings. We got the musicians lined up for the night, went over all the food and drink details at the club, worked out a guest list, and threw a heck of a bash for Elvis.

The night had some wild moments—Jerry Schilling got into a spat with his girlfriend and ended up punching a wall hard enough to knock over a few shelves' worth of bottles in the liquor store next door. (Elvis was good enough to pick up the tab.) But the image that sticks in my mind from that night is a tender one: Elvis holding Priscilla gently in the center of the dance floor and slow dancing. For all the moves I'd seen him make on a stage, I'd never really seen him just dancing with a partner. But there he was, holding her, gently swaying and looking like a man who'd found exactly what he'd always been after.

The other powerful memory from that night was produced a little later.

Young Priscilla, overwhelmed by the new surroundings and the celebration, evidently had a glass of champagne or two too many. Elvis wanted her to be safe and comfortable, but he still had a party to host, so he asked Barbara and me to drive her back to Graceland.

Even at the time, I couldn't help thinking that there probably weren't too many guys Elvis would trust to take care of his new love for him. But he trusted me. So I began 1963 by stepping out of Elvis Presley's private party with my new love and his new love. I got behind the wheel of my trusty Impala and headed down Highway 51 toward Graceland, with Barbara beside me and a tipsy Priscilla curled up in the backseat.

CHAPTER NINE

Bright Light City

The fireballs came rocketing through the dark, hitting the running, helmeted figure square in the chest. Sparks flew up and bounced off the heavy visor that protected his face. As the figure prepared to return fire at his targets, another volley of colorful flames and sparks cut through the night, with one fireball coming perilously close to singeing the hair off the top of my head.

Slowly, I inched my way off the battlefield, hearing Elvis's laugh come from within that helmet as he clutched a Roman candle in each hand and fired at Richard Davis and Jimmy Kingsley.

Happy Fourth of July, Graceland style.

The tradition of fireworks on the lawn in back of the house had started while Mrs. Presley was alive. She and Vernon would sit safely in the den while Elvis and Gene Smith and a few others of us would put on our own fireworks show. Elvis loved doing that, and even after Mrs. Presley was gone, the Fourth of Julys got bigger and bigger, until Elvis was sending guys down to the Mississippi roadside stands to buy huge supplies of firecrackers and bottle rockets and cherry bombs and Roman candles and anything else with a fuse on it. Somewhere along the way, we stopped putting on a fireworks show and started having fireworks wars. Like the roller-skating games, or climbing out of the roller coaster at the Fairgrounds, this was the kind of dangerous fun Elvis loved. But after a couple of trips to the emergency room when guys got hit in the face or somebody had a shirt burned off, we talked Elvis into wearing a motorcycle jacket and helmet when war broke out.

The fireworks weren't just a danger outside, though. Vernon Presley had a habit of taking a taste of whatever food was out whenever he walked through the Graceland kitchen. One day, there was nothing on the stove, so he scooped up a handful of M&M's from a glass bowl and filled his mouth. He did that quickly enough that the couple of us who were sitting there didn't have time to tell him that it wasn't a bowl of M&M's—it was a bowl of the little impact firecrackers that made a loud pop when you threw them against the ground. I've never seen Vernon looking more surprised than when wisps of smoke started drifting out of his mouth. One of us got him over to the sink to spit the stuff out, while someone else went upstairs to get Elvis. When it was clear that Mr. Presley was going to be okay, we were able to laugh about it, and Elvis had a word of advice for his daddy: Take a minute to look at what you're getting ready to eat before you throw it in your mouth.

That summer, I had more than the Fourth to celebrate. I was back hosting a rock 'n' roll show at WHBQ, the station where I'd started. I'd come over from WHHM, where I'd again had the chance to work for my old mentor Bill Grumbles. Grumbles put together a great lineup of on-air talent at WHHM, including Dewey Phillips, who I did manage to patch things up with. But the station never made money, and when I had the chance to get back to WHBQ, the hottest station in town, I took it. Pop music was starting to get some energy back, with the surf music of the Beach Boys and Jan and Dean on the charts, and Motown producing a steady stream of hits. The great guitarist Lonnie Mack had a hit with a rockin' instrumental of "Memphis," and even though Elvis was mainly doing soundtrack work, he stayed on the charts with cool tracks like "(You're the) Devil in Disguise." I was excited to be in the thick of things at WHBQ, in the prized six P.M. to nine P.M. shift. Just as important as having a good shift at the station was having the right time off, though. As I had been doing for years, I carefully requested my two weeks' worth of vacation days so that I could be with Elvis in Los Angeles while he worked on a film. In the summer of '63, I headed out to join him for the making of *Viva Las Vegas*.

"Okay, boys," said Elvis. "Listen up. Ann-Margret is coming over for dinner tonight."

We Memphis Mafia members were hanging around the main den of a beautiful house on Perugia Way in Bel Air, which Elvis had recently begun renting rather than checking in for an extended stay at the Beverly Wilshire. At the mention of Ann-Margret, we all began to hoot and holler. Elvis had just met the actress at some wardrobe fittings for the film, and while most of us had not seen her in person yet, we knew she was the hottest starlet in Hollywood.

Priscilla Beaulieu had just graduated from high school in Memphis— she'd finished her schooling there after Elvis had appealed to her parents, who were still stationed in Germany as part of Colonel Beaulieu's air force tour of duty. She was supposed to be living in the home of Vernon Presley and his second wife, Dee Stanley (whom Vernon had met in Germany during Elvis's army years). But, slowly and steadily, she moved into Grace-land itself, and the more time she spent with Elvis, the more they looked like a couple that was meant to be together. He loved the fact that she was younger—she was eighteen and he was twenty-eight—and that he could welcome her into his world as an innocent, open soul he could teach and guide. He didn't talk about his feelings or his plans for Priscilla with us, but it was pretty clear he wanted her to be a central part of his life.

Elvis's life wasn't an ordinary one, though, and life at Graceland was something very different from life in Hollywood. I'm sure he and Priscilla hadn't worked out any explicit agreements, but she was certainly aware that millions of women wanted to get closer to Elvis. And while he definitely wanted a future with Priscilla, that didn't mean he might not enjoy himself in the here and now with somebody else.

As far as somebody elses went, it didn't get any better than Ann-Margret.

"Man, is she fine," somebody called out in the Perugia den.

"She's got a body that won't quit," added somebody else.

"I can't wait to get a look at her," came another call.

"You ain't getting a look at her," said Elvis. "You guys are gonna get lost tonight."

This suggestion did not go over well, and we let Elvis know how we felt in the strongest possible terms. He didn't budge.

"I'll say it again. I want you guys to get lost tonight. When she comes up, I want one guy to go to the door and bring her to the den. Then I'll come in. And then that one guy can get lost, too. I don't want to see any of you guys hanging around here tonight."

Elvis headed back to his bedroom, and Richard Davis leaned over to whisper something to me: "Bullshit on that."

Elvis was going to be entertaining Ann-Margret in the house's main, larger den, which had a circular layout and was completely glassed in on one side. While Elvis was getting ready for his evening, Richard, Jimmy Kingsley, Alan Fortas, and I came up with a strategy. There were heavy drapes around the glassed-in side of the den, which Elvis had pulled shut for privacy. We went around and separated all the drapes an imperceptible half-inch or so, just enough so that someone on the other side of the glass could peep in.

We all stayed out of sight until Ann arrived. Billy Smith was the one designated to show Ann in, and when we figured he'd had time to get her to the den, we all crept outside and took up our peeping positions.

Ann-Margret was absolutely stunning. She had a great figure, and whatever she was wearing that night really showed off her beautiful legs. But she also just had a real glow about her. We'd seen all kinds of Hollywood starlets made up and done up and dressed up to look attractive. But Ann just had a natural beauty that knocked you out. And she had a fantastic smile, too, that lit up as soon as Elvis joined her in the den. When he put some music on, we felt it was safe to speak to one another in the quietest of whispers.

"Look at those legs."

"What a body."

"She's better looking than in the movies."

Ann and Elvis laughed and talked for a while, then sat down for a dinner that was brought in by the house cook. We tried as hard as we could to stay still and not make any noise. When the couple was through with dinner, Elvis turned up the music a little, and we saw him do something we'd only seen with Priscilla: He slow-danced with Ann-Margret. That sight shocked a couple of chuckles out of us.

They kept dancing and laughing and really seemed to be having a great time together. At some point, Elvis headed out toward his bedroom, leaving Ann behind. We didn't know what kind of move he was making, but we didn't care because we only wanted to look at her.

"Ahem."

We all jumped and turned at once to see Elvis standing there behind us, not looking very happy at all. There was just a moment when everything was quiet, then he began hollering at us and cussing us out and firing karate kicks at us and shooing us like a pack of dogs. We all scattered and took off running, though I got a good karate kick in the ass before I got away. I was at full speed looking for a way to get back into the house when I saw where I could head into an open door that led to a hallway toward the front of the house. I would have made it, too, except that the door wasn't open—it was just very, very clean glass. I smashed my face right into that door, fell backward on the ground, then popped right back up again like a damn cartoon. I took a moment to check my nose—the one Elvis had bought for me   which felt like it was broken but turned out not to be Then I took off like a jet one more time, trying to avoid being on the receiving end of any more karate kicks.

The next morning, Elvis wasn't smiling, but he wasn't kicking anybody either. He gave us a little speech about how he meant business: When he wanted to be alone, he wanted us to respect that. The more I thought about that, the worse I felt that we'd invaded his privacy the way we did. It truly was pretty juvenile of us (then again—Ann-Margret!). But eventually Elvis started laughing about the situation, and I think he really enjoyed the fact that while we were all head over heels for Ann-Margret, he was the guy who was with her. Later that day he sent Richard Davis out to the hip clothing store Fred Segal to buy twenty blue shirts and twenty pairs of blue slacks. Ann-Margret had said she thought he looked good in blue.

When I was alone with Elvis at some point, I couldn't help but pry a little more, and I asked him how the rest of the night with Ann had gone. Instead of a kick, I got a great big smile from Elvis.

"GK, she's a wild, sexy, sensuous woman," he said.

"Come on, Elvis, be a little more specific than that."

He just kind of shrugged and said, "Well, she almost sucked my thumb off."

I didn't know if this meant exactly what it sounded like, or if it was Hollywood slang for something I'd never heard about. But I figured I shouldn't press Elvis for any more private details. I walked away, a little confused— but with my imagination racing.

I got to know Ann-Margret a little better when the cast and crew of *Viva Las Vegas* moved to the Sahara Hotel in Las Vegas to do some location shooting, and I quickly discovered that in addition to being beautiful she had a warm, wonderful personality. As successful and great-looking as she and Elvis were, neither one had the typical Hollywood star attitude I'd seen in other celebrities, and they just hit it off tremendously. From his earliest days, Elvis had been a little reticent about getting seriously involved with women in show business—one of the things that drew him powerfully to Priscilla was that she was from outside of that world. But Ann was fun-loving and down-to-earth, and, though she was a star, she didn't have the inflated ego that a lot of much less talented actresses suffered from. While

Elvis stopping by to visit during one of my shifts as a disc jockey at WMC radio.

(George Klein Collection)

Elvis hadn't heard his second album until I delivered a copy that I'd received at my radio station to his home on Audubon Drive in Memphis, fall 1956.

(George Klein Collection)

Together at a preshow press conference in Toronto, 1957. Note the silver shoes, which were made to go with his gold-leaf suit.

(George Klein Collection)

Posing on Elvis's Harley-Davidson, fall 1956.

(George Klein Collection)

ABOVE: Elvis and Anita Wood ride a dodgem car at the Mid-South Fairgrounds.
(George Klein Collection)

ABOVE RIGHT: Publicity shot of Elvis and Ann-Margret for *Viva Las Vegas*.
(George Klein Collection)

RIGHT: Elvis in a custom-made shirt, with me and actress Venetia Stevenson, whom one magazine dubbed "The most photogenic girl in the world."
(George Klein Collection)

Elvis showing off the Hollywood prop gun he used to get us out of a scrape with some angry marines in Memphis.

(Reprinted with permission from Commercial Appeal)

Success brings new girl friends. Elvis Presley introduces Judy Tyler to Anne Neyland and sparks fly.

M G-M Presents **"JAILHOUSE ROCK"** in CinemaScope

Lobby poster for *Jailhouse Rock*. That's me on the couch—this film was my movie debut.

I was a groomsman at Elvis and
Priscilla's wedding, May 1, 1967.
Only fourteen guests attended the
actual ceremony.

(George Klein Collection)

A special toast from Elvis and
Priscilla on my wedding day, in
Elvis's suite at the International
Hotel in Las Vegas.

(George Klein Collection)

The Memphis Mafia together at my wedding, December 1970.

(George Klein Collection)

Elvis meets one of his idols, Roy Hamilton, during the 1969 sessions at American Sound Studios. That's producer Chips Moman on the right. Elvis recorded "Suspicious Minds" that night.
(George Klein Collection)

"Miss Teenage Memphis" —better known as Cybill Shepherd—appears on my *Talent Party* TV show. The show helped launch her modeling career, and years later she had a brief romance with Elvis.
(George Klein Collection)

American Bandstand's Dick Clark makes an appearance on my *Talent Party*.
(George Klein Collection)

The "Hardest Working Man in Show Business" —James Brown—rests awhile on *Talent Party*. We became very close friends and I had the chance to introduce him to Elvis.
(George Klein Collection)

I had the pleasure of serving as emcee when Sam Phillips was honored at a University of Memphis event. That's Jerry Lee Lewis and singer Brenda Lee with us.
(George Klein Collection)

My wonderful wife, Dara, and I visited Neil Diamond backstage at a concert in Memphis.
(George Klein Collection)

My dear friend and a very classy lady, Priscilla Presley. We're seen here at the Memphis Blues Ball.

(George Klein Collection)

My best man.

(George Klein Collection)

anyone close to Elvis knew he was absolutely smitten with Priscilla and sincerely wanted to build a life around her, it was also obvious that he was honestly overwhelmed by the feelings he had for Ann-Margret. With success had come a complicated life for Elvis, but Ann's humor and energy made it easy for him to enjoy himself. That meant a lot to him.

I ended up spending a lot of time with Elvis and Ann in Las Vegas and Los Angeles. One night we went to see one of Elvis's favorite gospel groups, the Clara Ward Singers, at the Frontier Hotel, where Elvis had played his first Vegas engagement in 1956 to less than enthusiastic middle-aged casino crowds. It was there I saw a rare occasion when Elvis lost his temper in public, after a cocktail waitress refused to serve Ann-Margret unless she produced ID.

Back in L.A., just before I returned to Memphis, I had one other notable experience with the pair of stars. Elvis was considering moving to a phenomenal celebrity's home in the Hollywood Hills that was now for sale. It had all sorts of crazy modern features, like TVs that would descend from the ceiling at the push of a button, and Elvis wanted Ann to see it. While he and Ann and Richard and I were out for a drive, we decided to stop by the place. The house was locked up, but Elvis didn't want to wait the hour or so it might take for a real estate person to show up. Richard had picked up a knack for getting into locked premises, and, sure enough, he found some sliding doors around back and was able to unlatch the lock on them using a credit card. He came around to the front door and let the rest of us in. We started looking at the spectacular layout and the amazing architecture, and Elvis pointed out one of the prime features—a secret "panic" room hidden behind a closet where the homeowners could go for protection if they needed it.

All of a sudden we heard a pounding on the front door. Elvis told me to go see who it was, and I opened the door to see a puzzled Los Angeles police officer standing there. It was only later we realized that by stepping on the carpet near the front door, we'd tripped a silent alarm.

"Do you have permission to be here?" the cop asked.

"We're just looking at the house," I answered. Richard came up beside me.

"How'd you get in?" the cop asked.

"The doors were open," said Richard. "We just walked in."

The cop looked skeptical. Then he heard some voices behind us in the house.

"Who else is here?" he asked.

"Well sir," I answered, "Elvis Presley and Ann-Margret."

"Bullshit," said the cop.

"Is there a problem?" asked Elvis, appearing behind me, with his arm around Ann.

The cop's eyes almost popped out of his head, and he changed his attitude very quickly. He started apologizing to Elvis while stealing as many looks at Ann as he could, and he finally said we could stay as long as we liked if we just locked up when we left.

Back in Memphis, I added yet another job to my own showbiz résumé: wrestling announcer. Professional wrestling was starting to get popular, and on weekends, WHBQ's TV station brought costumed wrestlers into the studio to do a show. TV program manager Lance Russell was the host, and when he needed a new cohost, he tapped me for the position. My interest wasn't so much in the wrestling but in just being on television. Working with Lance, I began to learn all the intricacies of what it took to work in front of a camera rather than just a microphone—how to play to the different camera angles, how to talk, how to move. It wasn't as easy as it looked. And, as it turns out, the wrestling wasn't always as phony as it seemed.

As a new face on TV, I figured that the best way to get myself noticed was to be edgy. I thought it might be good television to get the wrestlers a little agitated. One day I was interviewing a stockily built, very powerful guy named Treacherous Phillips, and when he started to say something about his fans, I cut him off.

"You ain't got no fans, Treach," I said.

"I get fan mail," he said, a little defensively.

"Are you crazy? Nobody writes you."

He reached into his pocket just as if we'd planned this and pulled out a letter. "Read this," he growled.

I took the letter and saw right away that it really was a fan letter. But I said, "You know what, Treacherous? I think you wrote this yourself." With a flourish, I tore it up right in front of him.

We were sitting on a pair of folding chairs and I was to his right. In a flash, he took his meaty right arm and backhanded me so hard across the chest that I flipped over backward and landed on the floor. Then he was on top of me—his 225 pounds against my 140.

Lance and the crew came running over to pull us apart, and after things calmed down, Lance said maybe I needed to tone down my interviews a little bit. I admitted that he was probably right. Oddly enough, Treach and I got along just fine after that. He went on to a career as a Memphis prison guard, and I can honestly say that the only guy who ever knocked me out of a chair became one of my closest friends.

I went back out to L.A. in June of '64 for my regular trip to see Elvis in Los Angeles, when he was making *Girl Happy*. The ranks of the Memphis Mafia at this point were filled by Richard, Jimmy, Alan, Billy Smith, Joe Esposito, Charlie Hodge, Lamar, Marty Lacker, Red and Sonny West, and sometimes Gene Smith. And, with Elvis at the center of things, we really did function well as a kind of rock 'n' roll fraternity house.

Elvis had Priscilla, and I was still going steady with Barbara. Red West and a couple other guys had gotten married, and most guys had some kind of steady girlfriend back in Memphis. When we were there, around Graceland, the guys, the wives, and the girlfriends generally got along well with one another. You did have to be a little careful around Priscilla—she was young and still finding her way as a part of Elvis's world, and he didn't want her treated as just "one of the guys" to be kidded around with. But she and the other women were often a part of what we did as a group in Memphis.

Out in Hollywood, though, it was a boys' club, and the boys wanted to have some fun. Elvis worked incredibly hard on his film sets, and he wanted to play hard, too, so nights at Perugia were sometimes like those old Graceland parties, with a group of girls from the film sets or from around town coming up to party with us. Things could get a little racy then. Elvis had a two-way mirror installed in one bedroom so that anyone in an adjacent closet could watch what was going on. (I can remember being jammed in that closet with Elvis, trying to stop from laughing as we watched someone or another put the moves on a date.) One night Alan Fortas said that he'd convinced a particularly pretty pair of girls to go skinny-dipping with him and me in the big beautiful pool out back. It felt safe to disrobe in the dark back there, and we all laughed as we jumped into the dark water. But we'd only been swimming around for a minute or so when all the pool lights came on, including some that lit us from underwater. I was out of the water in a shot and wrapped in a towel, listening to the guys above us on the terraced hillside laughing away.

"GK," Elvis called out, "I've never seen you swim so fast."

But for all the wild nights and all the laughs, I could sense a certain frustration in Elvis. At the start of his film career, there'd been an effort all around to get him into good vehicles to develop his talents, and he'd done all the work he was asked to do and made necessary compromises to get that career started. Elvis really enjoyed making movies, but he wanted better scripts and better supporting actors and he didn't want to have to sing all the time. Now his films were following a dreary formula—a mediocre script became a mediocre production with mediocre songs shoehorned into it. When I asked Elvis what one of his mid-sixties films was about, he said wearily, "Same story, different location. I get the girl, I beat up a guy, and I sing twelve songs."

Elvis continued to do what was asked of him professionally and never took out his frustration on the cast or crews he worked with. But sometimes we could see how those frustrations wore on him. One day, during the production of *Girl Happy* on the MGM lot, Elvis, Alan, Richard, Jimmy, and I rode in Elvis's Rolls-Royce from the soundstage to his permanent dressing room on the lot, the one that had been Clark Gable's. As we walked toward the building, a voice from above called down to us, "Hey guys! Hey Elvis, how you doing?"

We looked up to see the popular actor Steve McQueen hanging out a second-story window. There was a studio gym on that floor, and McQueen was getting in shape for his role as a lean, mean gambler in his next film, *The Cincinnati Kid.* To us, Steve McQueen was about as cool as they come, and Elvis had screened *The Great Escape* about a dozen times at the Memphian. But while the rest of us excitedly said hello back to the actor, Elvis just gave him a quick nod and then went into the dressing room. We asked Steve if we could come up to where he was, and he said sure. The four of us went up and sat on the floor of the gym with McQueen for about an hour, asking him all kinds of questions about his movies. He was friendly and easy to talk to, and when it was time for us to get back downstairs he said, "Guys, I really would like to meet Elvis. I'm such a big fan."

We said we'd bring Elvis up, and as we got downstairs, Elvis was just coming out of his dressing room, reading a book. We all began telling him that Steve McQueen was a big fan who wanted to meet him and all he had to do was look up at the second-story window again. Elvis didn't break stride and didn't look up. He just got in the Rolls. We looked up at Steve and just kind of shrugged and he waved it off with a smile. None of us could figure it out—Elvis was usually so nice to everybody he met, and here was a movie star whose work he admired, who was a fan of his, and Elvis was actually being rude.

Elvis and McQueen crossed paths a few more times, and Elvis never responded to him warmly. We just couldn't understand what the problem was—until we finally saw *The Cincinnati Kid.* McQueen's costar in the film was Ann-Margret, in a role that was a lot sexier and adult than what she'd played in *Viva Las Vegas.* I'm sure Elvis wasn't thrilled about the fact that a girlfriend of his was spending her days in lingerie, jumping into bed with Steve McQueen, even if it was just for the cameras. But I don't think his jealousy was only romantic. McQueen and Ann-Margret were making a dark, serious film for adult moviegoers, and they were working with a hot director—Norman Jewison—and a cast that included such talents as Edward G. Robinson, Karl Malden, Tuesday Weld, and even Cab Calloway. I think Elvis's problem with Steve McQueen was that McQueen was enjoying the kind of film career that Elvis had always wanted (and getting to do some great acting work with Ann in the process). Showing up at the studio to work on *Girl Happy,* I think Elvis was feeling down about the kind of career he was having. Even if the lucrative contracts the Colonel had wrangled made Elvis a much better paid star than Steve McQueen, McQueen was enjoying a couple of things that the Colonel would never have considered an important part of negotiations: creative freedom and artistic satisfaction. That's not an excuse for Elvis's rudeness, but it does offer an explanation for a behavior that really was out of character for him.

Elvis never took his feelings out on his fans, though. I remember pulling off the MGM lot one day, and as usual we slowed for a moment so that Elvis could wave to fans of his who had been waiting at the gate. One guy approached our open window and shouted, "Elvis, I wrote a song for you!" Alan yelled back, "Sing it! Sing it!" As the car started to pull away, this guy was running alongside trying to sing his song. Alan and I started laughing, but Elvis shot us the dirtiest of looks and told us to stop. "That's a guy who buys my records and goes to my movies," he said. "Don't make him feel bad about it."

If Elvis was having doubts about a career path that had seemed to drift out of his control, the Colonel was having the time of his life. He rarely came up to the Perugia house, as he rarely came out to Graceland, but he was always a larger-than-life presence on the film sets, holding court for cast, crew, and Mafia. He'd become looser about talking up some parts of his mysterious past, and he'd have us all listening raptly to the tales of his carny days. He'd made a lot of money with a sideshow attraction called "Colonel Parker's Dancing Chickens," though paying customers never suspected that the reason the chickens danced wildly when the Colonel turned on some music was that he also turned on a large hot plate beneath the sand the chickens stood on. He'd raked in more money selling spray-painted sparrows as rare canaries, and, when he worked at a pet cemetery, by charging bereaved pet owners for weekly flowers on their pets' graves—flowers that actually came cheap from the trash bins of local floral shops. When money was tight, he'd eat well by slipping a piece of broken glass onto a nearly finished plate of dinner at a restaurant, then making a fuss about his "discovery" until the management picked up his check.

The Colonel liked to recount an incident from Elvis's early tour of the Northwest: When an outdoor show was threatened by approaching thunderstorms, the Colonel guaranteed his profits by securing the license to sell raincoats and umbrellas at the stadium. He made a big deal out of his self-created "Snowmen's League" for talented swindlers and con men, and sometimes even claimed to have powers of hypnosis, which he'd demonstrate by coaxing members of the Memphis Mafia into getting down on all fours and barking like dogs.

I never got down and barked for the Colonel, but I had to admit that being around him was entertaining. On one set, someone came up to him and asked him if he was the man who had promoted the Hadacol shows. Hadacol was a patent medicine whose most effective medicinal ingredient was simply alcohol. The stuff had been promoted and sold with big traveling country jamborees that also featured some big Hollywood talent of the forties. Admission to the shows could be gained with Hadacol box tops.

"Hadacol—yep, that was me," said the Colonel.

The guy who'd asked said they were great shows that he remembered fondly, thanked the Colonel for the good times, then stepped away. I knew for a fact that Hadacol wasn't part of the Colonel's past. The medicine and the shows had been thought up by a Louisiana state senator named "Cousin" Dudley LeBlanc.

"Colonel, you had nothing to do with Hadacol," I said.

"George, let me give you some advice," he responded. "If it's good—take credit for it."

That actually wasn't bad advice (and it's something I've recalled when anyone's suggested that I came up with "the King" as a nickname for Elvis). But when I think back on those times with the Colonel, I'm not as entertained as I was back then. All of his stories were about charging as much as he could for a show that he put on as cheaply as possible, and, in retrospect, I don't think he ever stopped thinking that way when he managed Elvis.

The Colonel had certainly helped Elvis to achieve everything he'd desired when he'd first begun singing. From beautiful homes and beautiful women to limousines and private planes to the love of millions of fans around the world, Elvis's life was, in so many ways, all he'd dreamed for. But what really drove Elvis wasn't the love of the rewards he'd ended up with, it was the love of what had gotten him there: singing, performing, and entertaining. He'd been steered away from the exciting rock 'n' roll music he'd started with in order to accommodate a film career. He'd wanted so badly to be considered a serious acting talent and to be a part of great movies like the ones he grew up loving. But with *Girl Happy*, he'd just done his seventeenth movie in eight years—including the two years away in the army—and as lousy scripts kept turning into cheaper and cheaper productions, he must have had the sinking feeling that the Colonel was not about to line up a *Rebel Without a Cause* or a *To Kill a Mockingbird* for him. Elvis needed more than just top billing and "boffo" box office: He needed something to keep his creative spirit fired up. He needed an artistic challenge that he could rise to.

The Colonel was lucky enough to be working with one of the greatest talents of the twentieth century, and, in too many ways, he treated that talent like just another dancing chicken.

CHAPTER TEN

Talent Party

1964 was a year of rock 'n' roll surprises. An unknown garage band from the Northwest called the Kingsmen scored a top-ten hit with a cover of Richard Berry's "Louie, Louie"—though the barely decipherable lyrics were suspected of being so obscene that an FBI investigation was launched. A scrawny folksinger named Bob Dylan released his first album of all original material, *The Times They Are A-Changin'*, demonstrating just how much social commentary could be packed into a folk song. And the Singing Nun and Bobby Vinton were swept off the pop charts by four long-haired British kids in matching suits—though the Beatles had to make way for a while when none other than Louis "Satchmo" Armstrong scored a number-one hit with a romp through the title theme of a hot new musical, *Hello, Dolly!*

Back in Memphis, I got a nice rock 'n' roll surprise of my own. Everything that I'd been working at—the radio shifts, the drive-ins, the drag races, the wrestling—came together in a big way: I got my own TV show.

Wink Martindale had given up hosting WHBQ's *Dance Party* television show in 1959 to pursue his career in Los Angeles, and a series of other hosts had helmed it for a few years after that. But by 1964, the station had gotten nervous about who was dancing on *Dance Party*. As the musicians and audience for rock 'n' roll became increasingly integrated, the station felt that the sight of black couples and white couples dancing side by side as part of the studio audience might offend viewers. And apparently some higher-ups felt that if the unthinkable ever happened—if a black boy asked a white girl to dance or a white boy asked a black girl to dance—well, it would scandalize the show and the station.

To avoid that kind of scandal, the station decided to cancel *Dance Party* and repackage it as *Talent Party*. *Talent Party* would have a dancerless format, simply featuring a deejay playing records and interviewing recording artists who would then lip-synch to their latest hits. WHBQ wanted to bring someone over from the radio side of the company to be the new show's host, and I was ready and eager to audition: My year of experience interviewing (and sometimes being struck by) professional wrestlers had gotten me comfortable in front of TV cameras and gave me an advantage over all the other radio guys.

Elvis was really excited for me and was very supportive. The show's sponsor was Coca-Cola, and Elvis called some Memphis-based executives of the company to put in a plug for me. And on the day I did an on-camera audition for the host job, I received a very encouraging telegram:

> Dear George. I know you'll do great at your audition. Good Luck. Best Wishes—Your Friend—Elvis.

I got the job, but I also knew I was becoming captain of a sinking ship. Nobody really wanted to spend an hour watching a deejay on TV, and *Talent Party*'s low ratings reflected that. I thought hard about what might be done to reenergize the format of the show, then went to the show producers and laid out my plan. First of all, it seemed silly to have acts come in to do their lip-synching live on Saturday afternoons when the show aired. I thought that if the station would let me keep the camera crew on after the ten o'clock news, I could bring in a bigger range of stars on any night of the week, tape them at a time that was probably going to get a better performance out of them, then mix the live and prerecorded elements on the show. Then I suggested that if we were not going to have couples on the show, we still needed some sex appeal. I thought we ought to do what had been done on shows like *Shindig!* and *Hullabaloo* and have our own in-house troupe of beautiful girls who'd dance throughout the show. They would be called the WHBQuties, of course.

I also thought we could make the show more than just music, and wanted to book interviews with beauty-pageant queens and star athletes. From being out in Hollywood I knew that a lot of movies were now being promoted with "open end" interviews, where a celebrity's answers were prerecorded and mixed with a local radio host's live questions. I thought we could have a "Starline" section on the show, where'd I'd be seen in silhouette on the phone speaking with a movie star or pop star.

I guess my biggest idea was that instead of having *Talent Party* seem like a little show that was trying to act big, it should be proud to be a local show celebrating everything cool about Memphis. I didn't see why we couldn't feature high school cheerleading squads and homecoming kings and queens—the idea being that if you focused on a local school, you were almost guaranteed that every family of every student in that part of town would be watching. Last, in a town so rich in music, it seemed crazy just to focus on national acts. I wanted to make local garage bands a part of every show.

People around the station got excited about the changes, and as we put all the pieces in place, ratings began to pick up and I could tell that the show was starting to generate some excitement among young fans around town. It wasn't long before we had a real hit—something that every rock 'n' roll fan wanted to tune in to as part of their Saturday. All the road managers and record companies I'd made contacts with through the years were happy to get their talent on the show; Sears department store agreed to underwrite a fashion show segment; schools went crazy whenever they were spotlighted; and we had everybody from Miss Teenage Memphis to Miss Dixie to Miss Fire Safety show off her charms. I sent local garage bands to Sonic Recording Studio, where they worked with a producer named Roland Janes, a former Sun session guitarist who played on most of Jerry Lee Lewis's hits. For twelve dollars, bands could record two songs with Roland, then lip-synch to those recordings on *Talent Party.*

As the show took off, one thing bothered me a great deal. Records by black artists might get played, but the station's general feeling was that having a black artist performing—with the white WHBQuties dancing along—was just too shocking a sight for Memphis's delicate eyes. All around me, though, I saw evidence that my city was a lot more open-minded than that. Black and white players worked together at Sun, making records that appealed to a black and white audience. The same was true elsewhere in Memphis, like at Stax Records, where Booker T and the MG's had casually obliterated any color lines by becoming a biracial, hit-making house band. I decided I wanted to do what I could to erase the color line on Memphis TV. But I knew that if I was going to risk a move like that, it had to be done in a big way with a big star.

Fats Domino seemed exactly big enough, and when he came through town for a performance at Ellis Auditorium, I got the ten o'clock news camera crew to stand by while I headed off to the venue. I managed to get backstage and get to Fats after his show. We'd never met before, and though he said he'd heard of me, he wasn't interested when I offered him a spot on my show.

"Baby, I don't do no local TV," he said.

"I respect that, Fats," I said. "I know how big a star you are. But can I be straight with you?"

"Yeah, baby."

"If you come with me, you'll be the first black entertainer to do this show, and you'll open up the door for everybody else."

He thought a minute, then said, "Baby—let's go."

He headed out with me so I could drive him to the studio, but he laid down one condition for his appearance. He wanted something to drink while he played, and asked that we stop at a liquor store so I could run in and pick him up a pint of his beverage of choice. I figured if we were going to break down the color line, we may as well violate the station's no-alcohol-on-air policy as well. Back at the studio, I got him set up at a piano and discreetly placed a paper cup of Fats's beverage where I didn't think the camera would see it. Fats had a good taste, then knocked out four fantastic songs in one take each and was out of there.

The segment aired the following Saturday, and, lo and behold, there wasn't one bit of negative reaction. Not a letter, a telegram, or a phone call. My city, at least the part of it that watched *Talent Party*, had come through for me.

And, boy, did that open the doors. The word got around that if you were in Memphis, you ought to do Klein's show, and I got to work with great stars like Otis Redding, Jackie Wilson, Al Green, and Sam Cooke, along with Sam and Dave, the Drifters, and the Spinners. I was the first host to put James Brown on in the South, which began a wonderful, long friendship with him. I had a great interview with Patti LaBelle, whose group the Bluebelles was getting a lot of attention as the opening act for the Rolling Stones. (I didn't have any luck getting an interview out of the guy who accompanied Patti to the studio—Rolling Stone Brian Jones. In making my case to him I made the mistake of saying that I'd "made" "Satisfaction," meaning that I'd been the first deejay to play it heavily in Memphis. His chilly response was, "You 'played' 'Satisfaction.' *We* made it.")

One of my favorite *Talent Party* moments occurred in my first year as host, when, with the help of Wink Martindale, I got Sam Cooke booked to do the show. He was coming through Memphis as part of a coheadlining tour with Jackie Wilson, in which they'd take turns city-by-city as to who opened and who closed that night's show. I'd met Sam before at a show at Ellis, and we got along well enough that I decided to ask him a favor: I wondered if he would invite Jackie Wilson to come along with us. Sam did, and Jackie said yes, though Sam gave me a firm warning: "Jackie loves the ladies, and if you don't lead him by the hand out of here after the show, you can forget about seeing him again tonight."

I worked hard to get them both to the studio quickly after the show, and couldn't wait to shoot a couple songs each with such great talents. But as Sam was doing a practice take of his song "Everybody Loves to Cha Cha Cha," I noticed that Jackie was mouthing along with every word and I got an idea.

"Jackie, you really know Sam's stuff," I said.

"Man, we're like brothers. I know everything he's ever done."

"Well, tell me what you think of this. When we start really shooting this one, why don't you sneak around back, and when Sam's done with the first verse, you pop through the curtains and take over the song."

Jackie loved the idea, and while he certainly surprised the heck out of Sam, Sam loved it too, and they were both having a ball as they tried to match each other line for line and dance move for dance move. Footage of that magical moment is still out there on the Internet, and you can't help but smile when you see the smiles on their faces.

Unfortunately, there's a sad postscript to that great moment. Sam really liked the British boots I was wearing when he did the show, and I took down his mailing address and his shoe size and promised to send him a pair. I ordered them and shipped them to him, but by the time they arrived at his home, he was gone. On December 11, 1964, as a result of some still very shadowy circumstances, Sam Cooke was shot to death in the office of a Los Angeles motel.

Talent Party became a big enough hit that when the first holiday season rolled around after I'd been on the air, I hosted a George Klein Christmas Charity Show rock 'n' roll concert, the first of what would become a forty-year holiday tradition in Memphis. The shows always featured stars (Jerry Lee Lewis, Charlie Rich, Billy Lee Riley, the Box Tops, the Gentrys, Paul Revere and the Raiders, and many others) as well as a lot of local acts, many of whom had been on the TV show. The money we raised was handed over to a couple of charities: the Mile of Dimes, which distributed food to needy people, and the Good Fellows organization, which staged an event at Ellis Auditorium at which bags of clothing, gifts, and goodies were handed out to the long line of needy folks that turned up. I was partly inspired to put on the Christmas charity shows by Elvis, who always gave so generously to so many causes. It meant a lot when Elvis told me he was proud of me for doing the charitable work, and it meant even more when he told me something I hadn't been aware of: When his family had been suffering through some tough times, he'd stood in the Good Fellows line at Ellis to receive one of those holiday bags.

Elvis was an avid reader, and one of the topics that interested him most was spirituality. (When he was once asked why he wore both a cross and a Jewish chai around his neck, Elvis said, "I don't want to miss out on getting into heaven on a technicality.") He had a great hunger for all kinds of knowledge, and was greatly inspired in his spiritual seekings by one of the newest and most improbable members of the inner circle, Larry Geller. Larry was a Hollywood hairdresser who'd left Jay Sebring's salon to become Elvis's personal barber, and in the time they spent together they'd quickly bonded over discussions of religion, philosophy, and the meaning of life.

Elvis enjoyed reading the Bible, but he wanted to explore other religions and beliefs as well, and was particularly taken with Khalil Gibran's *The Prophet* and *The Impersonal Life* by Joseph Benner. In Los Angeles, he'd become fascinated with the teachings of the Self-Realization Fellowship, a meditation-based spiritual organization founded by Paramahansa Yogananda. I was never too interested in exploring that kind of stuff, and Elvis never pushed it on me. But I do remember him doing a couple of demonstrations for me that came straight from some of his mind-science books.

Once, outside of Graceland, he held his hand over some bushes and asked me to watch carefully. His hand stayed still, but damned if the bushes didn't start moving a little bit. Then he told me to focus on a cloud, and he did some hocus-pocus with his hands and it seemed like he was making the clouds move. Elvis didn't make a big deal out of it—he wasn't trying to show me that he had special powers, just that there were powers we all had that we didn't understand. I wasn't so sure. I figured if you stared hard enough at anything long enough, you'd start to see it move. Still, it was a convincing exhibition of what he was picking up from his books.

Elvis also enjoyed sharing some of the nonspiritual sorts of things he was picking up in his readings. One day we were sitting around Graceland when he said, "GK, you know what a fer-de-lance is?"

"I don't know, Elvis."

"What about a black mamba?"

"Don't know, Elvis."

"Well don't step on either one. Those are two of the deadliest snakes in the world."

With my bump up to TV personality, I made a few changes in my lifestyle. I finally moved out of the little house near Humes I'd grown up in and got a real nice apartment of my own in Midtown, and I traded up cars so that I was driving a new Chevrolet. Barbara lived close by in her own apartment and we still saw each other as much as we could. That was sometimes difficult: My radio and TV schedules were demanding, and she worked regular hours in a full-time job at a medical clinic. But while being a part of Elvis's group might have put an unworkable strain on some relationships, Barbara was very understanding and supportive when it came to my spending time with Elvis (although I have to admit that I did not fully inform her about everything that went on at the Perugia house).

So, even with a radio shift, a TV gig, and a steady girlfriend, I was still able to juggle my calendar so that I could spend vacation time in Los Angeles with Elvis as he made more movies. I was out there in June of '65 while Elvis was shooting *Frankie and Johnny,* one of the eight films of his I got a walk-on part in. And it was during that trip that I started thinking about making a permanent jump to the West Coast. *Talent Party* was hot and my radio show got top ratings too, but after spending so much time in Hollywood over the years, I couldn't help but think that a job in Los Angeles would be a great next step in my career.

I'd gotten in the habit of bringing tapes of my shows out to L.A. when I visited Elvis, and I'd make the rounds of all the big rock 'n' roll stations— KFWB, KRLA, KHJ—but I never had any luck getting a job offer. One day the program director at KFWB, Don French, called me to say that a jock had called in sick and they wanted someone who could fill in for a day. They thought maybe I'd like to do a special Elvis-oriented show.

I had a blast doing it, especially knowing that I'd be heard by all the Mafia guys up at Elvis's Bel Air home. (He'd moved from Perugia Way to Bellagio Road.) Jerry Schilling had become a part of the Mafia, and when he bought a Triumph Bonneville motorcycle to get around L.A., Elvis liked the model so much that he bought about a dozen of them for the rest of the guys (though he kept riding the big Harley-Davidsons he favored). I played Elvis tunes dedicated to "the Bel Air Bonnevilles" or "El's Angels" and threw in all kinds of inside references I thought the guys would get a kick out of. The KFWB executives enjoyed the show, too, because the next day Don French did in fact offer me a job—a weekend shift at the station with a promise to move into weekdays when something opened up—for better money than I was making in Memphis.

Sometimes getting what you think you want can really throw you, and I was now faced with a decision that was harder than I'd thought it would be. For advice, I turned to the sharpest dealmaker I knew: the Colonel. I explained my situation to him, and he mulled it over.

"George, you're a great big fish in a little pond back in Memphis, and that's not a bad thing to be. You're number one on the air, you've got yourself a TV show, everybody knows you and loves you. Out here, you're not going to have much juice. I'm not sure I'd give up what you have just for some weekend work."

I realized that the Colonel was saying exactly what I was thinking. I called Don French back, told him how flattered I was, and turned down the job. But just a day or two before I was to head back to Memphis, I got one more call from Don. One of KFWB's wildest, most exciting jocks, Don MacKinnon, had been killed when his car swerved off the road and plummeted down a cliff in Malibu. French wanted me to take over KFWB's midday slot. I ran the offer past the Colonel again, though this time he was with Elvis in Elvis's dressing room. Elvis was excited about me taking the job: He liked the idea that we'd spend more time together in

L.A., and I think he just naturally enjoyed hearing that good things were coming my way. But the Colonel told me I still needed to think hard about it, and, again, the Colonel was right. I was going to be a lot happier in my own little pond. I turned down the L.A. job offer that I'd thought I wanted so much, and headed back to Memphis.

Being the big fish on *Talent Party* did have some undeniable benefits, like the great friendship I developed with James Brown. I didn't get close to him right away—the first couple times he did *Talent Party*, it was clear that I was to address him as "Mr. Brown," and he called me "Mr. Klein." The very first time I had him on the show, he was red-hot with the success of "Papa's Got a Brand New Bag" and "I Feel Good," and I considered it a major score when he agreed to get into my car so I could drive him to the studio for a taping. But as I drove around to the back of the station building to get to the studio door, Mr. Brown had a problem.

"Mr. Klein," he said. "I don't go in no back doors."

I explained that the whole building was shut down—that I'd kept the late-night news camera crew waiting for us, and it was just easier to get to them through the back studio doors.

"I'll say it one more time. I don't go in through no back doors. We go through the front or I'm out of here."

It might have seemed like a strange request to some, but I knew exactly where he was coming from. Before I'd had Bo Diddley on my show, I noticed that he had set up a hot plate and some pots and pans in his hotel room. I asked him if he liked to cook. Bo laughed and said that it was just a habit from his years on the road: He'd gotten so tired of being told he had to use the back doors to restaurants that he preferred eating simply in his room rather than giving up a bit of his dignity.

That night, James Brown went through the front door of the studio.

Early in his career James had established a reputation as a wild man on stage, but in person he was one of the smartest, sharpest, most focused people I ever met. Watching him backstage after his shows was a revelation—

as wild as he'd been onstage, he was aware of every little thing that had happened around him. He actually fined band members for mistakes, and more than once I heard him yell, "Bring me the books. Player missed a note—that's a twenty-five-dollar fine." He knew exactly what he wanted in his music, and everything you heard coming from his band was from his ideas.

By the third or fourth time James Brown did the show, we were "James" and "George." He was always with a different beautiful woman, though, and I asked him how I should address them.

"George, George, George," he said. "Just call 'em all Mrs. Brown and you'll never be wrong."

Often, after I finished a show, I'd spend the night with Elvis at the movies, alternating between the Memphian theater and the Crosstown. One of the most memorable introductions to Elvis I ever witnessed occurred in the lobby of the Crosstown. Richard Davis and I had gotten friendly with a wild-man soul singer named Roy Head, who, at the end of 1965, had the biggest hit of his career with "Treat Her Right." (That song was only prevented from being a national number one by the success of the Beatles' "Yesterday.") Richard and I saw Roy perform one night at Memphis's Thunderbird Lounge, where the singer lived up to his reputation as the one white guy who could move like James Brown or Jackie Wilson. After the show, Roy reiterated to us that he really wanted to meet Elvis sometime. We told him he should join us over at the Crosstown after his performance at the Thunderbird the following night.

Roy made it over to the theater, and Richard and I were talking to him in the lobby when Elvis happened to come by us on his way from his seat to the candy counter. I told Elvis that our guest was Roy Head, who'd cut "Treat Her Right."

"Man, I love that record," said Elvis, extending a hand to Roy.

Roy didn't shake Elvis's hand. Instead, he fell to the floor, grabbed Elvis's leg, and bit his ankle. Elvis went into a karate stance as if he were ready to kick Roy Head's head off and shouted, "What's wrong with you?"

Roy stood up, dusted himself off and said, "I'm sorry, Elvis. You really are an idol of mine. But if I just shook hands with you, you'd never remember me. Now I know you're never going to forget the guy who bit you on the ankle."

Roy had a point—Elvis never forgot him.

I was back in L.A. in the summer of '66 while Elvis was making *Double Trouble*. The more significant memory from that visit started with an announcement I saw in the papers: Jackie Wilson was doing a headlining engagement at the Trip, a hot little Hollywood nightclub. I told Elvis about it, and he set it up so that he and the Mafia could get to a show. Elvis really was never much of a partygoer or club hopper during his moviemaking years, so a lot of the Mafia guys were skeptical that he'd actually go to see Jackie. But I knew how much Elvis loved Jackie's work and was pretty sure he wouldn't miss this night out.

James Brown happened to be in town as well, and Elvis agreed that James should be our guest at the show. James was a big Elvis fan, and I'd been trying to get the two of them together in Memphis, but the timing had never worked out—the couple afternoons James was free to come to Graceland, Elvis was asleep.

I got to the Trip early to make sure that all the arrangements were set and that a table for James and a table for Elvis and Priscilla were taken care of. Jackie Wilson was attracting a star-studded crowd, and that night members of the Rolling Stones and the Buffalo Springfield were in the house, as was up-and-coming Irish rocker Van Morrison. (Somebody told me he was the lead singer for Them, and I asked the unhip question, "Them who?") James arrived first with his road manager and a bodyguard. "Where's Elvis?" was the first thing he said to me. We were making small talk when I saw that Elvis and Priscilla had arrived. I excused myself and went over to greet them. I told Elvis that James was just a few tables away, but knowing how all eyes in the room, including some press eyes, were watching Elvis, and knowing how the press sometimes made a big deal of the hierarchy of stars, I wondered if he wanted to take his seat and have me bring James over to him.

"No," said Elvis. "Take me over to James."

Priscilla took a seat at their table. Elvis and I worked our way through the crowd, and then I made the introductions between the two most electrifying performers I'd ever seen. The first thing James said was, "Elvis, you sure do sleep a lot."

"Aww, James—you know how it is," Elvis said with a laugh. "If you're up all night, you got to sleep all day."

From that night on they were fast friends, and over the next couple of years James did get to spend quite a bit of time at Graceland. Sometimes if he was in town he'd just cold-call and try to catch Elvis, and I was lucky enough to be there a few times when James and Elvis spent the night singing gospel songs together.

Jackie Wilson put on a phenomenal show, and afterward Elvis and I went backstage so I could make introductions between those two. Elvis had always said that Jackie was one of his favorite singers, and when they finally met and had a few laughs together, Elvis invited Jackie to his movie set—an invitation Jackie took him up on a couple of days later. Before we left the club that night, Jackie said, "You know they call me the Black Elvis?"

"I hope that's a compliment," said Elvis.

"Damn straight it is," responded Jackie.

As the summer wound down, I was back in Memphis, where, in August 1966, I had the pleasure of meeting the Beatles. They were doing an afternoon and an evening show at the Mid-South Coliseum as part of their third U.S. tour, and I was asked to emcee the earlier show. They were very much at the top of their game as a recording act, releasing great songs like "Day Tripper" and "Nowhere Man" and hitting number one on the charts in the months before the Memphis show with both "We Can Work It Out" and "Paperback Writer." But some folks in Memphis were not entirely happy to see the Beatles come to town.

John Lennon had done an interview with a British newspaper in which he talked at length about his own celebrity, remarking that it was absurd to him that people seemed more excited about the Beatles than they were about Christianity. Just weeks before the Beatles came to Memphis, the interview broke in an American teen magazine, with Lennon quoted out of context and seeming to boast that the Beatles were "more popular than Jesus." A lot of people were outraged, especially in the South, and a number of radio stations, many of which had been happy to build up their ratings playing the Beatles' music, now turned anti-Beatles and organized events at which Beatles records would be smashed and burned. Memphis's mayor, William Ingram, and the Board of Commissioners released a proclamation that they officially disapproved of the band. But even with the scandal lingering, about twenty thousand Memphis citizens were happy to pay to see the Fab Four play.

I had a little history with the Beatles. I was one of the first deejays at WHBQ to get excited about them, and, in 1964, I covered one of their first big press conferences in Atlanta. The following year, I answered the phone in the Graceland kitchen and found myself speaking to Paul McCartney: He and John were calling to thank Elvis for the evening the band had spent at his Bel Air home. (I missed that amazing summit meeting of rock 'n' roll talents, though Alan Fortas proudly told me he'd smoked a joint with George Harrison.) And I'd been planning on traveling with the band throughout the '66 tour as a member of the press until my *Talent Party* sponsor, Coca-Cola, said that, in light of Lennon's "Jesus" comments, they would not underwrite my travel expenses.

I ended up just emceeing the Beatles' afternoon show in Memphis, though I'm very proud to say that, as far as I know, I'm the only person to ever introduce both Elvis and the Beatles onstage. Security around the show was tighter than anything I'd ever seen in the city, and there were angry protesters outside the venue. The atmosphere was tense, but when I got to meet the Beatles backstage I was struck at how they stuck together and maintained a calmness and a sense of humor amid all the craziness.

The Beatles' opening acts included the Ronettes; a great, hard-rocking Boston band called the Remains; R&B singer Bobby Hebb, who had a big hit at the time with "Sunny"; and the Cyrkle, a band that had a hit then with "Red Rubber Ball." But it was clear what the crowd really wanted to hear. When it was time, I went out onstage and got the crowd revved up a little more, then led them through a cheer to spell out "Beatles." As the crowd got to *S* the band took the stage, and I'll always remember that as I ran off John Lennon was running by me, and he slowed down just long enough to say, "Great intro—thanks, GK." For a guy who was right then having his records burned, he was awfully considerate.

"George Klein, WHBQ, coming at you with more hot sounds for a cold November day. That was Tom Jones's 'Green Green Grass of Home' back-to-back with '96 Tears' by Question Mark and the Mysterians, coming at you now with the Beach Boys and 'Good Vibrations' . . ."

I put the record on and settled back for a quick break during my six-to-nine shift at the station. I'd dropped the "DJ-uh-GK" tag and my crazy rhymes when I returned to WHBQ: That stuff had sounded fresh in the fifties, but as rock 'n' roll grew up, all of us deejays had to adapt to the changes in style or risk becoming dinosaurs. The Beach Boys' new hit had just started playing when a call came through for me. It was one of the Mafia guys, at some road stop where Elvis had parked the custom bus he'd had designed for his Memphis-to-L.A. road trips. Elvis had been away for several months, having spent a stretch of time in Palm Springs after completing the production of *Easy Come, Easy Go.* He got on the phone.

"Hey GK, we just pulled out of Little Rock and we're on our way home. We just picked up your station."

"Well, it's great to hear your voice, Elvis."

"We'll see you soon, GK, but—you just played that record by Tom Jones, didn't you?"

"'Green Green Grass of Home'—yeah, Elvis, it's doing pretty good back here."

"Man, GK—I've got to hear that again."

"Uh—well, Elvis, I just played it a few minutes ago. We're not supposed to repeat songs so quickly."

"I know, GK, but just play it again for me, would you? We'll see you in about an hour and a half."

The song was kind of heavy for a pop record—about a prisoner on the eve of his execution who's dreaming of a few more moments in his loving home. Jerry Lee Lewis had cut a country-style version of it, and Tom, with Jerry Lee's blessing, had gotten a hit out of it. I didn't know at the time that Red West had previously tried to get Elvis interested in the song, to no avail. But he liked it now, and I played it again. I wouldn't ever tell my listeners that I'd just gotten a call from Elvis, but I dedicated the record with some kind of code—something like, "This one is for the Hound Dogs in Arkansas who want to hear it again."

Thirty minutes later I got a call from another one of the Mafia guys.

"GK—Elvis wants to talk to you."

He got on the line. "GK—play it again, would you?"

I ended up playing the record five times, and when I got off the air I took a copy straight over to Graceland. Elvis and the guys were just pulling in themselves. As soon as Elvis stepped off the bus, I approached him with the record.

"Here, Elvis—now go play the damn thing yourself."

He laughed and said, "Thanks, GK. I just couldn't get enough of it. The song kept making me think about how much I missed this place."

A few weeks later my workday was again interrupted by a couple of Memphis Mafia guys. But this time it wasn't over the phone. I was just about to begin my six-to-nine radio shift when a receptionist told me that a couple of Elvis's guys were downstairs waiting to see me. I went down to find that Richard Davis and Jerry Schilling were in the station lobby.

"What's going on?" I asked.

"Elvis needs to see you right now," said Jerry.

"What?"

"We don't know what it's about," said Richard. "But he sent us over in the limo to get you."

All of a sudden it felt like a real Mafia moment: Two big guys wanted me to step into the limo to go see the boss.

"Guys, I can't just leave—I'm on the air in twenty minutes. The guy who's on now has been on for four hours. I can't hang him up."

Richard and Jerry were quiet a moment, then Richard said, "Elvis says it's pretty important. You better figure out a way to go meet him."

I ran back upstairs and quickly explained to the station manager what was going on. He'd said it was okay to leave—he'd have the jock who was on go an extra hour to cover for me. I got back to Richard and Jerry, jumped in the limo, and we all took off. But, in another strange turn that felt like a real Mafia moment, I realized that we were not driving toward Graceland.

"Uh, guys—you're going the wrong way," I said, starting to wonder if I really should be worried.

"We know where we're going," said Richard.

"Well, what's going on?" I asked.

"Elvis is downtown and he's getting a new car for himself," said Jerry. "He said it would be easier to meet at the Cadillac dealership than to go to Graceland."

Downtown didn't seem that much closer to the station than Graceland, but I went along with it. A few minutes later we pulled up to a Cadillac dealership that didn't have a single light on. The place looked completely closed up.

"There's nobody here, man," I said.

"Well, he's got to be in there somewhere, GK," said Jerry. "He told us to meet him here."

I got out of the car in the dark parking lot and approached the building with Jerry and Richard hanging a few steps behind me. I didn't know how I was going to get into the place, but they told me to try the main showroom door and, sure enough, it was unlocked.

I stepped into the dark showroom and took a few tentative steps forward. All of a sudden, every light in the showroom came on, and the whole place lit up like a movie set. There was only one car sitting right there in the middle of the showroom floor: a yellow '67 Cadillac convertible. My first thought was, "Elvis sure is going through a lot of trouble to show off his new car."

And then there he was, strolling toward me from one of the back offices with a sly smile on his face.

He stood by the car and said, "Come here, GK." I took a few steps toward him.

"Stick out your hand," he said.

I did, and he dropped some keys into my hand.

"Merry Christmas, GK."

The yellow '67 Cadillac convertible was mine. A gift from Elvis. The best Christmas present I'd ever gotten, from the best friend I'd ever had.

I was absolutely stunned, and as I stared down at those shiny new keys in my outstretched hand, I could hear Elvis and Richard and Jerry laughing as they saw me struggle to come up with something to say. I actually started feeling a little weak in the knees.

Finally, I looked square at the guy who'd given me this gift, the guy who meant the world to me.

"Elvis, as a man who gets paid to talk, I really ought to be able to make a great acceptance speech. But I just don't know what to say."

He took another step toward me, put his arm around my shoulders, and spoke softly.

"GK," he said, "what's fame and fortune worth if we can't share it with our friends?"

CHAPTER ELEVEN

Home on the Ranch

On a cool February night in 1967, Barbara and I were driving south to go party with Elvis. But we weren't headed to Graceland. Instead, we were driving past the house, across the state line, and through the middle of nowhere to get to Horn Lake, Mississippi. Elvis had just bought himself a ranch, and he wanted to celebrate.

Elvis's main Christmas present to Priscilla that year had been a beautiful horse that she could ride around the grounds at Graceland. But since he knew she might not enjoy riding by herself, he also bought a horse for Jerry Schilling's girlfriend, Sandy Kawelo, a lovely Polynesian girl Jerry had fallen for during the making of *Paradise, Hawaiian Style*. Then Elvis decided that Graceland needed some improvements to become more horse friendly and initiated some large-scale renovations on the grounds and on the run-down barn at the back of the property—renovations that included him getting up on an industrial-size bulldozer to mow down some structures out back. Then he began buying more horses for Mafia members and their wives, and finally tracked down a beautiful golden palomino for himself, which he named Rising Sun.

Elvis was a guy who, when he wanted to play touch football, rented out the five-thousand-seat stadium at Whitehaven High. The Christmas before, when Priscilla gave him a slot-car track as a gift, he became so passionate about slot-car racing that he filled an addition over one of the

Graceland patios with a massive, arcade-style track. Now his passion was horses, and almost every day I was hearing a new report of horses or stable gear being purchased.

That afternoon, Alan Fortas told me that while he and Elvis, along with Priscilla, Jerry, and Sandy, were out looking for a Tennessee Walker to purchase for Vernon, Elvis had spied a for-sale sign on a piece of property that must have looked like a horseman's dream. Right away, Elvis had Alan get in touch with the seller.

A deal was quickly worked out with the property owner, Jack Adams, who also ran the nearby Twinkletown Airport. Elvis would pay full asking price for everything on the property, including the furnished ranch house and the cattle that were already grazing on the land, on the condition that he could move in that night. Adams agreed. He got his ranch staff to clear out, and in the space of a few hours, Elvis became the owner of a ranch in Horn Lake, Mississippi.

After work, I picked up Barbara and we headed down to Elvis's new property. The little ranch house was packed with Memphis Mafia members, spouses, and girlfriends. I guess I'd initially been a little grumpy about having to make the drive down to this unfamiliar spot, but my mood changed as soon as I stepped into that party. Everyone seemed to be in an exceptionally good mood, and Elvis was beaming with a glow I hadn't seen for some time.

"GK! You made it," he shouted when he saw me.

"Elvis, I can't believe this. You bought yourself a ranch?"

"Bought it in a day, GK," he said. "We'll have some good times here."

He was right. In becoming a ranch owner and turning the Memphis Mafia into a bunch of ranch hands, Elvis had given himself a tremendous challenge, which he threw himself into fully. Making plans for the ranch, Elvis seemed more energetic and in-charge than he had for a long time, and that rubbed off on all of us. Elvis may have been having trouble steering his career the way he wanted it to go, but he now had a place where he could live the way he wanted to, surrounded by the people he wanted around him, far from the call of Hollywood or the influence of the Colonel or even the needs of the fans at the Graceland gates. By driving just a few miles into Mississippi, he could really get away.

When the idea of naming the place was raised, a lot of suggestions got tossed around. Alan came up with Circle G, and Elvis started to object, thinking the *G* was for Graceland. But when Alan explained that he was thinking of *G* for Elvis's mother, Gladys, the name took. Within a week or so, Elvis had turned a good portion of the Circle G into a sort of Memphis Mafia trailer park, with house trailers for him and Priscilla, Jerry and Sandy, Billy Smith and his wife—just about every couple in the group. Alan Fortas moved into the little ranch house, and Elvis gave him the new responsibility of working as ranch foreman. I had an apartment in Memphis to drive back to, and, frankly, I preferred heading back to the city than staying at the ranch, so I didn't really push for my own trailer—though Elvis kept promising that it was going to turn up soon on my own little corner lot of land.

Elvis conquered an initial uneasiness with horses to become quite a rider, and he rode hard enough to develop some pretty serious saddle sores. When he decided that they needed some medical attention, he had Charlie Hodge get in touch with me. Barbara worked at a medical clinic, so Elvis thought she might be able to refer a doctor. I thought Elvis might be best off with the doctor Barbara actually worked for, a talented, trustworthy physician with a great, easygoing demeanor. I could personally recommend him myself, because he'd become my own primary physician. I asked Barbara to call the doctor and see if he'd meet Elvis at Graceland to treat the sores. Barbara made the call, the doctor made the trip, and that's how Dr. George Nichopoulos—Dr. Nick—became a part of Elvis's world.

Even with all the good times at the Circle G, there were a couple of problems with the place. For me, the main problem was the horses. I much preferred a Cadillac to a palomino and never felt comfortable being up in a saddle, though Elvis did insist that I get up on a horse a couple of times. The bigger problem was that Elvis wanted so much to create something special at the Circle G that he just wouldn't stop spending on the place. After buying horses for everybody, he started buying brand-new trucks for everybody, including the handymen he had working to get the trailers set up. (I saw him ask one worker for a dollar. When the startled guy reluctantly handed him a crumpled bill, Elvis tossed him the keys to a Ford truck.) Elvis paid a small fortune to have a high wooden fence put up around the property. And he just kept buying more and more horses and more and more gear. There were so many horses that even just naming them became a challenge, though Elvis did have some fun with that. At the time, Mayor Ingram of Memphis was pushing to have the Mid-South Coliseum renamed the Elvis Presley Coliseum. Elvis returned the favor by naming one of the horses Mare Ingram.

The Colonel had recently renegotiated and extended Elvis's contract with RCA to guarantee him three hundred thousand dollars a year as an advance against royalties. But even with that sum, plus the movie money he made, Elvis was now spending money faster than he was earning it. It almost seemed that, in spending as much as he did on the ranch, Elvis was trying to buy himself out of the career concerns that were weighing increasingly heavy on him.

His next film up was scheduled to be *Clambake,* which, from the look of the script Elvis was sent, was going to be as uninspired a production as the past few films had been. Elvis dragged his feet about heading back to Los Angeles to begin work on the movie, a development that had both the Colonel and Paramount studios extremely upset with him. The situation became more complicated when Elvis fell during the night in his bathroom at his Los Angeles home and was diagnosed with a mild concussion. The fall seemed to be a true accident, but Elvis didn't seem to mind that his injury pushed the film production schedule back even further.

I wasn't in L.A. when Elvis took that fall, but I heard right away what happened in its aftermath. The Colonel called all the guys together and basically read them the riot act. Expenses were going to be severely cut back, and anybody who wasn't pulling his weight as an employee was going to be out. The Colonel considered Larry Geller's interest in spirituality to be an unnecessary distraction for Elvis, and essentially drummed Larry out of the group. The whole thing was a power play on the Colonel's part that

a strong Elvis would have never stood for. But Elvis at that time was hurt
and frustrated. He knew what he wanted from his career, but nobody was
listening to him, and I think he'd reached a point where he just didn't feel
like putting up much of a fight anymore.

Clambake didn't do anything to ease Elvis's doubts about his career, but
maybe it did help him focus on what he wanted on a most personal level.
As that production came to a close, a very hush-hush piece of information
worked its way through Elvis's inner circle: Elvis and Priscilla were getting
married.

Elvis called to invite me to the wedding, which would be held at the
Aladdin Hotel. When the time came, Elvis flew me from Memphis to
Palm Springs to join up with him and Priscilla and other members of the
wedding party. Elvis had asked me to keep quiet about the wedding, but
rumors were still swirling in the press, and when Joe and I went out to a
Palm Springs convenience store to pick up some toiletries, we found ourselves tailed by a very persistent journalist—Rona Barrett. When she
approached us, we played dumb and didn't give her any information, but
she still ended up being the first reporter to break the story of Elvis's wedding in the national press.

Just after midnight on May 1, the wedding party snuck out the back
door of Elvis's Palm Springs home, climbed over the backyard wall, and
got into a car to head to the airport. Elvis had been loaned Frank Sinatra's
private jet for the occasion, and he and Priscilla, myself, Joe and Joanie
Esposito, and a pair of pilots boarded that to fly to Las Vegas. The rest of
the entourage (family members, a few Mafia guys, and Harry Levitch, one
of Elvis's favorite jewelers) boarded a separate plane that Elvis had leased.
I was deeply honored that Elvis wanted me on the plane with him.

The wedding day was a beautiful one for Elvis and Priscilla, but it also
showcased a lot of the problems in Elvis's world at the time. For one thing,
on a day that was such a personal celebration, the Colonel—who had
vowed never to interfere in Elvis's personal life—ran the show. The reason

the wedding was at the Aladdin was that the Colonel was friendly with the hotel's owner, Milton Prell. And, because the Colonel wanted an event that could be tightly controlled and kept from the media circus, the ceremony itself was held in Prell's small private suite. Elvis, the guy who loved doing things in a big way, was getting married in a room that felt crowded with fourteen people in it. And the Colonel even seemed to have a hand in deciding who those fourteen would be, setting things up so as to exclude most of the Memphis Mafia guys.

Elvis had named Joe Esposito and Marty Lacker as co–best men, and he wanted me to be there, too, as a witness to the wedding vows. I felt privileged to be included, but when most of the other guys heard that they would only be at the reception and not the actual wedding, there were a lot of hurt feelings. Red West was both furious and heartbroken, and at one point exploded at the Colonel, threatening to break the big man's cane over his head. Red then stormed out of the hotel, not bothering to stick around for the reception.

At the reception, I could see the hurt on the faces of guys like Jerry Schilling and Charlie Hodge, and I think we all had mixed emotions. On the one hand, Elvis and Priscilla were happily focused on each other, and nobody wanted to spoil the day for them. But none of us could quite believe that the Colonel had stuck himself in the middle of this day. It just didn't feel like the kind of wedding Elvis and Priscilla would have wished for, and what could have been an event that was grand, romantic, and wonderful for everyone felt like it was being done on the fly and on the cheap.

I do remember one funny, unexpected moment after the wedding. The Colonel had invited his own list of people to the reception, and one of his guests was comedian Redd Foxx, who was appearing in one of the lounges on the Strip. I was sitting at the head table with Elvis and Priscilla when Redd approached to convey his congratulations. When Elvis asked if he was having a good time, Redd said, "Yeah—but I'm the only spook here."

After the wedding, a small group of us spent a few days back in Palm Springs with the newlyweds, and then it was back to Memphis, where a lot of time was again spent at the Circle G. This time around, Elvis was able to relax enough that the whole atmosphere of the ranch became a lot more pleasant for everyone. Instead of the mad buying spree he'd been on before, Elvis gave himself a chance to enjoy the place. I still didn't like horses any better, and much preferred nights at Graceland, the Fairgrounds, or the Memphian, but it was nice to see the group come together around Elvis and Priscilla and be a part of their happiness.

Elvis and Priscilla were very much in love, and even as Priscilla got more and more beautiful as she grew from a girl into a woman, we knew Elvis didn't just love her for her looks: The two of them were loving partners who also shared a great friendship.

I hadn't been the most faithful of boyfriends to Barbara, but I'd come to treasure her as a friend and companion, and the idea of building a life together with her started sounding a lot more satisfying than skinny-dipping with strangers out in Hollywood. Jerry and Sandy were deeply in love, Joe Esposito was devoted to his Joanie, and all around us the group seemed to be discovering the pleasures of domestic commitment, right there on that ranch. Picnics, cookouts, ballgames, snake hunts—no longer the rock 'n' roll frat, we were now living at the coolest coed summer camp imaginable. The ranch period was brief—by the summer of 1969 the property would quietly be sold off. But it really was a wonderful time, and I think everyone who was a part of those days and nights has special memories of the Circle G.

In general, Elvis Presley loved being Elvis Presley, but there were a few moments when even he was surprised at who he was. I remember one rainy evening he and I were driving back to Graceland from a night out somewhere. He'd been battling with some broken windshield wipers on the ride, and halfway up the Graceland driveway, he suddenly stopped the car.

"GK, you see that big house up there?" he asked.

"Uh, yeah—I see it, Elvis."

"And you see this fancy car I'm driving. You see these diamonds I'm wearing?" He held out a hand to show off some of his large rings.

"Yeah, Elvis."

"Man, I sure hope it's not a dream."

He wasn't kidding around. It seemed like a serious moment of reflection for him. I thought about all the very real changes in my life that had happened because of him, then gave him an easy answer.

"It ain't no dream, Elvis," I assured him. "Believe me, it ain't a dream."

For the few times that Elvis really did want to get away from being "Elvis," he had a special vehicle: a beat-up old black panel truck. The truck got used for utility work around Graceland, but occasionally Elvis would try to make himself unrecognizable by putting on a black yacht cap and some sunglasses. He'd fill up a jug of iced tea, climb into that old truck, and drive it all around Memphis. It was a way for him to revisit some of the old spots that meant a lot to him—Humes High, places he'd lived, parks he'd played football in—without drawing any attention to himself. But sometimes the disguise worked a little too well.

One early evening, just as the sun was setting, I was driving my car past the Memphis airport, on one of the shortcuts I took to get to Graceland. Through the dusk, on the side of the road, I saw a guy next to a truck with its hood up. The guy waved, and I waved back, and I remember thinking, "Hey—he sort of looks like Elvis." But there was no reason Elvis would be out in that part of town, and when his panel truck had broken down before, he hadn't stayed with it: He'd found a phone and called Richard Davis or one of the other guys to come get him.

I made it to Graceland, parked in back like I always did, and went in the house. "Where's Elvis?" I asked the first guy I came across.

"He's out in the black panel truck," was the response.

Oh, shit.

I started telling the guys what I'd seen on the way over, when all of a sudden Elvis burst in the front door.

The first thing he said was: "Where's Klein?" And when he called you by your last name, you knew you were in trouble. He targeted in on me and started throwing some play punches at my arms and shoulders.

"You son of a gun—why didn't you pick me up?"

"Elvis! Elvis—I swear I didn't know it was you."

"You waved at me, man," he said, punching a little harder. "You waved at me and you kept going. I gave you that damn Cadillac and you drove right by me in it. Man, am I mad at you." He said it with a smile, but I knew I was lucky that some anonymous driver a minute behind me had been kind enough to pick up the guy in the black yacht cap and give him a ride to Graceland (a ride that earned that driver a hundred-dollar tip).

I went out to L.A. during the summer of '67 to make my usual Hollywood visit. Elvis was filming *Speedway*, his twenty-seventh movie, in which he predictably played a race-car driver who fought the bad guys, got the girl, and sang a dozen mediocre songs. Elvis did have a great relationship with his costar, Nancy Sinatra, though it was more of a big brother–little sister dynamic than anything romantic. He even helped me set up an interview with her for my radio show, something he hadn't done with any other costars. Elvis was working again with choreographer Alex Romero, who'd worked with him on *Jailhouse Rock* all those years back, and that added a little energy to some of the dance numbers. But, though there were some pranks and joking around on set, it seemed pretty obvious to me that Elvis could be doing much better work than what he was doing. One afternoon, I found myself with the Colonel in his office on the MGM lot, and I decided to ask some of the questions that had been bothering me.

"Colonel," I started. "Why don't you let Elvis do something different—the way Steve McQueen or Paul Newman do all kinds of films. Secret agent films are big—Dean Martin has fun doing the Matt Helm movies, James Coburn did *Our Man Flint*. Elvis would love doing something like that and he'd be good at it."

"George, George," the Colonel practically shouted as he leaned back in his chair. "Frankly, we don't give a shit. We don't have to. My boy's getting a million dollars up front and fifty percent of the picture every time he works. None of those people get close to that. Brando doesn't get it, John Wayne doesn't get it. But my boy does."

"But, Colonel," I said, trying to keep things loose and conversational, "couldn't Elvis get some better casts, better songs—some better scripts?"

"George," he barked, his expression darkening, "we don't give a shit about scripts. If we had to read the damn script, we'd charge them another million dollars. There are guys walking up and down Hollywood Boulevard with Oscars in their hands. They had a great script, and now they can't get arrested. My boy is getting a million dollars up front, fifty percent of the picture, and top billing. That's all Hollywood cares about—making money. Elvis doesn't have to ask anybody out here for any favors."

"He doesn't need any favors," I answered, this time with a sharper edge to my voice. "He's a star and he can demand better support, better casts, better directors, and better movies."

"If he asks for all that and the movie bombs, he's gone cold," the Colonel roared back. "If we do it their way and the movie bombs, it's their fault. Elvis still comes out on top."

I knew it wasn't going to help to push the conversation any further. The Colonel had a point that Hollywood often operated on a what-have-you-done-for-me-lately basis, but Newman, McQueen, even Brando had taken some chances—had even been in some bombs—and they were still working as A-list actors. Frank Sinatra's movie career had gone cold for a while, but then he came back strong with *From Here to Eternity* and a long string of hits. I remembered what our Hollywood friend Nick Adams had once told me: that he preferred taking little parts in great movies than big parts in lousy movies. Elvis got top billing every time out and was still one of the highest paid actors in town. But the Colonel just couldn't see the bigger picture. He'd made Elvis a rich celebrity. But Elvis the artist was starving.

Despite Elvis's dissatisfaction with his work, the holiday season in 1967 was a sweet one. For one thing, Elvis was going to be a daddy. Priscilla was in an advanced state of pregnancy at Christmas, which made what was always a special time around Graceland even more so. Elvis, always generous by nature, had a holiday tradition he'd started with his post-army Ellis Auditorium concert: He would hand out at least fifty thousand dollars' worth of checks to fifty needy charities. Graceland itself was transformed, a magical place becoming even more magical. Elvis started a tradition of setting up eight big Christmas trees outside, four on each side of the front door, each done up in its own color of lights. (I asked him once where he got that great idea and he said it came from a department store in Beverly Hills.) He always loved having the long Graceland driveway done up in blue lights, and we heard more than once that confused local pilots sometimes thought they were looking at a landing strip when they flew over the house.

For a guy who could buy anything he wanted for himself, Christmas presents were a big deal to Elvis. He didn't care what you gave him, but he wanted to get something. One year I gave Elvis a giant starburst clock. He could have bought the same clock dipped in gold if he wanted to, but he appreciated the gift so much he had it hung over the fireplace mantel in the Graceland living room. (It's still up there.) He also gave out some wonderful, personal gifts: In 1964 he gave me a Lucien Picard gold watch engraved GK EP 10 YEARS, meaning we'd both logged ten years in show business.

That year I was particularly proud of the gift I'd come up with for him. Every time Elvis traveled between Memphis and Hollywood, there was always trouble finding a way to pack and organize the pile of books he wanted to bring with him. I had the idea to build him a rolling bookcase—a kind of cabinet on wheels, covered in black leather, with EP written on the doors in white. When he opened it up that Christmas Eve, his eyes lit up like a kid's. He stopped the whole process of gift-giving and gift-opening and had somebody go up to his bedroom and bring down a stack of books so he could test it out. It was a great feeling to watch him roll a couple dozen books around the first floor of Graceland, knowing that in some small way, I'd been able to make him happy.

My favorite part of Christmas Eve at Graceland came after the presents, around midnight, when other members of the Memphis Mafia would begin to leave to get ready for their own Christmas mornings at home.

Often, that would just leave Elvis and Priscilla and Barbara and myself, and we'd usually all end up going for a long ride, because Elvis loved seeing what everybody else's Christmas decorations looked like. Those late-night rides are still some of my fondest memories with Elvis.

The Christmas good cheer stretched through to New Year's Eve, with Alan Fortas and me still in charge of setting up a private party for Elvis at the Manhattan Club. (In later years we moved it to the Thunderbird Lounge and then to T.J.'s, a club run by my friend Herbie O'Mell.) But just weeks into 1968, Elvis looked like he was feeling ten Christmases rolled into one. On February 1, Priscilla gave birth to a daughter, Lisa Marie Presley.

"You want to hold her, GK?"

I'd spent the day at the hospital with Elvis, watching him run around like a crazy man to burn off all his nervous energy. But now I stood in Priscilla's hospital room with the new parents and their new baby. Elvis was delighted, remarkably loving, and incredibly comfortable as he held his baby close to him. He wanted to hand her to me and share the happiness.

"No, no, Elvis, that's okay. I'm afraid I'll drop her."

"GK, you're going to hold her." He took a step toward me.

"No, Elvis, no . . ." Too late. I had a baby in my arms.

It was a nice feeling to know that he trusted me with the thing that was now most precious to him—but I could only hold her barely a minute before my nerves got the better of me.

"She's beautiful, Elvis. Priscilla. But—you better take her back."

They both laughed at my jitters with little Lisa, and Elvis quickly scooped her back up. Watching the parents with their new child, I thought I'd never seen Elvis and Priscilla looking so much in love, and so full of complete, simple joy.

Elvis was a real family man now, and things had never been so happy and tranquil around Graceland. But in 1968, the world beyond those Graceland gates was in turmoil. I was on the air at WHBQ, toward the end of an afternoon drive-time shift, when I learned that the nation's turmoil had touched Memphis in a terrible way. A news bulletin came in announcing that Martin Luther King Jr., in our city to offer support to striking sanitation workers, had been shot dead on the balcony of his room at the Lorraine Motel. The whole city was in shock. Memphis was a place where there had been real harmony between the races, musical and otherwise, and nobody quite knew what to make of the fact that such a disgraceful act of hatred had happened here. I felt I needed to get out in the city to try to make sense of it all, so a couple of days after the shooting Herbie O'Mell and I drove down to the Lorraine Motel. The place seemed unnaturally still—it was hard to believe it had been the scene of an assassination only days before. There were just a few other people milling around the motel parking lot, looking as confused as we felt.

News reports had said that the shot was fired from a nearby building. Herbie and I figured out which building it was, and were shocked to discover it was completely open and unattended: There were no police around, no FBI, not even any crime scene tape. The place was a real low-class flophouse, the kind favored by hookers and winos. We went to an upper floor and in the hallway we recognized a guy named Charlie—who had been on the news as one of the residents who saw the shooter running through the building after the shots were fired. Charlie pointed us to a communal bathroom at the end of the hall where the shooter had stationed himself.

In the dank little bathroom was a small window that gave a perfect view of the balcony at the motel where Dr. King had been standing, and we were struck that the killer had found such a perfect vantage point for a direct shot. Somebody had been in there dusting for fingerprints, and you could still see the ghostly imprint of the shooter's left hand on the wall next to the window. We didn't stay long, and weren't sure what to make of everything we saw. Mainly, we just couldn't believe that, given the national impact of the bullets fired from that flophouse window, we could walk right into the scene of the crime.

After that strange moment of calm, Memphis did erupt. There were marches and memorials. There were riots down on Beale Street, and a citywide curfew was imposed. The flophouse and the motel were cordoned off and under police watch. Charlie was even taken into police custody to protect him as a material witness. I remember driving home from the radio station and seeing tanks and jeeps on Memphis streets. Something beautiful and fragile in my city had been shattered, and I wondered if it could ever be put back together.

In many ways, the death of Dr. King changed the way America looked at itself, and it certainly had an impact on popular music. The sweet, optimistic soul music that had come from artists such as Wilson Pickett and Otis Redding gave way to music that was stronger and angrier, and my friend James Brown was one of the leaders in pushing in that new direction. I remember talking with him in his dressing room after a Memphis show sometime in the year after Dr. King's death. James was getting ready for me to take him to the studio to do my TV show, and at some point in our conversation I used the word "colored." He cut me off instantly.

"George," he said gruffly, "we don't use that word no more."

"What do you mean, James?"

"Colored—nah. We don't use that word. It's 'black' now, George. Black."

"But James, my mother always taught me to be nice and use the word 'colored.' I thought that was okay."

"I know, I know, but times have changed. It's 'black' now."

I just nodded, and was glad that I'd learned this new lesson straight from James Brown. But then something occurred to me.

"James, what about the NAACP? They still use 'colored.'"

James didn't miss a beat. "I'm working on that, too, George," he said. "I'm working on that, too."

With all the social upheaval in the air in the summer of 1968, Elvis began a project that would have a great effect on his career. The Colonel had made a deal with NBC for Elvis to do a one-hour television special, with the original understanding that it would be a fairly typical celebrity Christmas show. But Elvis, encouraged by a young director named Steve Binder, decided to use the opportunity to get back to his rock 'n' roll roots and give his fans something they hadn't had much of in almost a decade: some real, rockin' Elvis. I got almost daily reports from Alan Fortas as the show was taking shape, and heard all about the battles for creative control between the Colonel and Elvis. It sounded like Elvis was winning.

Almost as soon as Elvis finished working on his TV special, he flew out to Arizona for a location shoot of his next feature film, a Western titled *Charro*. Toward the end of September, Elvis was finally back in Memphis, and plans were made for nights at Graceland and at the Memphian. But some sadder plans had to be made as well. On September 28, 1968, Dewey Phillips, the deejay who had been such an important part of the birth of rock 'n' roll and the start of Elvis's career, died of heart failure. He was forty-two years old.

Dewey had ridden out years of decline to his early grave. And in a sense, rock 'n' roll's success is what did him in. He was a unique wild man who helped popularize the music, but as it became popular, the stations that played it became more and more smooth and formatted, until there was no place for a voice like Dewey's. His drinking increased, and by the end he became more of a Memphis street character than a significant radio figure.

Elvis had kept a warm spot in his heart for Dewey, as did Sam Phillips, and both tried to look out for him even when Dewey didn't make it easy. Elvis often asked me to make sure Dewey had enough money, though he never wanted me to let Dewey know the cash was coming from him. He thought it might hurt what was left of Dewey's pride. I was a pallbearer for Dewey, and Elvis and Priscilla and some of the guys made a point of coming to the funeral to pay their respects. I was a little puzzled when it seemed like Elvis and Alan were actually laughing during parts of the service, but they explained themselves afterward. The more they'd thought of the crazy phrases Dewey had used in his prime—"mother," "loverboy," "wheelbarrow full of pissants"—the more they laughed about what a crazy, one-of-a-kind character Daddy-O Dewey had been.

On December 3, 1968, Elvis was back in Los Angeles for the production of another film, *The Trouble with Girls*. I was in my Memphis apartment, and nothing could have pulled me away from my television that night.

After hearing from everybody else how good a job Elvis had done on his TV special, I finally had a chance to see for myself.

I was blown away.

The *Elvis* special began with him just glaring straight into the camera and singing, "If you're looking for trouble, you came to the right place." From those opening moments right on through to the final song, the show was nothing but pure, red-hot Elvis. The pleasant guy from all those lame movies was gone: This Elvis was lean and mean, not looking to be nice and not answering to anyone but himself. He was tanned and handsome and looked fit and full of fire—especially when wearing a suit of black leather.

There were hip, full-scale production pieces built around Jerry Reed's "Guitar Man" song, and some favorite gospel numbers that Elvis approached with an intensity that had rarely showed up on the big screen. There were stand-up concert sequences in which he delivered renewed oldies such as "Heartbreak Hotel" and "All Shook Up"—you could practically feel the adrenaline rush of a master performer finally allowed to cut loose the way he wanted to. And there were those great sit-down segments, the prototype for the "Unplugged" concerts. Elvis—with Scotty, D.J., Charlie Hodge, and Alan around him—gave one of the rawest, most honest performances of his life, working through favorites such as "One Night," "Lawdy Miss Clawdy," and "Baby, What You Want Me to Do." Over the years, I'd wondered if Elvis could still rise to the level of performance he'd been at in the early days. Now I had my answer. Yeah—he could hit that level and zoom far beyond it. He wasn't just returning to form, he was setting a whole new rock 'n' roll gold standard for himself.

At the end of the show, Elvis sang "If I Can Dream," a newly written song of hope that had a special poignancy at the end of a year that had contained so much strife and loss: the assassinations of Martin Luther King Jr. and Robert F. Kennedy, the escalation of the war in Vietnam, riots in the streets of American cities. Elvis delivered that final, simple plea for peace and understanding with such overwhelming conviction that it gave me goosebumps.

By the time that TV special was over, I was prouder of Elvis than I'd ever been, and once again completely in awe of his talents. Frankly, I was just as happy as hell.

The king of rock 'n' roll had put his crown back on.

CHAPTER TWELVE

•• • •• • •• • ••

American Music

"What a funky place. I like it. It reminds me of Sun."

That's the first thing Elvis said as he stepped into American Sound Studios at 827 Thomas Street in North Memphis, just about five blocks away from Humes High School and right across the street from a drive-in barbecue place we Humes kids used to hang out at. It was the second Monday in January 1969, just a few days after I'd made my pitch at the Graceland dining room table for Elvis to get ahold of some stronger material and to record here at American.

The North Memphis neighborhood where the studio was located was now slightly run-down and a little on the seedy side—you didn't fear for your life, but you made sure to lock up your car. Back in the Humes days, the American premises had been a shoe-repair shop, and the storefront building was still humble in appearance. Inside, the place was indeed funky. Comfortable, but still funky. It looked "lived-in," to put it nicely, and there wasn't anything impressive about the small recording room that would lead you to suspect that some of the most popular records in the country had come out of there over the last couple of years.

Producer Chips Moman, American's owner, and his studio's house band, who became known as the Memphis Boys, had become some of the hottest hitmakers in the country, creating chart-climbing hits for the likes of the Box Tops ("The Letter," "Cry Like a Baby"), Merrilee Rush

("Angel of the Morning"), Joe Tex ("Skinny Legs and All"), B. J. Thomas ("Hooked on a Feeling"), and Dusty Springfield ("Son of a Preacher Man"). While Elvis had begun launching his "comeback"—a phrase he never liked—with his TV special, the guys at American were at the top of their game.

Elvis hadn't ever crossed paths with Chips or any of the Memphis Boys before, but he was cautiously optimistic about working with them. The guys at American were fans of Elvis's fifties work but didn't know what to expect from him now. Still, when Elvis walked into American that January night, these hotter-than-hot hitmakers rose to their feet like they were coming to attention. Elvis was in their house, and even for these seasoned pros, that was something worth getting excited about. For his part, Elvis made it clear he was ready to work. The time, the place, and the chemistry were all perfect for some great music to be made.

I'd first met Chips Moman through another one of my side jobs. For a year or so in the early sixties, I'd taken a shot at starting my own record label with a couple of partners—Wimpy Adams, my Memphis State friend who'd ended up managing the Fairgrounds, and "Sambo" Barrom, a local Golden Gloves boxing legend who had a hand in a number of night-club and entertainment interests. Klein, Adams, and Barrom added up to KAB Records, and our smartest move was to recruit Chips as our in-house producer. He'd made a name for himself as an L.A. session guitarist, a member of Gene Vincent's touring band, and also as an engineer and pro-ducer for Stax Records in Memphis. Chips produced some of the early Stax hits for Carla Thomas, Rufus Thomas, Booker T and the MG's, and the Mar-Keys, but when he felt he wasn't being treated fairly by the label, he struck out on his own.

KAB Records didn't pan out, but I stayed close with Chips. At one point we took a shot at cashing in on the surf-instrumental craze and got some time in Scotty Moore's studio to record a track. When I showed up at the studio, I was surprised to find that Chips and I were the only ones there—I had expected that he'd pull a group of musicians together. Instead, he had me help run the studio board as he overdubbed himself playing every instrument on the track, something I'd never seen anybody else do. When we decided to add a sound effect of the ocean's roar to the track, Chips came up with the idea of recording the flushing of a studio commode. My main contribution was to come up with a name for the song and the artist. The tune became "Goin' to L.A.," and the group—even though it was really just a lot of Chips—became the Hitchhikers. It was released on one of the record labels run by Texas rock 'n' roll entrepreneur Huey P. Meaux. We failed to climb the charts, although a couple of reviews did comment on the cool ocean-surf effect.

Soon Chips opened American and began to assemble his outstanding studio group: guitarist Reggie Young, bassists Tommy Cogbill and Mike Leech, keyboardists Bobby Emmons and Bobby Wood, and drummer Gene Chrisman. Chips also hired a staff songwriter, a childhood friend of B. J. Thomas's named Mark James. As I scouted local bands for *Talent Party*, I also became a kind of unofficial talent scout for Chips. Some of my WHBQuties were dating members of a popular local act named the Gentrys, and when I ran into the band at a Memphis barbecue joint, I suggested they get over to Chips to do some recording. The result was "Keep on Dancing," a national top-five hit in 1965.

I also started doing some songwriting with Mark James. I'd never been able to play an instrument or read a note of music, but the rhyming skills that had gotten me started as a deejay made me useful as a co-lyricist with Mark. I'd also played enough hit records through the years that I had a good sense of what kind of storytelling worked well in a song, and what kind of song titles would appeal to a listening audience. Mark and I got along great together and eventually came up with a number of songs that were recorded, including "Stone Cold Soul" for Jackie DeShannon, "Love Ain't Easy" for Flash and the Board of Directors, and a couple of "Angel of the Morning" follow-ups for Merrilee Rush: "Sunshine and Roses" and "Love Street." On his own, Mark had just had some big hits writing for B. J. Thomas—"Eyes of a New York Woman" and "Hooked on a Feeling." Mark had also worked with Chips to record some of his songs himself, and

I was particularly taken with one, a soulful number called "Suspicious Minds."

By the time Elvis came to American to record, I'd spent a lot of time there. The place had some drawbacks—occasionally the recordings of quieter songs were ruined by the sound of rats in the ceiling. But Chips and his players had a group spirit very similar to that of the Memphis Mafia. Once, after a couple of the musicians' cars had been broken into, the Memphis Boys decided to send a message. They had somebody go out in the woods and catch a bunch of snakes, and then put the mess of reptiles in a great big gift-wrapped box, which was placed on the backseat of an unlocked car in the American parking lot. I was at the studio the night that a car cruised into the lot and a couple of its passengers hopped out and quickly found the easily grabbed gift. They pulled it into their vehicle and made it back out to the street to the closest intersection before the car screeched to a halt, the doors flew open, and snakes and would-be thieves scattered in all directions. The American parking lot was pretty safe from then on.

Chips was a no-nonsense guy who always told it like it was. He was focused on getting great recordings of great performances of great material and had very little patience for anything getting in the way of that. He was never rude, but he was direct in a very Southern way. It would have been natural for Chips to wonder whether the Elvis coming to him was still a vital talent or simply a star resting on past glories. But as soon as Elvis and the band got to business cutting the country weeper "Long Black Limousine," a great working dynamic was set. Chips wanted to get the best he could out of Elvis, but he was supportive and diplomatic about whatever suggestions he made, and I think he found that Elvis usually knew what to fix in a vocal even before he heard a playback. Elvis appreciated the fact that somebody was just dealing straight with him, musician to musician.

There was another producer at the sessions—Felton Jarvis, the RCA staffer who Elvis had come to trust as a friend and musical colleague. But Felton was an easygoing guy who understood that he was mainly there as an RCA representative and as a form of moral support for Elvis. While Felton might occasionally make a suggestion or answer a question Chips had, he understood that Chips was running the show at American. So Elvis was giving his all, Chips was in charge, and the only objective that mattered was cutting some great songs.

That was the ingredient that had been missing from Elvis sessions for a long time, but at the American sessions, the usual protocol for song selection had been tossed away and, for the first time in a long time, Elvis had a shot at some really strong material. Mac Davis had written "Memories," a standout ballad in the TV special that Elvis had loved singing, and Felton brought in a number of new demos from him. Chips had access to the great work from Mark James and some of his other staff writers. And even the songs coming through the usual Hill and Range channels were stronger, in part because Lamar Fike was now working with the publishing company. Lamar thought "Kentucky Rain" by a young country writer named Eddie Rabbitt would be just right for Elvis.

Neil Diamond had recently been in American cutting "Sweet Caroline" and "Brother Love's Traveling Salvation Show." I'd come to that session and then taken Neil to the WHBQ TV studio to be on *Talent Party*. I learned that Neil was a big fan of Elvis's and that he dreamed of writing something for him. He'd given me his private phone number just in case any such opportunity ever arose. When Elvis booked time at American, I called Neil and asked him if he had anything Elvis might record there. He sent by special delivery an acetate of "And the Grass Won't Pay No Mind." When I played that for Elvis upstairs at Graceland, he got excited about cutting it.

Some of the material didn't get picked until we got into American. On the first night there, when we took a break to listen to some demos, I found myself in the studio control room with Chips, Felton, Elvis, and a few others. Felton put on a tape of the stuff that he'd gotten from Mac Davis and the first song we heard was one about the cycle of violence in the inner city.

It was called "In the Ghetto." When it was over, there was silence, then Elvis said, "Play that again."

We all listened again, and when the song was over there was silence once more.

Finally I spoke up. "Elvis, that's heavy, and it's good, but it's kind of a message song and that's never been your thing."

He said, "Yeah, I don't know. But put a hold on that one. We'll listen to it later."

Chips gave me a kind of funny look, and then we went on listening to some more songs before Elvis went back to recording. I got home after the session and all that kept going through my head was that "Ghetto" song. The night of the next session, I went up to Graceland before we all headed to the studio. I came in through the back door and found Elvis and some of the guys hanging out in the back den.

I approached Elvis right away and said, "I think I made a big mistake."

"What are you talking about, GK?"

"Elvis, I said that 'In the Ghetto' song wasn't right for you. But I can't get it out of my head, and I think it's actually perfect for you. It's a great song."

I saw a hint of a smile flicker on his face. "No shit, GK," he said. "Damn straight it's a great song, and I'm cutting it tonight." Apparently it had been stuck in his head, too.

And when Elvis did record it, I found out what the funny look Chips had given me was all about. One of Elvis's favorite artists in the fifties had been Roy Hamilton, a black singer with an incredibly smooth sound, who brought an almost operatic style to such pop records as "Unchained Melody" and "Hurt." Roy's career had cooled off in the sixties, but just months before Elvis came to American, I'd seen Roy perform in a Memphis club and was blown away at what great chops he still had. I'd brought him to Chips, who promptly signed him to his own record label and began recording with him at American. Chips had been hoping that Elvis would pass on "In the Ghetto" so that Roy could record it.

Roy didn't get that one, but when Elvis heard that Roy would be recording at American on an afternoon before one of Elvis's evening sessions, he asked me to check with Roy to see if it was okay for Elvis to visit him there. Roy was thrilled, and when the two got together, I could see that it meant a lot to Elvis to be able to pay his respects to an artist he had admired for so long. Elvis surprised everyone in the studio by offering Roy one of the songs he was planning on recording that night, a great Barry Mann–Cynthia Weill tearjerker of a tune called "Angelica." Roy, deeply touched, accepted the gift. Sadly, it was one of the last things he recorded: He died not too long after his time at American, done in by a massive stroke at the age of forty.

The first couple of nights at American were energetic and productive, but it was when Elvis and the band cut "In the Ghetto" that the chemistry in that studio really became something extraordinary. As good as those Memphis Boys were as players, it seemed they got even better for Elvis. They loved the fact that he didn't like to rehearse songs part by part and section by section—instead, he wanted to work out an arrangement once with Chips and then just go for it until they got the right take. Watching Elvis's TV special, I'd felt I was watching a kind of magic as Elvis revealed to us that he was the same fierce performer he'd always been. Now, in the studio, I was watching that magic happen again. And I could see the effect it had on everyone in that studio—I remember seeing the look of awe on Priscilla's face as Elvis recorded "Kentucky Rain" with all his heart, soul, and passion.

About halfway through the sessions, Chips said he had something he wanted Elvis to hear, and he played him Mark James's recording of "Suspicious Minds." Chips was a great writer himself—he'd cowritten "Do Right Woman" for Aretha Franklin—and had a reputation for using his great ear to put the right song with the right act. Chips thought "Suspicious Minds" was perfect for Elvis but hadn't wanted to push one of his own songs at the first sessions. Now that Elvis had cut "Kentucky Rain" and "Don't Cry Daddy" and so many other strong tracks, Elvis and everyone else was in a great mood, and Chips decided to play the song for him in the control room. Elvis listened, surrounded by me, Freddy Bienstock from Hill and Range, RCA executive Harry Jenkins, and Tom Diskin—as always, the eyes and ears of the Colonel.

When it was over, Elvis said, "That's not bad. Can we put a hold on that?" Chips said he'd hold it.

Elvis walked back into the studio to talk to the musicians, and as soon as he was out of the control room, Freddy Bienstock and Tom Diskin zeroed in on Chips. They started hitting him with all kinds of talk about how business was done with Elvis's music companies and how, since "Suspicious Minds" wasn't officially presented at the start of the sessions, Hill and Range was going to have to take half the publishing and part of the writer's percentage of profits as well. They said the wrong thing to the wrong guy. Chips had street smarts and a country temper, and he launched into a tirade. I think I'd warned Chips that he might run into this kind of thing, but I'd never seen him as mad as he was then.

Chips cussed out Freddy and Tom in ways I know they weren't used to hearing, but, frankly, it was exactly what they deserved. Chips let them know how disgusted he was that, at a session in which things were going so well, these guys were raising nickel-and-dime concerns over publishing and trying to grab money away from a songwriter. I can't remember the exact phrases Chips used, but I think he made it clear where Freddy and Tom could stick the session tapes, then proclaimed that the recording session was over.

Harry Jenkins jumped up and tried to be a peacemaker, asking everyone to calm down. "Things are going well here," said Harry. "We don't want to ruin the session. Let's talk about all this later."

That wasn't good enough for Chips, who was still shaking, he was so mad. He made it clear again in the strongest terms that the matter was not open for discussion now or later, and that there wasn't a chance in hell that Tom and Freddy were going to get a piece of the publishing.

Harry sent Tom and Freddy out of the control room, following them out the door. Chips gave a quick look in my direction, still shaking his head in disgust. I knew he had every right to be as angry as he was, but I also knew that Bienstock and Diskin weren't speaking for Elvis. I had a feeling if Chips and Elvis could deal with the situation one-to-one, it could be worked out and more great music could be made.

"Chips," I said, "before those guys get to Elvis or to Colonel Parker and everything gets bent out of shape and told ten different ways, ask Elvis to come up to the control room right now. When he walks in, you ask me to leave because you want a private talk with Elvis. That way Elvis will know it's important. Then explain to him exactly what just happened—the plain simple truth of it."

Chips used the studio intercom to call Elvis up to the control room, then asked me to leave. I went out to the studio, but I kept shooting looks over at the glass of the control room to see what was going on in there. Chips had calmed down, and as he talked I could see Elvis smiling. Chips was gesturing and making his points, and Elvis started laughing. After a minute or two, they both looked happy and Elvis came back, ready to go to work again.

When I had the chance, I asked Chips how the discussion had gone. He said that he'd told Elvis that if Elvis started his own personal publishing company right then, Chips would give him half the rights to "Suspicious Minds," but he didn't want a penny going to Hill and Range.

"Don't worry about those sons of bitches," Elvis said to Chips. "You just worry about me. I don't want half your damn publishing. It's your song, and the writer gets his share, that's fine by me. I just want some good material, man. I want some hits."

Elvis did cut a lot of hit-quality material at American, but by the last scheduled session, "Suspicious Minds" had still not been recorded. Elvis and Joe Esposito and I and some of the other guys were sitting in the small outer lobby at American. Elvis was reading a copy of *Billboard*, waiting to do a few vocal punch-ins with Chips, and everyone else was relaxed. But Joe noticed that I was in a nervous, fidgety state.

"What's wrong with you, GK?" he asked.

"Joe, I'll put my whole show-business career on the line for one song—'Suspicious Minds.' Mark wrote it and I had nothing to do with that one, but I know it's a smash hit for Elvis. I've been waiting all through these sessions for him to cut it, and now I'm afraid it's going to get overlooked."

"You really believe in that song?" asked Joe.

"I'm no genius, Joe. But that song and Elvis are a natural smash together. I know it."

Joe suggested we walk over to Elvis together to give the song one more pitch. I tried not to sound too worked up, but I think I just about promised to Elvis that the song would go to number one. I didn't need to give it too hard a sell, though, because almost as soon as I mentioned the song's title, Elvis snapped his fingers and said, "Yeah—'Suspicious Minds.' We forgot that one. Let's cut that thing right now."

Chips got excited about doing "Suspicious Minds" as the final song at the sessions, and the musicians had no trouble kicking into gear, as they already knew the arrangement from having recorded it with Mark James. Elvis spent some time working over the lyrics, and then, after just three or four takes, nobody could think of any way the track might be improved. Chips played it back over the loudspeakers, and the studio just went nuts. It was a great song, given an awesome performance by Elvis; it was one of those magical moments when everything had gone right. There were high fives all around, and Chips said, "Elvis, we cut some fine songs here, but this tops them all."

After the American sessions, Elvis had a busy schedule to jump back into. He went out to Los Angeles to shoot his final feature film, *Change of Habit,* which costarred Mary Tyler Moore as a very pretty nun. Then Elvis began selecting material and putting a band together for his upcoming return to live performance with a debut four-week engagement at the Las Vegas International Hotel. The good feelings we all had about the American work were validated by the public when "In the Ghetto" was released as a single in the spring and rose to number three on the *Billboard* charts. The reaction to the TV special had let Elvis know that he'd never really lost his connection with his original fans, but he was particularly happy to put out a record strong enough to win over new, younger fans.

I kept writing with Mark James, and we were excited about coming up with something for one of the artists who recorded at American right after Elvis, British singer Petula Clark. Clark had had some monster hits with "Downtown" and "Don't Sleep in the Subway," and now wanted to work with Chips, blending her voice with a country-soul sound much the way Dusty Springfield had. I came up with a title—"Loving You's a Natural Thing"—a background story, and some lines of lyrics, and Mark went to work pulling it all together into a song. We were both happy with what we came up with. However, when we played it for Chips, he said he liked it but he wanted to hold on to it. We didn't understand: The Pet Clark session was coming up and we knew she needed some material. Chips explained that he'd just signed a new artist, Ronnie Milsap, who'd been creating a lot of excitement as the house act at the downtown club T.J.'s. Chips thought our song could be the hit that would help launch Ronnie's career.

Well, Ronnie did record the song, and did a good job with it. But it wasn't a career-making hit, and just briefly cracked the bottom of the top one hundred on the pop charts. Still, it's the closest I ever came to writing a hit, and every so often I get a check for about five dollars' worth of royalties from "Loving You's a Natural Thing."

After the American sessions, I knew without a doubt that the King was back. Elvis Presley had been responsible for some of the happiest moments in my life, but I don't think anything filled me with the kind of complete joy and satisfaction I felt the night of August 1, 1969, as I sat in the Las Vegas International for the first time and watched Elvis return to live performance.

I'd been planning on being there for Elvis's July 31 debut performance, but he had requested I come the second night: He felt that would be the first "real" show after the VIP-packed opening-night gala. It was a real show, all right. From the opening explosion of "Blue Suede Shoes" to the wicked groove of "Mystery Train" to the high-energy heartbreak of "Suspicious Minds," I was in a state of absolute euphoria. Elvis threw himself into his performance with a mix of confidence and wild abandon that was more powerful than anything I'd seen back on tour in 1957. He looked fantastic, thin and fit and dressed stylishly in a simple white karate-style suit with a rope belt. His voice was as strong an instrument as it had ever been, but he hardly ever just stood there and sang. He was all over the stage, rolling on the floor, doing karate moves.

Elvis had a lot of musicians onstage with him: a backup band, a small orchestra, a white male gospel quartet, and a black female vocal quartet. (Elvis had wanted the Darlene Love–led Blossoms, who had backed him for his TV special, but when they weren't available I suggested the Sweet Inspirations, who had done some great work at American.) During final rehearsals, Elvis had turned to Sam Phillips for some advice on how to organize all the musicians onstage. Elvis told me that when he was explaining to Sam how the stage would be set up, Sam cut him off.

"Stop right there, Elvis. I don't need to know where the violins are. Where's your guitars and bass and drums?"

"Well, right behind me, Mr. Phillips," said Elvis.

"Good, and that's where you keep 'em," said Sam. "You keep that rhythm section backed right up to your ass, Elvis, cuz when that rhythm section is kicking your ass, you're gonna put on a good show. You just let 'em kick you."

The band did indeed kick, and complemented Elvis's wild energy perfectly. James Burton was a respected session guitar player, but hearing him play Elvis's hits onstage, I started thinking he was the best rock 'n' roll guitarist that had ever picked up the instrument. Jerry Scheff was as solid and inventive a bass player as you could ever want, and drummer Ronnie Tutt played with a ferocity that was truly awesome. Watching Elvis that night, I was so happy for him and so proud to be his friend. I wanted to hang on to every great moment of the experience as it roared by, and yet the next moment always seemed even better.

The thing that really stood out for me was the spark and the spirit Elvis brought to the stage. He was enjoying the hell out of what he was doing, and those of us who loved him almost couldn't believe that he'd turned things around for himself so beautifully. A few times that first night I was there, he looked down at me in my booth and gave a little wink or a nod, and in those moments I think I realized that no matter how close to this guy I was as a friend, nothing was ever going to stop me from being an absolute fan, too.

Elvis at the top of the charts. That's what I'd been hoping for when Elvis recorded at American, and that's what I impulsively promised him before he recorded "Suspicious Minds." I don't think my promise had anything to do with it, but when that single was released just after the first Vegas run, it steadily picked up more and more radio airplay and generated more and more sales until, by the end of the year, Elvis had a number-one record again.

The song that was released sounded a bit different than what had been recorded at American, though. In his Las Vegas shows, Elvis was getting such an enthusiastic response to the new song that he would stretch it out, having the band come way down and then slowly bringing it back up to a climactic finish as he repeated the first three lines of the lyrics. Producer Felton Jarvis thought it would be cool to incorporate that ending into the record and took the master tape back to a studio to rerecord some horn parts and adjust the volume of Elvis's vocals to create the false fade and repeated ending section.

The song's new ending didn't hurt its success, but it pointed at a sad epilogue to the American sessions. Elvis had completed some great recordings there, but once he was out of the studio, the politics and game-playing between the Colonel and Chips Moman never stopped. When "In the Ghetto" charted, Chips's name was not on it at first, and it seemed that the Colonel and Hill and Range and RCA were going to do everything they could to deny the role Chips had played in Elvis's return to recording success. Chips and Felton had started out as friendly colleagues, but now there were hurt feelings and strained relations between them. I had hoped that American might become a new studio home for

Elvis, but after the 1969 sessions there was just too much ill will between Chips, the Colonel, and RCA. Elvis would go on to record at Stax, in Nashville and back in L.A., and even at Graceland. But the material, the performances, and the recordings would never be as strong as they were at American. Of course we didn't know it at the time, but "Suspicious Minds" would be the last number-one record of Elvis's career.

Elvis was back at the Las Vegas International at the end of January 1970, setting up what would become a regular schedule of winter and summer engagements there. He again did two shows a night, and at his dinner show on February 1, he began another tradition by performing for a special guest in his audience: Lisa Marie, who was there with Priscilla to celebrate her second birthday in high style. For the next several years, Lisa Marie rarely missed a Las Vegas birthday show, and those nights were always an emotional highlight for her beaming father.

Throughout that second Vegas run, there were sold-out shows and rave reviews, and Elvis continued to deliver incredibly energetic performances. And it was at this engagement that Elvis started wearing the famous one-piece jumpsuits designed by Bill Belew. This wasn't to hide any weight gain, as would be the case in later years, but so that Elvis could be as physical and active as he wanted to be: He kept ripping through anything else he wore onstage.

The Colonel seemed to be fully in his element in the wheeler-dealer environment of Vegas. It became clear pretty quickly that he had a real fondness for the action at the casino tables, but, despite his great bargaining skills, he didn't come out a winner too often. I also saw the Colonel do something in Vegas that puzzled me at first: He had Tom Diskin go up and down the Strip, stopping in every hotel to have the Colonel paged. I asked him why he did that, and his response was classic Colonel: "Now everybody knows I'm in town, George. I don't have to call them on my dime—they can call me."

The International, which had opened for business just before Elvis's first run there, was thrilled to have such a hot draw. I did see one moment of friction, though. One night Elvis decided to have some fun at the gaming tables, but he didn't want to just play blackjack—he wanted to be the dealer. A buzz went through the casino and pretty quickly there was a crowd lining up to play at Elvis's table. Nobody was going to bet small in front of Elvis, which made the casino managers happy. The problem was that Elvis didn't really know the game very well. He was dealing out cards with Joe Esposito trying to whisper the rules to him. Elvis being Elvis, he didn't want anyone to leave his table a loser, so he started finding ways to let everybody beat the dealer, even if it meant throwing cards away until they got the ace they were after. Finally some casino people got up to Elvis and quietly made it clear to him that he was giving away a sizable amount of the International's money. Elvis's career as card dealer came to an end, and the odds at the blackjack table went back to favoring the house.

In Memphis, Elvis had the family and the home life he'd always wanted: He and Priscilla were devoted to each other and to Lisa, and Elvis couldn't do enough to spoil his little daughter rotten. (I think Priscilla probably had to work as hard keeping his parenting under control as she did taking care of Lisa.) In Las Vegas, Elvis was making the kind of music he wanted to make and had returned to being the world's greatest entertainer. Now it only made sense to start thinking about taking his act on the road again.

And if he was going to do road gigs, why not kick them off with a concert at something as spectacular as the "Eighth Wonder of the World"? That was the phrase being used to describe the first domed sports stadium in the world, the Houston Astrodome, which was just a few years old at the time. Elvis wanted to perform for a wider public than the people he was drawing to Las Vegas, and the Colonel arranged for him to make six headlining appearances at the Houston Livestock Show and Rodeo, held at the Astrodome.

The first afternoon show at the Astrodome was not a great one, though it was no fault of Elvis's. He didn't like being on the rotating stage that had been built for him, and the sound in that sports stadium just wasn't very workable for a concert. Everything Elvis said or sang took about seven seconds to bounce around the building, and he and the band had a terrible time trying to hold things together. Elvis also found himself performing to a lot of empty seats. Back at the hotel before the first evening show, he was really upset, feeling that outside of Vegas he just didn't have the wide appeal he used to have and that it had been a mistake to book himself into such a large venue. We all pointed out that people were still on their way into town for the event, and someone called Elvis over to a window to show him a sight that cheered him a great deal: Stretched out as far as we could see were lines of traffic working their way toward the Dome. The rest of his shows set higher and higher attendance records for the venue.

Several months later, in the summer of 1970, Elvis had another great run at the International, much of which was filmed for the documentary *That's the Way It Is*. The Colonel had laid down some pretty strict guidelines for the film crews. They could have access to follow Elvis around, but they were to remain observers: Elvis wasn't going to give them any interview time or do anything special for the cameras. Elvis himself might not have gotten that note, though, because at one of the first shows, on a night when I had again flown out to be with him, he did something I hadn't ever seen him do before. After a few songs he just casually stepped up to the edge of the stage and asked for a drink of water from a front table, then stepped down into the audience. He began to walk through the crowd, slowly making an arc across the entire floor. None of us knew what he was doing, and we rushed to give him some protection—the bigger guys stayed right behind him and I tagged along to offer whatever extra security a guy my size could. Elvis was engulfed by adoring fans as he slowly made his way, shaking hands, kissing faces, waving, talking, and smiling. When he finally got through the crowd and hopped back up onstage, he said, "You didn't think I'd make it, did ya? I didn't either."

That spontaneous moment in the crowd seemed even more notable after Elvis received a death threat toward the end of the Vegas run. The threat turned out to be an empty one, but Elvis had been concerned enough to call in Red and Jerry to rejoin him for extra security. Elvis was touched by the loyalty and concern we all showed him in that situation, and had Priscilla pick out about a dozen gold rope bracelets for us guys. Each bracelet had our name on the front and a nickname on the back. Joe Esposito was the Brain, Richard Davis was Beer Brain, Dr. Nick was Needles Nick, and Jerry was Twinkletoes (from a picture Elvis had seen of a very young Jerry dressed up for a dance recital). Billy Smith was Scatter, the name of a pet chimpanzee that Elvis had kept at Graceland for a while. The back of my bracelet said "Rockin' 50s." I started wearing that bracelet every day, ready to let the good times roll again. I knew Elvis was ready, too. The back of his bracelet said "Crazy."

With Vegas and the Astrodome conquered, Elvis was ready to really take his act on the road. The Colonel set up a six-city minitour as a test of a new partnership with a couple of sharp young promoters, Jerry Weintraub and Tom Hulett. I knew Tom from times he'd come through Memphis with some of the other acts he worked with, such as Creedence Clearwater Revival and Three Dog Night, and I knew he'd deliver top-quality stage productions for Elvis. I also knew that I was going to do whatever it took to get back on the road as a travel companion.

I'd taken too much time in Las Vegas and Houston to ask for more vacation days from WHBQ. But I came up with an idea of filing live concert reports to the radio station as I traveled with Elvis. It was the kind of idea that probably should have been run past the Colonel, but I went straight to Elvis with it. He approved, and WHBQ loved the idea of getting insider reports of Elvis's first real tour in years. So, with Elvis's welcome and the blessing of both Barbara and WHBQ, I was on the road again.

The second show of the tour was at St. Louis's Kiel Auditorium, and that's where we met up with Tom Hulett. Just as I knew he would, Tom wanted everything around Elvis's performance to be top quality, and he had arranged for a state-of-the-art sound system to be used at Kiel Auditorium. This was something new for Elvis—up until then he'd been performing through venue PA systems rather than his own setup. I saw Tom Diskin visibly flinch when he heard about Hulett's system: I'm sure he and the Colonel considered it an unnecessary expense. But it made a huge difference to Elvis, who raved after the show that it was the first time he'd ever really been able to hear himself and everything that the band was doing. The great sound system became a requirement from then on.

There was tremendous energy and excitement in Elvis's group about being on the road, just as there had been back in 1957. But on one plane ride, when he and I were sitting together, Elvis asked me a question I hadn't expected to hear from him.

"GK, do you get nervous when you come out to do your TV show?"

"Well, Elvis, I make a point not to give myself enough time to get nervous. The show goes on at five, and from the moment I get there at three, I'm running around like crazy trying to get everything organized. I don't really think about being in front of the camera until the last couple minutes before showtime and then, yeah, I always do get nervous. As long as I've been doing it, I still get nervous."

"Good. That's what I want to hear."

"What do you mean?"

"If you're going to put on any kind of a show, it's good to have that nervous energy, otherwise you come out flat. That's one of the reasons I don't want to get to any of these venues early. You've got to meet everybody and shake hands with the president of this and that, and by the time you go onstage you're too comfortable. You got no edge. You've got to let your nerves work for you."

As in the early days, the Colonel had meticulously mapped out routes from airports to hotels to venues so that Elvis never had to waste a minute before showtime. He'd spend ten minutes before the show in a dressing room in which the only items he asked for were a case of Mountain Spring bottled water and a full-length mirror. Then, with his nervous energy at its peak, he'd hit the stage full force.

· · ·

Offstage, we started partying like the old days, although with so many of us committed to wives or girlfriends, the parties sometimes took on the feel of a spectator sport. In Tampa, some of the guys—who shall remain nameless—picked up a couple girls who I guess could be described as falling somewhere between groupies and hookers: They were big Elvis fans who were willing to do just about anything for cash. The guys got them set up in a hotel room, and the word was that they were going to put on an explicit girl-on-girl show for us. I'd never seen anything like that, and I have to admit I was curious. It was getting close to showtime when I heard a knock on my hotel-room door. It was Elvis's daddy, Vernon Presley.

"George, where is everybody? Nobody's in their rooms and I can't find Elvis anywhere."

My mind raced, but I couldn't come up with anything other than the truth. "Oh, they're all in a room down the hall, Mr. Presley. There's going to be a show down there."

"A show? What kind of show?"

Again, before I could think of a workable lie, I found myself stating the facts. "Well, they got some crazy girls who are going to do some wild sort of things, I guess. I'll tell Elvis you're looking for him."

"That's all right, George. I'll walk down with you."

I can't even describe the look Elvis shot at me when I walked into that room with his daddy. But his anger at me didn't stop the scheduled entertainment. Vernon just found a place to stand with the rest of us and watched as Elvis began directing the girls like a certain kind of movie director: You touch her here; you kiss her there; hang on to that; hold still . . .

It really was a heck of a show. And Vernon stayed right to the end of it.

On one of the last flights on that tour I was sitting across from a young LAPD officer the Colonel had hired for some extra security—one of the Colonel's very smart moves was to travel with people who had valid credentials with a real police department to help smooth things along in each city. I asked the young guy how he managed to get time off from the Los Angeles force to tour with Elvis, and he explained that he'd needed to get out of town after having completed an undercover drug bust. There'd been trouble with drugs coming into Hollywood High School, so this cop had been asked to pose as a high school student to try to figure out where the supplies were coming from. He started living the life of a high school senior again, taking classes, going to dances, even dating. He thought he might get some useful information from one particular senior girl and took her out in his car. At some point he got close enough to her to see that under her blouse she wore a gold lightning bolt on a gold chain necklace—the symbol of the West Coast Mafia. The more he asked her about her family, the more he was sure that her father was at the center of the drug deals. The drug bust came down, and, using the cop's information, several mobsters were arrested, along with several teachers and students at Hollywood High.

I thought this was an incredible story and asked the young guy to repeat it to Elvis, who was sitting across the aisle from us. Elvis thought it was a great true crime story, too, but he seemed especially interested in one detail—that gold lightning bolt on a chain.

Not too long after that, I went to see Elvis and he greeted me by saying, "GK, come here. I've got something I want to show you." He opened up the special case he kept his own rings and jewelry in, and pulled out a necklace that he proceeded to put around my neck. "You got one of the first twelve of these," he said.

At the end of a gold chain was a pendant that Elvis said he and Priscilla had designed together. The design incorporated the West Coast Mafia's lightning bolt with a Southern expression that had become popular among members of the Memphis Mafia: "Takin' Care of Business." Across the bolt, that expression was written in a more direct, condensed form: TCB.

● ● ●   ● ● ●   ● ● ●   ● ● ●

Exclusive Engagements

"Why don't you just marry that girl, GK?"

"Oh, I don't know, Elvis. I'm working on it," I answered. "Maybe we'll do it when Barbara gets well."

I'd gotten a call from Elvis when I got home after visiting Barbara at the Vanderbilt University Medical Center up in Nashville. She'd become seriously ill with some ailments that weren't easily diagnosed, and, at Dr. Nick's recommendation, we checked her into the top facility at Vanderbilt to receive treatment. She was still in critical condition and was going to remain at the hospital for a few days, so I was making a daily trip to see that she was being well taken care of.

By 1970, Barbara and I had been together for most of a decade, through all the unpredictability and crazy schedules of life around Elvis. I was more serious about her than I'd ever been, but I was just plain gun-shy about getting married. Elvis kept bringing it up, though. He liked Barbara a lot, he could see how devoted to her I was, and he wanted us to be husband and wife.

After another day's visit to Barbara, I got another call from Elvis.

"GK, how's Barbara?"

"I just got back from Nashville, Elvis. She's doing a lot better."

"GK—I'm a married man. Most of the guys are married now—ain't it about time you got married?"

"Well, Elvis, we've talked about it a little, but no heavy plans yet. It's a big step for me."

"You been with her ten years, man—how long you need to take a step?"

"I don't know, Elvis."

"Well, I'll tell you what I'll do, GK. If you'll get married, I'll pay for the entire wedding and I'll be your best man."

Once again, this friend of mine had me speechless. I tried for a moment to think of reasons why Elvis's offer shouldn't be accepted, but there weren't any. I couldn't imagine anyone but Barbara being my wife, and I wouldn't have wanted anybody else but Elvis standing beside me as my best man. "Elvis—I don't know what to say. But you don't have to put on the wedding. Just having you as my best man would be enough."

"No, no—I want to pay for this thing. If you're going to do it, let's get it done right. That'll be my wedding gift—the wedding."

I called Barbara at the hospital right away, and we both agreed that the time was right and that the offer was amazing. Cupid Elvis had given us the final push we needed, and now we couldn't wait to be married. Barbara recovered from her illness and was out of the hospital a few days later, and we began making wedding plans.

Elvis wasn't performing at the International in December of 1970, but he had access to the beautiful thirtieth-floor VIP suite he used during his engagements. So, just about six weeks after he made his offer to be my best man, Elvis paid to fly Barbara and me to Las Vegas, where we were married in Elvis's suite. He flew out all the guys who were in L.A., and we brought along guests in our plane from Memphis, including a law-enforcement figure that Elvis and all of us had gotten very friendly with, former Shelby County sheriff Bill Morris. Elvis put all of us up at the International. We didn't bring a lot of family: My mother, an old school Orthodox Jew, had a hard time accepting the fact that I was marrying a gentile. Barbara's sister was her maid of honor, and Dr. Nick walked her down the aisle.

As we got ready to start the ceremony, Elvis realized that one detail had been overlooked: There was no music for the bride's processional. He told

Charlie Hodge to get over to the piano that was in the suite to start playing "Here Comes the Bride."

"But I don't know it, Elvis," said Charlie.

"Fake it, Charlie, fake it," Elvis said emphatically.

Charlie took a shot at the song, and did a pretty good job of it, too. As I took my position with my bride-to-be on one side and Elvis on the other, it really did feel like a perfect moment. But for some reason a pair of rabbis had been lined up to perform the service together, and it started to seem like each wanted to out-talk the other. I didn't really know my way around a Jewish wedding—maybe I'd been to one or two as a kid—but it felt like there was a lot of ritual, and that was taking twice as long with two rabbis. As meaningful as the moment was, I could tell that Elvis was starting to get a little fidgety. I looked over at him once as the rabbis worked their way through the service. He gave me a wink and I winked back, but I could tell what he was thinking: "This is nice, but let's move it along . . ." Finally the moment came when Elvis handed me the ring, and I slipped it onto Barbara's finger. I was a married man.

We had the reception right there in the suite, and it was a great party, with everyone, especially Elvis, in a very happy mood. At times I thought he was even happier than I was. But I think we were all able to feel a warm, wonderful togetherness that we hadn't been able to have at Elvis's wedding because of the way those arrangements had been mishandled. I looked around that room and there was my beautiful bride, Elvis and Priscilla, and all the guys who had been such a part of so many great times: Jerry, Joe, Alan Fortas, Richard Davis, Charlie Hodge, Red, Sonny, Lamar Fike, Marty Lacker, and Dr. Nick. Many of the happy moments were captured by a special photographer: Joe had hired the NBC photographer who'd shot all the stills for the '68 special, figuring that he'd be unlikely to leak any shots to the press. Elvis arranged for everyone who attended the wedding to get a beautiful album of every photo that they were in.

Generally, Elvis didn't take a lot of personal pictures with us, but he did that day. And it turned out he had an additional wedding present for

Barbara and me: a matching pair of gold-plated derringer handguns. There were a lot of jokes made about how a married couple would eventually put those guns to use. Then I came up with something I thought would make a cool photo for our album. Ever since Elvis had received his death threat in Las Vegas, he had wanted to be armed, and he wanted that fact to be made public. (When I asked him about that, he said, "I want the crazy SOBs out there to know that if they take a shot at me, I'm going to shoot back.") Now, even dressed to the hilt for my wedding, he was carrying a gun in a shoulder holster under his jacket. With the idea of a "shotgun wedding" in mind, I asked Elvis to hold his gun to my head as we posed for the photographer. The picture we got out of that moment is one of my all-time favorites of us together.

Back in Memphis, my life didn't feel too different, except that Barbara moved into my apartment, and now the group could tease me about being a married man. Elvis liked to put Priscilla up to asking me a question that always made me blush: "GK, you had any strange lately?" At that time "strange" had become a Southern slang expression for adventurous sex, and Elvis always laughed at my embarrassed response to the question. That was the big punchline around Graceland for a while—"Had any strange, GK?"

Elvis had a very busy month following my wedding. Just a couple of weeks after the event, he got into an argument with Vernon and Priscilla over his spending habits. He stormed out of Graceland and set off on the famous "lost weekend," traveling by himself on commercial flights for the first time in his life. He headed to Los Angeles, where he convinced Jerry Schilling to accompany him on a flight back to Washington, D.C. For years, Elvis had great relationships with the police departments who provided security for him in various cities, and he was always excited if he could secure a badge or credentials from them. Now he wanted to get a hold of a federal drug-enforcement badge he'd seen. On his flight with

Jerry, Elvis wrote a personal letter to President Nixon, which the two of them then hand-delivered to what I guess was a very surprised guard at the White House gates. I think Jerry was understandably skeptical about what Elvis was trying to do. But you could never underestimate Elvis Presley: That trip ended with him and Jerry and Sonny West standing with President Nixon in the Oval Office. Elvis got his badge.

By Christmas Eve, Elvis was back in Memphis. He was in his usual high spirits for the holidays, and was particularly excited about having the chance to shower more Christmas toys and gifts upon little Lisa. It was again a real pleasure for Barbara and me to spend a late Christmas Eve with him and Priscilla at Graceland. Eventually we all went out for a ride to look at the lights around the city, as we had in years past. But when Elvis figured we'd seen all the best Christmas decorations that Memphis had to offer, he had an idea for one more stop: the Shelby County Jail.

In our early years together, when Elvis and I were out late at night, he would sometimes stop at funeral homes—his logic being that they were the only place open in the wee hours of the morning. I'd walk in with him to the lobby of some mortuary and wouldn't go any farther. But he'd head off to find the mortician and ask about the bodies that had come in that evening and sometimes get a full tour of the facilities. Now, I figured a jail on Christmas Eve was much better than a funeral home, so I didn't raise any objections. We pulled up to the Shelby County Jail and walked in through the back door. A sergeant at the main desk looked up and, without missing a beat, asked, "Elvis—what are you doing here?"

"Nothing else is open on Christmas Eve, so we thought we'd come visit you guys," Elvis responded.

The cops on duty were thrilled and started gathering around our group. We talked with them for a while, and then Elvis put in a special request: He wanted someone to contact Sheriff Roy Nixon and see if it was okay for us to visit the prisoners in the jail to wish them a Merry Christmas. We got the okay, though for obvious reasons the women weren't going to be allowed back in the cell area with us.

I didn't really like being near those cell doors, even if I was on the right side of them, but Elvis seemed perfectly relaxed and even happier than he'd been opening Christmas presents. We started walking slowly down a long corridor, and the guys in their cells started springing to life and yowling with delight:

"Hey Elvis!"

"Merry Christmas, Elvis!"

"Elvis, can I have a Cadillac?"

"Elvis, will you be my lawyer?"

Elvis was laughing and shaking hands with the guys through the bars of their cells (something he'd been asked not to do). And when somebody asked if he'd sing a little Christmas song, he broke into a goofy version of "White Christmas" that they loved. We were slowly working our way past the rest of the cells when another voice rang out.

"George Klein!" I couldn't imagine who'd be calling for me instead of Elvis, but the voice continued.

"Humes High, Elvis—it's me! Harold Poole!"

It was indeed Harold Poole, a former Humes student who was then well on his way to earning the distinction of being one of the most arrested men in the history of Memphis. He'd been four or five years ahead of us in school, but everybody in North Memphis knew Harold Poole.

"Aww, Harold," said Elvis. "What are you doing here?"

"Well, I got in a little barroom fight, Elvis, that's all," said Harold. "But Elvis—could you please help get me out of here?"

"Well, you've got to behave yourself, Harold."

"I will, Elvis, I will."

"GK," Elvis said to me, "go tell the guys out front that I'll put up Harold's bond, and they can let him out."

I was back in a few moments to tell Elvis what I'd heard: Harold couldn't be processed out that night, but they'd let him go in the morning.

Elvis went back over to Harold's cell. "You're settled up, Harold. They'll let you out in the morning. You can be home for Christmas."

"Thank you, Elvis, and God bless you," said Harold.

I know that was one of the most appreciated Christmas gifts that Elvis ever gave, and I think it was one of the ones he most enjoyed giving.

In January of 1971, Elvis received an honor that was particularly meaningful to him. The national Junior Chambers of Commerce organization, the Jaycees, had named him as one of the Top Ten Outstanding Young Americans of the year, an honor that in previous years had been bestowed upon people such as Leonard Bernstein, Orson Welles, Jesse Jackson, and Richard Nixon. Elvis was constantly being offered various awards and honors, and the Colonel was usually very suspicious of them. The Colonel figured that the organizations giving the awards wanted Elvis for publicity purposes more than they wanted to pay actual tribute, so he usually told the groups to mail the award, then he'd send out a thank-you letter signed by Elvis. But Elvis was moved that the Jaycees wanted to honor him, and he agreed to accept it in person at an event held in Ellis Auditorium. He also attended the honorees' breakfast at the Rivermont Hotel in Memphis.

Accepting his award in person meant that Elvis would have to speak, and for a guy who was such a natural onstage, he was very nervous about public speaking. All of us who knew him could hear that he was nervous as he accepted his honors at the Ellis event, but he rose to the moment with some brief, heartfelt remarks. He said that as a child he was a dreamer, and that while reading comic books, he'd imagined himself to be the hero of the comic book stories. Now, he told us, all of his dreams had come true a hundred times over. He concluded with some lines of the lyrics from "'Without a Song," a tune that he'd first heard sung by Roy Hamilton in 1955: "Without a song, the day would never end/Without a song, a man ain't got no friend . . . So I keep singing a song."

Frankly, in the early years of the seventies, Elvis was still the strongest guy I knew—a guy who at times really did resemble a comic book hero. He was an incredible workhorse who never seemed run down by a punishing schedule that included the Vegas engagements, tour dates, recording sessions, and back-and-forth travel between his Memphis and Los Angeles homes. Some of the guys around Elvis occasionally spun out of control, but he always seemed to keep things together, and there were times when he demonstrated an almost superhuman physical toughness. When he needed to be treated for an eye ailment during a recording session in Nashville, he toughed out an injection straight into the eyeball without benefit of anesthesia: He insisted on using some karate-based meditation techniques instead. I may have been naïve, but for a long while I wasn't worried about the medicines he was taking to keep himself going.

I think all of us had been more worried during the movie years, when his weight would yo-yo and he'd suffer from some awful mood swings. But now he was in the best physical shape of his life and was happy about his career. Whatever he was taking just didn't seem to be a problem. I had heard some whispers about the high number of prescription pills Elvis was taking for a long list of very real physical ailments, and there was some concern about the number of doctors he was seeing to get those prescriptions. Dr. Nick oversaw Elvis's care in Memphis, but there were doctors and dentists in Los Angeles and Las Vegas who seemed to write prescriptions for Elvis just to be able to say that they had him as a patient.

Looking back, I have to admit that it took me a long time to figure out just how big a part of Elvis's routine those pills were becoming. The guys who worked for him might have been much more aware of what was going on, but Elvis always seemed to make a point of not taking the pills or talking about them around me. I've thought about that a lot over the years: For all the things we shared with each other and for the amount of time I was in his home, he must have made a conscious effort to keep that part of his life separate from our friendship.

On one occasion, though, Elvis was willing to share a nonprescription substance with me. While nobody in Elvis's group would have qualified as a real "stoner," a few of the guys did enjoy smoking marijuana occasionally as a way to relax, and I'd heard that one of the guys had brought a small stash of it to Graceland. Elvis and I and Priscilla and Barbara and a couple other guys were sitting in the den off the kitchen late one night when he said, "Hey, GK, have you ever smoked pot?"

I hadn't. I'd certainly been around the stuff. I'd dealt with a number of acts on *Talent Party* who seemed to enjoy it, and I'd been to plenty of parties where the distinctive smell of marijuana was in the air. I wasn't particularly against it, I just hadn't ever smoked it myself.

"Would you like to experiment?" Elvis asked.

I thought a moment. Brother Dave Gardner was the first guy I'd ever seen with a joint, and I'd turned down the offer to smoke with him. But that was back in 1960, when the drug had seemed scarier. Things were different now, and enough people I knew had smoked it that I figured it was worth a try. "Yeah, Elvis—I think I would. I'd like to see what everybody is talking about."

Somebody brought Elvis a joint, and we sat there in the den and smoked it. At first it didn't seem like any big deal—not much more to it than inhaling and blowing smoke, just like with a regular cigarette. Then it hit me. I shifted in my chair and was aware of every little movement my body was making. My head felt heavy, and it seemed like all the familiar objects around me, Elvis included, were now part of some strange film I was watching. My heart was racing but time seemed to be slowing down to a crawl. I kept trying to be in the moment with Elvis instead of being so caught up in my head, but I couldn't get a hold of the crazy thoughts that were racing through my mind. I'd lose track of what Elvis was saying, or lose track of what I was saying to him.

I do remember being tickled by the idea that my friend had become a street. The Memphis City Council had just voted in favor of renaming a section of Highway 51 after Elvis, so Graceland's new address was 3764 Elvis Presley Boulevard. We started talking about that, and Elvis joked about some of the things we might start hearing on the radio traffic reports: "Dead dog found on Elvis Presley"; "Farm truck dumps turnips on Elvis Presley." Pretty soon I was laughing like a little kid.

It was the strangest mix of euphoria and panic I'd ever felt. The euphoria was nice: I could see what all the fuss was about. But the stabs of panic, like when I realized I had to drive home—those were not so much fun.

Back at Graceland the next night, I wasn't sure if Elvis knew just how powerfully the pot had affected me, but I was not looking forward to another smoking session.

"GK," he said to me. "Driving home last night—did it take a long time for the traffic lights to change?"

"Shit, yeah, Elvis—I thought I was going crazy."

"And how fast did you drive home?"

"I was worried I was going to get a speeding ticket, Elvis. Then I looked down at the dashboard and saw I was going twenty-five miles an hour."

He started laughing. "Weird stuff, ain't it, GK?"

"I've got to be honest, Elvis. I don't think I like that feeling."

"I don't like it either," he said. That was the end of my career as a pot smoker, and as far as I know, Elvis didn't smoke after that either.

While Elvis continued to be a top draw in Las Vegas and at concert venues around the country, I kept working hard on *Talent Party*. I was extremely proud of the show for its unique mix of local interest and national acts. I still gave garage bands a shot every week and still made a fuss over local high school kids of note. (Sometimes the local talent went national: I had a cheerleader named Gail Stanton on the show when she was crowned Miss Frayser High. She went on to be a very popular Playboy Playmate.) I was also proud that *Talent Party* was still often ahead of the curve in booking up-and-coming stars—Otis Redding had made his first big TV appearance on my show. Other national acts that we featured in the sixties and early seventies included the Zombies, Ray Charles, Chuck Berry, Stevie Wonder, Al Green, Isaac Hayes, Paul Revere and the Raiders, the Beau Brummels, the Standells, the Shirelles, Roger Miller, Tony Joe White, Billy Joe Royal, the Spinners, the Coasters, the Drifters, the Four Tops, the Ides of March, Tommy James and the Shondells, Black Oak Arkansas, and Peaches and Herb. I still got excited every Saturday about meeting new artists and putting on a great show for my Memphis audience.

My TV success led to my being in further demand as an emcee at concerts, and I got to meet a lot more greats doing that job. In particular I remember a few quiet moments I got to spend alone with Jimi Hendrix backstage at the Mid-South Coliseum in 1970. I'd first heard about Jimi from the jams he had with some of the musicians at Stax studio, including bassist Roland Robinson. I'd emceed Jimi's 1969 Memphis show at Ellis Auditorium, but this time, at the Mid-South, we really had time to talk. I asked him about some of the wild things he'd done onstage, like lighting his guitar on fire. He said he was through with that kind of showmanship and wanted to focus more on the music he played. I also asked if he was aware of some of the crazy rumors that were going around about his drug use, like that he shot heroin into head and neck veins. He laughed and said that while he'd heard all the rumors I'd heard and then some, none of them were true. He was a real gentleman and a pleasure to talk to, and he put on a phenomenal show that night. You could see how some of the rumors might start—it didn't seem humanly possible for anyone to do what he was able to with a guitar. But while the crazy rumors may not have had any truth to them, Jimi did have his demons, and just three months after I talked with him, he was dead from an overdose of sleeping pills.

One of the challenges of the *Talent Party* show was to keep it fairly hip as styles changed in music and fashion, and sometimes I had to take some emergency measures to prove to a hot act that they weren't stuck with a square host. I booked the Doobie Brothers to play live on the show when they were first starting to get hot, but the band got hesitant to perform when they came to the studio and decided just before airtime that the set looked too slick for their image. No problem—I simply had the *Talent Party* crew rip the set into tatters, then asked the band if they'd perform amid the destruction. They loved it, and went on to do a great show for me.

There were a couple of stars I couldn't get on the show no matter how nicely I asked: Louis Armstrong and Aretha Franklin just wouldn't do a local TV show. But the only star I ever had a really negative experience with was soul singer Brook Benton. Elvis and I had a little history with him, as we'd met him in the late fifties backstage at a WDIA Goodwill Revue—one of those shows at which Elvis and I were just about the only two white faces. Brook was just an up-and-coming singer and songwriter then, but I'd known his name because he'd put out a song called "I Wanna Do Everything for You" that Elvis and I both really liked because it was patterned after "Don't Be Cruel." I introduced Brook to Elvis, and Elvis said that if the singer had any material that would be right for Elvis to cut, he should send it in to Hill and Range. I gave Brook all the contact information, and he eventually submitted a song by his writing partner Clyde Otis called "Doncha Think It's Time," which Elvis released as the B-side to "Wear Your Ring Around My Neck." As far as I knew, it worked out well for everybody.

Brook Benton got very hot again in 1970 with the single "Rainy Night in Georgia" and headlined that year's Goodwill Revue at the Mid-South Coliseum. I got to him backstage to try to get him on *Talent Party*. He was being kind of difficult, so I reminded him of our connection.

"Come on, Brook, don't you remember me? I'm the guy who introduced you to Elvis Presley."

"Fuck Elvis Presley," he said.

It only took me a second to come up with the proper response. "No— fuck Brook Benton," I said. I walked away, and never played another one his records on any of my radio shows.

While all of this was going on with *Talent Party*, I was continuing to do my radio show for WHBQ, and around this time I had an experience that gave me something in common with Elvis and a lot of other celebrities— I got my first stalker. At first, "Crazy Betty" seemed to be a dedicated listener, regularly calling the station's deejay request hotline during my shows to talk to me and ask for her favorite songs. But the calls started to become a nightly event, and her side of the conversation became uncomfortably personal. She started sending gifts to the station, often home-baked pies (which the radio staff, having dealt with crazies before, promptly threw out). I realized Betty really was crazy when she called me one night and said, "I'm going to freeze you to death tonight." When I asked her to explain, she said, "I'm going to put my radio in the attic."

She became more of a problem when she got my home address and phone number. I began to receive long, rambling letters from her and started getting phone calls in the middle of the night. If I hung up the phone, she'd just call back over and over again. I started leaving the phone off the hook after she called, but I'd find that when I picked up the phone in the morning she was still on the line talking away. She was married to a Navy pilot stationed at the Millington base, and I finally took the step of contacting him and asking if he'd get his wife to leave me alone. He said, "I think you two got something going on." He was crazier than her.

Crazy Betty started waiting for me outside of clubs or events I emceed and would follow me in her car, bumping the back of my car at every stoplight. One night I got a call at work from my landlady, who wanted to know if she should let my "aunt" into my apartment. I asked her to describe the aunt—it was Betty. It was creepy and maddening to get that kind of attention, and I went from being polite to letting her know that I didn't want anything to do with her. I didn't think the police could be much help, but I wasn't sure what to do. The problem finally came to an end with another call from Crazy Betty. She let me know that her husband, the pilot, was being transferred, so she wouldn't be around anymore. I don't know how many celebrities ever get that kind of courtesy call from a stalker, but I appreciated it.

I got a different kind of unwanted attention one night when I parked my car at a closed gas station down the street from my home. A couple of girls called me by name over to their car. They said they liked my show, then asked if I'd sit in the car with them. It was a strange request, but I wasn't sure how to say no, so I got in the car. I didn't get more than a word or two out before they really pounced on me, tearing at my clothes and making their intentions obvious. I don't know if they really liked me that much, or whether I was being set up in some way, but I squeezed my way out of the car fast, thanked them for their interest, and got the hell home.

When Elvis returned to Las Vegas for his August run in 1971, his familiar showroom was under new management; the International was now the Las Vegas Hilton. In the fall he did a twelve-city national tour, and in January he was back in Las Vegas to begin another engagement. Throughout this period I got out to join him as much as I could. I always loved the parties up in Elvis's suite after a late show, and at a couple of these I saw Elvis impress his guests by reciting word for word the speech that George C. Scott delivered at the beginning of *Patton,* a recently released film that we'd repeatedly watched with Elvis at the Memphian.

Being the movie buff that he was, he had always enjoyed quoting lines from films. Early on he'd loved a little exchange from *Jailhouse Rock,* which we'd act out in all kinds of situations. I'd say, "I'm going to make you rich." He'd say, "I'm already rich," and I'd deliver the payoff—"You'll be richer!" Later, Elvis got a lot of mileage out of a favorite line from *Cool Hand Luke:* "What we've got here is a failure to communicate." But the *Patton* monologue wasn't just a quick line—it was a real performance, and there were times when he was giving that speech that I wished he'd had something that substantial to deliver in his own films.

Sometimes the good times we had in Las Vegas came from simply following Elvis through the hotel. Elvis and I were both thirty-six years old, obviously not kids anymore, but he'd never completely outgrown the fun-loving spirit that had once had him jumping out of the cars of the Pippin roller coaster. One night Elvis and I and a few other guys were walking through a service hallway to head back to his room when we heard the unmistakable sounds of Bill Medley of the Righteous Brothers singing "You've Lost That Loving Feeling." Bill was singing as a solo act in the Hilton lounge during the weeks that Elvis headlined, and they had a great respect for each other's talents. In the early sixties, I'd seen Elvis make anonymous calls to the *Shindig!* TV show to request that they play more Righteous Brothers. Now, when Elvis heard Bill's music, he walked a few paces down the hallway, then made a sudden U-turn and said, "Come on, guys—follow me." We followed him through a couple of doors, and all of a sudden we were walking right across the lounge stage.

"Hey, Bill," Elvis said as he passed the singer.

We got to the other side of the stage, but there was no exit over there, so we had to double back.

"Hey, Bill," said Elvis again.

As we walked off the way we came on, we heard Bill Medley say to his audience, "I don't know who that guy is, but if he wants to come on the road with me he's welcome to."

When we finally did get up to Elvis's suite, he started feeling bad that he'd stepped on another performer's stage. You didn't hear Elvis apologize for much, but he had Bill Medley up to the room and let him know he was sorry he'd interrupted his performance.

"Are you kidding?" asked Bill. "That was the happiest crowd I've ever sung for. You're welcome to step up on my stage anytime you want to, Elvis."

Word about Elvis's surprise interruption seemed to get around town, because Bill Medley had people lined up trying to get into his shows the rest of his run.

I wasn't sure exactly what kind of understanding Elvis had worked out with Priscilla, but I'd known since those *Viva Las Vegas* days with Ann-Margret that Elvis considered himself capable of loving the woman he'd left at home while devoting himself fully to the woman he happened to be with elsewhere. I'd been in his Las Vegas dressing room when he was visited by MGM studio head Jim Aubrey, whose date was a striking brunette starlet named Barbara Leigh. After the couple left, Elvis showed me a small piece of paper. While they'd been talking, Elvis had slipped Barbara the paper and a pencil under the dressing-room table and she'd written down her phone number. They began a romance, and she'd come to see him in Las Vegas, Los Angeles, or even in Memphis when Priscilla was at their home in L.A. At the same time, he'd begun a romance with a young woman named Joyce Bova, who worked in Washington, D.C., and who'd also met Elvis after a Vegas show.

The interesting thing was that while some of the guys around Elvis were happy just to rack up one-night stands, Elvis wasn't really interested in that kind of fleeting pleasure. He wanted someone to connect with and talk to—a much more intimate sort of traveling companion. And while some of the guys, myself included, had flings with women whose names we barely knew, it was always clear that the woman with Elvis was some-one he considered important.

I remember being in his Las Vegas suite at a party that was attended by singer (and future sausage maker) Jimmy Dean, who was headlining at the Desert Inn on the Vegas Strip. Jimmy had been an early supporter of Elvis and first met him when Elvis was a guest on Dean's 1950s TV show. The two saw a lot of each other when they both started playing Vegas; Jimmy was a familiar face in Elvis's suite. One night, Jimmy was doing some pretty obvious flirting with Elvis's date. Elvis walked over and put a small handgun to the side of Jimmy's head and said, "Leave her alone." I suppose Elvis was being half playful—but only half. Everybody tried to laugh it off, especially Jimmy, but the message was clear: You just didn't mess with Elvis's woman. That had never really changed—Elvis had put a shotgun to poor Arthur Hooton's head all those years ago for barely putting his hands on Yvonne Lime.

From my point of view, it didn't make much sense for Elvis to feel jeal-ous or threatened by anybody. But, knowing how Elvis felt about his women, I found myself in a very awkward situation when I was out on the road with him for some dates on the fall '71 tour. Toward the end of a weekend when Joyce Bova had been traveling with him, Elvis approached me with a special request.

"GK, would you do me a favor," he said. "Joyce here has to get back to work tomorrow morning. I've got a private jet lined up and a limo to meet her at the airport, but would you fly with her and make sure she gets home okay?"

"Sure, Elvis. I'd be glad to."

That tour was using Philadelphia as a home base, so Joyce and I got to the Philly airport and got on the plane that Elvis had chartered. We sat next to each other and started talking about Elvis, but she'd just had a weekend of keeping late Elvis hours and was exhausted. She fell asleep. She laid her head on my shoulder. And as she fell into a deeper sleep, she started snuggling up against me. I knew she wasn't flirting—she was just tired and wanted something to lean against. But I started flashing on Arthur Hooton and Jimmy Dean with guns against their heads. I thought to myself, "GK, if you shift in your seat and this girl wakes up and thinks you made some kind of a move on her, it's all over." I twisted my head as far away from Joyce as I could and kept my hands frozen on my knees. Joyce had a great nap all the way to D.C., but I had the most uncomfortable plane ride of my life. My neck was still sore when I got back to Philadelphia, but at least I didn't have to worry about whether Elvis was armed or not when I saw him.

There were still moments when I was struck by the kindness and generosity that were also a part of Elvis's nature. On that fall '71 tour, I was particularly excited about Elvis's performance at the Boston Garden. As a huge basketball fan, I loved the opportunity to be in that legendary arena before the crowds arrived to walk on the famous parquet floor. After Elvis's show, he came offstage and we started walking him fast to his waiting limo in the Garden's load-in area. As we made the walk, we passed an old black janitor who waved and said, "Hello, Mr. Presley."

Elvis didn't hear him, so I leaned over to him and said, "Elvis, give a wave to that guy over there."

"What did he say?"

"He just said, 'Hello, Mr. Presley,' and waved."

Elvis went from walking full speed ahead to stopping dead in his tracks. I noticed that I was getting the evil eye from some of the other guys—they just wanted to get him in the car and out of there. Elvis walked over to the old guy and introduced himself. The old guy had to put his broom aside so that he could shake hands with Elvis.

"Let me ask you something, sir," said Elvis.

"Yes, Mr. Presley?"

"You got any kids at home?"

"I got a few. A few grandkids, too."

"Do they like my music?" asked Elvis.

"I don't know everything they listen to, but I know they like your music, Mr. Presley."

"Do you like my music?" Elvis asked.

"Mr. Presley, I love your music."

"Okay," said Elvis, turning to me. "GK, you hold back and ride with the band to the hotel. I'm going to get out of here, but you get this man's name and address and I'm going to have RCA send him all my albums." He turned back to the janitor. "Is that all right with you, sir?"

"Why, thank you, yes, Mr. Presley," the old guy said.

It was yet another lesson to me about how important it was to Elvis to be nice to people and treat them well. There was the old showbiz line about "Don't step on people on the way up, because you'll see them on the way down." Colonel Parker had once twisted that around and announced to a group of us, "We can step on all the people we want on the way up, because we're not coming down." Elvis had never bought into that cruel approach at all. He was kind and generous with his time, even when it clearly took an extra effort on his part.

I stayed behind at Boston Garden and got the name and address of the old guy. I never saw him again after that night, but I put the request in to Colonel Parker and followed up until I was sure RCA had sent the man his Elvis records.

Elvis also had a forgiving nature, and I was reminded of that with one of the additions he made to his Las Vegas set list. Back in 1955, Elvis had been happy to meet singer Marty Robbins backstage at the Grand Ole Opry, but had felt betrayed when Robbins rushed out an Elvis-style cover of "That's All Right, Mama" that actually beat Elvis's version on some pop charts. Marty had gone on to have plenty of success on his own, and one of his most recent albums contained a song that Elvis was drawn to. "You Gave Me a Mountain" told the tale of a beaten-down man whose family life has fallen apart, and who now must summon the strength to face life's challenges. By now Elvis was starting to treat some of his early rock 'n' roll hits as almost throwaway songs onstage, but when he sang Robbins's song, he poured his heart into it and made it one of the dramatic highlights of his set. Elvis never forgot about Marty's "That's All Right, Mama" but he wasn't going to hold a grudge that got in the way of good music.

Elvis had a tremendous ear for songs, and he knew a great song for himself when he heard it. I knew right away he'd found strong material with "You Gave Me a Mountain," but I was less certain about another addition to Elvis's set. When I showed up from Memphis for one of the Vegas shows, some of the guys informed me that Elvis was now singing "My Way" in his show. Frank Sinatra had recorded the song a couple years before, and not only was it a huge hit for him, it had quickly become Frank's signature tune. As much as "Suspicious Minds" was Elvis's, "My Way" was Sinatra's. I said so to some of the guys, but they said I should hold off judgment until I heard Elvis sing it. I heard it that night, and damned if he didn't make it an Elvis song. Again, his instincts were right on the money.

I wasn't with Elvis at the end of his February 1972 engagement at the Hilton. But the big news in his world spread quickly back to Memphis: Priscilla was leaving him.

When I first heard the news, I immediately thought of the previous holiday season at Graceland, when the good cheer around the house had been cut through with an unmistakable tension between Elvis and Priscilla. There'd been some great laughs, like when Elvis got stunned doubletakes from all of us by handing out "bonus" envelopes that actually contained McDonald's gift certificates (once our shock wore off, he handed out thousand-dollar checks instead). But I thought there had been a nasty edge I'd never heard before in the way that Elvis and Priscilla joked with each other. And while they generally acted nicely toward each other, that was the thing—it seemed more like acting than genuine feeling. As sad as I was for both of them and for little Lisa, I have to say that it wasn't a tremendous surprise to hear that they were separating.

I knew quite well that Elvis had not been a faithful husband, and we soon heard that Priscilla had admitted to him that she was having an affair with Mike Stone, a karate instructor she had been studying with. But from my point of view, the affairs weren't the reason for the breakup. They were simply evidence of the larger problem: Elvis and Priscilla had grown apart. Priscilla was a gorgeous, intelligent girl who had grown up in a fishbowl—a beautiful fishbowl—but now that bowl was too small. She had matured and now she was a gorgeous, intelligent woman who wanted a life of her own.

I'd always had a good rapport with Priscilla. I genuinely liked her and considered her a friend, and I think she felt that way about me. I hoped that Priscilla would find the satisfaction and happiness she deserved living her life on her own terms. I hoped that Lisa would always know how much her father loved her. But even more so, I hoped that Elvis would be all right. I worried about him, and I wondered how he would face the mountain he'd been given—the mountain that, up until now, he'd only been singing about.

CHAPTER FOURTEEN

●●● ●●● ●●● ●●●

Burning Love

Aside from the TV appearances he'd made early in his career, Elvis had never performed in New York City. But as part of a spring '72 tour, Colonel Parker had Elvis booked into three nights at Madison Square Garden. This was something Elvis was nervous about, still unsure how the more sophisticated music fans of New York might feel about him. His worries were lifted a bit when his three scheduled shows sold out so quickly that a fourth was added. Elvis got himself into tremendous shape, and at the Garden he delivered some of his finest performances to date. Truly, nothing energized him more than taking on a new challenge, and this was another time when he rose to the occasion and delivered some of his best work.

The Colonel wisely arranged with RCA to record Elvis's Garden shows for release as a live album. That record went gold in weeks, the first Elvis album in years to sell so strongly. Elvis had also done some fine studio work, releasing a gospel record, *He Touched Me,* which would earn him his second Grammy Award. (He received his first Grammy for the 1967 gospel recording "How Great Thou Art.") He was excited about a new film project, a concert documentary that would make use of some cutting-edge film and sound-recording techniques. That film, *Elvis on Tour,* would go on to win a Golden Globe Award for Best Documentary of 1972. (I had a small part in that movie: I'm seen briefly at the microphone at WHBQ saying, "Here's my man Elvis himselvis" as an intro to "Suspicious Minds.")

Elvis was even at the top of the pop charts again. In the wake of his estrangement from Priscilla, he'd wanted to focus on recording material that captured his heartache, such as "Always on My Mind" and Red West's "Separate Ways." But with strong encouragement from Felton Jarvis, Elvis agreed to cut an up-tempo number that Felton believed had great potential as a single. That record, "Burning Love," made it to number two on the charts and was kept from reaching the peak only by the popularity of Chuck Berry's first-ever number one: the double-entendre-driven novelty tune "My Ding-a-Ling."

There was much that was going well for Elvis, but he was also feeling a terrible loneliness without Priscilla in his life. She and Lisa had moved out of Graceland and were living in Los Angeles, in what had been the family home.

I think Elvis knew he had lost something irreplaceable with Priscilla, but he did not want to feel lonely for long. So, just as he'd sent me out into the crowds at those fifties shows to find girls for our parties, he asked me now to help find him a woman that he might enjoy spending some time with. Again, Elvis wasn't just looking for women to pull into bed—and he certainly wouldn't have needed my help for that. He wanted to meet a woman he could relax with, open up to, and share some special time with. A woman who could help him forget, for a little while, what he'd lost.

Right away I thought about a girl I'd had on *Talent Party* a couple of times, a smart, fun-loving beauty queen named Linda Thompson. Linda was certainly a looker—she was Miss Tennessee in the Miss USA pageant—and she had expressed to me an interest in meeting Elvis. On one of Elvis's nights at the Memphian Theater, I extended an invitation to Herbie O'Mell and an RCA promo man named Bill Browder (who, when he later developed his own singing career, was known by his stage name, T. G. Sheppard). They showed up accompanied by a couple of girls they'd met earlier at dinner: Linda Thompson and one of her fellow pageant competitors, Jeannie LeMay. They all sat with me, and I reconfirmed with Linda that she wanted to meet Elvis.

When the time was right, I made the introductions between Elvis and Linda, and, minutes after the introduction, Linda was sitting in the most prized seat in the Memphian—the one next to Elvis. Over the next few nights she was back at the theater, and then came back to Graceland to be a part of our late-night parties there. She fit in with the group well and brought out a great side of Elvis. It was nice to see him able to relax and laugh with someone, and it seemed that with Linda he'd found someone who might become a steady part of his life.

With Elvis, though, "steady" was a relative term, and when Linda headed out of Memphis for a family vacation shortly after they'd met, Elvis wasn't going to let himself stay lonely. Again he gave me a call, but this time he called me while I was doing my *Talent Party* broadcast. Back in 1966 I'd had another beauty queen on my show, a recently crowned Miss Teenage Memphis named Cybill Shepherd. My fashion director and I thought Cybill had such a great look and strong sense of herself that we believed she could really make it as a professional model. We asked if we could take some photos of her to send off to a New York agency. She was more interested in going back to college than in modeling, but she consented. When the New York agency received her photos, they called back almost immediately, ready to sign her up. Her career was off and running and in 1968 she was Model of the Year. By 1972 she'd begun a film career with a strong performance in *The Last Picture Show* and had begun a romance with that film's director, Peter Bogdanovich.

I'd told Elvis about Cybill over the years and had talked up what a beauty she was and what a great sense of humor she had. When she was kind enough to make another appearance on *Talent Party*, Elvis was watching. We'd just gotten to the first two-minute commercial break in her interview when my director started signaling me.

"There's somebody on the phone who says he's Elvis."

I picked up the line right at my desk on the *Talent Party* set. "Hello?"

"Get her out here tonight," said the voice at the other end.

"Well, hang on now, Elvis, let me ask her if she wants to come out."

She did. We met Elvis at the Memphian that night, and he and Cybill got along great right away. They headed back to Graceland, and another brief but sweet romance began.

When Elvis performed his run at the Las Vegas Hilton in August 1972, he was visited by both Linda and Cybill. But during the couple weeks I spent at the Hilton, there was a week or so in which neither one was going to be around, and Elvis asked me again if there was anyone else I knew who might be right for him. Las Vegas was obviously full of beautiful women who'd be happy to have a fling with Elvis Presley, but, again, I knew that wasn't what he was looking for. I thought of a young woman Jerry Schilling and I had met on one of Elvis's recent concert tours. We had so much fun talking to her at a show in Cincinnati that we invited her back to our hotel for the postshow party. She'd briefly met Elvis then, and she and I had stayed in touch. Her name was Chris Pfaffman, and, as a huge Elvis fan, she was thrilled when I called and asked her if she'd like to come out to Las Vegas to be Elvis's guest.

Because I've remained a friend of Chris's through the years, I've heard some details about her time with Elvis, and I think they say a lot about what kind of person he was. On the one hand, Chris has substantiated what some of Elvis's other romantic interests have said—that he was a fantastic kisser. But Chris has also told me just how courteous and tender Elvis was, and how he truly went out of his way to make their time together special and meaningful for both of them.

Above all, what Chris told me confirms that, beyond physical intimacy, Elvis was always seeking a kind of spiritual intimacy with the women he chose to be with. Elvis and Chris spent a good deal of time together talking about the Bible and a range of spiritual matters. These were the kind of conversations that the Colonel had once sought to end by banishing Larry Geller and insisting that Elvis turn away from his philosophy books. I suppose they were now conversations that Elvis didn't think he could have with any of us Mafia guys. But with a willing, open soul like Chris, Elvis could feel comfortable sharing his deepest thoughts. Sure, Elvis liked having a pretty girl in his hotel room. But I think the ability to have a deep, honest conversation with someone was what gave him the greatest pleasure.

The morning Chris left Las Vegas to head back to Cincinnati, Elvis wrote her a note, addressed "My Dear Chris." It contained simple, heartfelt instructions on how to gain strength from a kind of Christian-based meditation. "Visualize yourself as strongly as possible, and surround yourself with the Christ-light—pure, white light," he wrote. "Keep yourself in tune with the Christ of God within, completely trusting in him . . . He will never let you down. Love, E.P."

I had always tried very hard to keep my friendship with Elvis entirely separate from my TV and radio career. But in the fall of '72, WHBQ began a radio promotion that I thought Elvis might want to hear about. WHBQ was owned by RKO, and RKO's chief radio programmer was a genius of a guy named Bill Drake who did a lot to create the top-forty format in radio. With football season in full swing, Drake had come up with the idea of having an imaginary all-celebrity football team, with listeners guessing who the players were from clues they heard on the radio. What really made it special was that when a player was identified, you'd hear them actually say their name and position. So the station was doing what it could to get brief celebrity recordings along the lines of "Burt Reynolds—halfback," or "Clint Eastwood—linebacker."

Station management felt there was only one possible celebrity who could be quarterback, and that was Elvis. I told them right away that, while it was a great idea, it wasn't the kind of thing he would go for. But they asked if I'd at least run it by him. I showed up at Graceland one night, came through the back door, and was a little surprised to see Elvis standing right there in the den. I noticed a couple of the guys were moving around as if they had some task to get finished, but that wasn't unusual.

"Look, Elvis," I said, "let me just get something out of the way so I don't have to sweat it out all night. I know you won't do it but I told my bosses I'd ask."

"What are you talking about, GK?"

I went into my explanation, telling him how they already had Burt and Clint and others for the radio team, but that they really wanted him.

"And you're saying I'll be quarterback?"

"Yeah. All you have to say is, 'Elvis Presley—quarterback.'"

"That's cool, GK, but I don't know if I can do it." One of the guys came back into the den and stopped for a moment behind Elvis, then walked on.

"Elvis," I said. "I know the use of your voice is contracted to RCA. I don't want to make any trouble for you. I just said that I'd ask you and I did, so . . ."

"Shut up," he said.

I wasn't sure what I'd done wrong. I thought I'd been taking his side in this. He brought his hand around from behind his back and opened it to reveal a small jeweler's gift box.

"Happy birthday, GK," he said.

It was indeed October 8, my birthday. The guys had seen me driving up, and when they reminded Elvis of the date, he'd sent them up to his room to fetch this gift.

"What?" was all I could say.

"Shut up, stop trying to sell me on some promo, and open the box," he said. Inside was the most stunning ring I'd ever seen: a huge green stone in a gold setting, surrounded by eighteen white diamonds and twenty yellow diamonds. I slipped it on and couldn't stop admiring it.

"Elvis, what a great gift. But now I feel even worse for asking you to do a radio spot."

"Well, you ought to, GK," he laughed. "You ought to."

Elvis didn't do the promo, but I'm still wearing that ring every day.

As cautious as I was about bringing my business to Elvis, it was a different matter altogether if he wanted me involved in his business. We were sitting around Graceland once when he said, "GK, I'm getting to the point where I need to start investing in some business stuff. I love what I do, but it'd be nice to make some easy money, too, and I want to get some business deals going. I want you to be on the lookout for some business opportunities for me."

"Elvis, I don't want to be your business guy," I said. "Every time I drive up that driveway you're going to say, 'Here comes GK with another deal,' and go upstairs to avoid me."

"No, no. I won't do that. I don't want you to bring me every damn deal that's out there. Just if you hear something that sounds like a good deal, something interesting, run it by me. I may not do anything about it, but I want to think about it."

The first idea for a deal ended up coming from Elvis. Cable TV was just starting out as a business, and he was interested in getting into it. I knew the interest wasn't strictly financial: Elvis had long been frustrated that the local Memphis TV channels signed off at night just as he was getting into a TV-watching mood. He'd once had me go to the management of WHBQ's Channel 13 to pass along his offer to buy up all of the midnight-to-six A.M. commercial time so that the station would never sign off, but the station didn't have the resources to run a broadcast all night. Elvis figured if he could own his own cable system, he could finally watch TV all night long.

I started doing some research for Elvis and found that the city's central cable office was in a little house not far from the Memphian. I went in there and found what was at the heart of the Memphis cable industry: one little old lady, a couple of tape machines, and a handful of movie tapes that she'd play over and over. I found out it was going to cost Elvis about a million dollars to wire his neighborhood for cable, and it might take ten years for him just to break even as a cable system owner. Of course today that initial investment would be worth a fortune, but back then it didn't look like the kind of "easy money" Elvis was after. We didn't pursue it any further.

We did try to make a go of another opportunity that came up not too long after that. FM radio was in its infancy: A lot of AM stations owned an FM signal, but few were doing much with it. I had a better sense of the future of

FM than I did of cable TV—I was sure its crystal-clear stereo sound would eventually make it the preferred signal for music stations. When WHBQ decided to sell off its FM signal, I made a pitch to Elvis, and he decided to put up $450,000 for the signal on two conditions: He wanted me to run the new station, and he wanted his initials in the call letters. I don't know if we would have had WEP, WEAP, or WTCB, but the signal was sold before we could get Elvis's offer in. What might have been a good rockin' Radio Elvis station instead became WEZI, an easy-listening station.

I liked the idea of Elvis making some easier money, but the deal that did go through for him was one that really bothered me. In March of 1973, the Colonel finalized a deal with RCA that sold all of Elvis's master recordings back to the label for a lump sum payment of $5.4 million. The record company now owned outright everything that Elvis had recorded up to 1973—from "Hound Dog" to "Heartbreak Hotel" to "Suspicious Minds" to "Burning Love." That $5.4 million was a lot of money, and it gave Elvis the influx of easy cash he'd been seeking. But it felt wrong to me to put a price tag on this amazing artist's entire catalogue and just cash it out. I didn't speak with Elvis about it, but I tried to raise the issue with Colonel Parker diplomatically.

"George, all them old records are just sitting on a shelf," he said. "They're not making any money for Elvis. People have already bought them—why would they buy them again? RCA's giving us millions, George—that's like found money."

I certainly didn't have the foresight to know that with every change to come in the music industry—from the popularity of oldies radio formats to the rise of classic rock to the advent of CDs to the birth of digital media—Elvis's catalogue would become one of the most valuable properties in the world. All I knew was that for all the great music Elvis had made, and all the great memories that music had created, $5.4 million felt cheap.

While pursuing "easy money," Elvis had also taken on a formidable challenge in early 1973. His January *Aloha* show in Hawaii was the first-ever worldwide satellite broadcast of a concert, and between live and delayed telecasts, he was able to reach over a billion fans with one performance. Elvis seemed excited about the concert in the weeks leading up to it, and those of us around him felt it was the kind of challenge, like the '68 special, that would drive him to a higher level of achievement.

I didn't make it to Hawaii, but when I saw the U.S. broadcast of the show, I was a little troubled. Elvis certainly delivered an entertaining show, but some of us could see that something was a little off. Up until now, when Elvis got himself into shape for a major event, he'd end up looking great. But now he looked a little drawn and tired, like he'd lost weight too quickly. His voice was fine, but he didn't bring any special spark to the stage like we might have expected at such a significant show. Between the Colonel's and RCA's promotions, this had been built up to be a historic event. But in some ways, Elvis seemed to be simply going through the motions of being Elvis.

The problems became more pronounced during the Hilton engagement that followed in February. Elvis missed several shows due to illness, and when four drunken fans climbed up onstage one night, he spiraled into an irrational rage, eventually claiming that the guys were hitmen sent by Priscilla's love interest, Mike Stone.

I know I wasn't the only one beginning to notice the times when Elvis seemed "off." Linda Thompson had become a steady, devoted girlfriend to Elvis and was in fact now living at Graceland. She enjoyed some great times with him and clearly enjoyed the mink coats and VIP lifestyle that came with being his love. But I think she also found that she sometimes had to take on the role of nurse or mother just to help him get along. Friends like Joe and Jerry and Red and myself were picking up on some of Elvis's lapses, but I think we all wanted desperately to make excuses for him: He's just been working too hard; he just needs to start working again; he's just reacting to a new medication.

Sometimes there really was no excuse that would explain Elvis's behavior. There'd been an uncomfortable incident at Graceland when Elvis seemed to want to offer some marriage counseling to Billy Stanley, one of the sons of Dee Stanley, Vernon Presley's second wife. Billy and his wife had been going through a rough patch, and Elvis gave the couple a ring that he said would bring them happiness—though to us it looked like a wedding band he'd said he lost back at the Circle G ranch. Later, when Billy was occupied doing something else, Elvis took the attractive wife out for a ride on his motorcycle, and when they returned, he surprised all of us by walking her up to his bedroom. When they emerged a while later, he had a funny expression on his face, and he kept singing a line from a Hollies song: "He ain't heavy, he's my brother." Nobody was sure what had actually happened, but the whole thing felt sour and out of character for Elvis.

I think now it's clear that he had developed a terrible chemical dependency on his prescription medication, but at the time it was harder to see. We all knew what a drunk or a junkie looked like, but that wasn't Elvis, and in 1973 there wasn't the openness about other kinds of addiction that there is now. With all the problems in his life and the pressures on him, he was still an amazing person most of the time, and it just didn't seem too alarming that he was a little off now and then. Nobody wanted to acknowledge that the most incredible, talented person we'd ever known was struggling.

Music was always a refuge for Elvis, and there were hopes that when he got back to recording, he'd shake off whatever was bothering him and get himself right. With all that had gone down in the wake of the American sessions, I didn't have it in me to try to push Elvis to record there again. But Marty Lacker had connections at Stax, another of Memphis's legendary studios, and sessions were booked there. Unfortunately, there wasn't the same magic in the air at Stax as there had been at American. Elvis got a few decent tracks out of his sessions there, such as "If You Talk in Your Sleep" and an energetic cover of Chuck Berry's "Promised Land," but nothing that felt truly special.

When Elvis returned to Las Vegas for his August '73 engagement, he got some of the worst reviews of his career, and it became almost impossible for anyone working with him not to notice that he was in a diminished state. But at the end of that engagement, when the Colonel was infuriated by remarks Elvis made onstage about the Hilton management, Elvis did something that required considerable strength: He fired the Colonel.

That was unsettling news for anyone who was a part of Elvis's world, but, although I didn't say it out loud, I was excited at the prospect that Elvis might finally part ways with the Colonel and start fresh with someone new. In the early days, Elvis was a one-of-a-kind talent who'd benefited greatly from a one-of-a-kind manager like the Colonel. But Elvis didn't become a star simply because he was well promoted: He became a star because he was Elvis. And now he had outgrown the Colonel.

Conventional wisdom had been that only the Colonel could handle Elvis. I'd always thought Sam Phillips would have done just as good a job. And Brando had a manager. Sinatra had a manager. Muhammad Ali had a manager. They all did fine without the Colonel. I felt there had to be someone out there who'd be willing and able to manage Elvis, and if the Colonel was now asking for something like a million-dollar payoff to walk away from Elvis, so be it. If Elvis approached a top manager and said, "You can have me as a client for a million dollars," then handed that money to the Colonel, everyone could be a winner.

It didn't work out that way, though. Within a couple of weeks the Colonel, in some of the sharpest negotiating of his career, wore down the resolve of Elvis and Vernon. Before long, Elvis and the Colonel were client and manager once more.

Not long after Elvis and the Colonel put things back together, Elvis and Priscilla made their separation final. And I know it's a strange thing to say, but Elvis and Priscilla had the most beautiful divorce I've ever seen. I think once the stress and strain of their marriage was lifted, they both realized what a loving bond they shared. From what I could see, after the initial uneasiness of the split-up, there wasn't any real bitterness or hard feelings on either side. There's a famous photo of Elvis and Priscilla leaving a Santa

Monica courthouse right after their divorce had been made official. They're arm in arm, looking more like a couple heading out to dinner than one that's just ended a marriage. I asked Elvis once what he was saying to Priscilla when that picture was taken. He said he told her, "We met as friends, and we part as friends. If you ever need anything, just call me. I'll always love you."

Elvis remained a doting father, and while he and Priscilla were able to maintain that wonderful friendship and to appreciate the role each of them played as parents to Lisa, you could see how it weighed on him that his daughter wasn't an everyday part of his life anymore. I can remember seeing how she'd run to him when she came for visits to Graceland, and how emotional he'd get when it was time to say goodbye and send her back to Priscilla. When he and Lisa were together, he took her almost everywhere he went (to the Stax sessions, for instance). He'd do whatever he could to bend his schedule to be there with her if he felt she needed him, like after she had her tonsils out at age six. And Priscilla continued to balance some of the harder, day-to-day work of parenting against Elvis's generous expressions of fatherly love—like when he presented his little daughter with a gift of diamonds and a fur coat.

I know it took a great deal of strength for Elvis to get through his parting with Priscilla, but in October 1973, almost as soon as he returned to Memphis after the divorce, the unthinkable happened: His strength gave out. He was having so much trouble breathing that Dr. Nick felt it necessary to check him into Baptist Memorial Hospital for extensive testing and a period of recuperation.

As scary as it was to hear that Elvis had been checked into the hospital, I was actually relieved to see him there. His health had obviously been declining, and in the days before the Betty Ford Center, there was really no other way to get addiction treatment than to check him in for an extended hospital stay. As proud a man as Elvis was, he didn't seem to fight the treatment. He knew he had to get his health back together, and he knew this was probably the only way to do it.

I think once he was admitted to the hospital, a lot of us around him finally came to terms with just how difficult it had been to see a guy we respected so much turning in performances that were so far below what he was capable of, and how painful it was to admit that a guy who was loved by people all around the world could act in ways that were self-destructive. For a long time, we'd simply accepted the idea that if Elvis was getting prescriptions from doctors, that medicine had to be necessary to treat some real physical complaint. But Elvis had a way of getting whatever he wanted from doctors, who were either unaware of how many other doctors he was going to or who just didn't care. Eventually, his body just couldn't handle all the substances he was putting into it. I wasn't happy that he needed to be hospitalized, but I was thankful that, under the watchful eyes of the hospital staff, he'd have a chance to get healthy again.

Of course, if Elvis was going to stay in the hospital, he was going to do it Elvis style. He had one private room with a second bed installed so that Linda could stay with him, and a second room across the hall where some of the guys would stay both for security and to keep him company. His favorite foods were cooked for him at Graceland and delivered to the hospital. Sometimes if a lot of guys had shown up to visit him, we'd wait in the second room and take turns going in to see him. Sometimes he really just wanted to be with Linda. But sometimes I'd go up there and nobody else would be around.

Once, he asked me to bring him a portable record player and some of the latest records so he could hear what kind of things other singers were cutting. (He didn't have much patience for listening to the radio.) I showed up with the player and a stack of records, and the two of us just sat there quietly listening to music. I remember playing him a new album by Charlie Rich, *Behind Closed Doors*. Elvis had always liked Charlie: He'd been playing Charlie's "Mohair Sam" when the Beatles had come to visit him in Los Angeles. Elvis liked Charlie's new title track, but he was really taken by another song, "The Most Beautiful Girl," and he had me play that five or six times in a row. We'd talk about the story the lyrics were telling—of a man who's driven away the love of his life and now regrets it—then play it again. Elvis didn't say her name, but I couldn't help but feel that each time we listened to the song, he was thinking about Priscilla.

Another visit during that hospital stay when the two of us were alone stands out in my mind. Barbara and I were still living in my Midtown apartment, and for a while, Elvis had been talking about buying us a house. He recruited Pat West, Red's wife, to help us house-hunt, and when we found something we really liked, Elvis had put down a one-thousand-dollar deposit to hold it while we worked out a deal. Now, in the hospital room, he had something to tell me.

"GK, you know my situation's changed. I've got some bad news, man. I can't get you that house at this time."

I can't say I wasn't disappointed, and I couldn't help but wonder if the Colonel or Vernon had done some more cracking down on expenses. This was the first time in my life that Elvis had ever backed out of anything he'd promised me, but that didn't mean much in light of everything he'd done for me over the years.

"Elvis, I'm just glad you're getting better in here," I said. "I'd rather have a friend than a house."

Elvis really did get better in the hospital. He looked better—much more himself. He lost weight and had some of his old energy and good humor back. Dr. Nick had the chance to sort out the wild mix of prescriptions Elvis had become dependent upon, and now had him on a greatly reduced and strictly monitored regimen of only the medications he felt Elvis truly needed. To help Elvis transition off some of the medications that weren't needed, Dr. Nick began substituting placebo pills. Dr. Nick also convinced Elvis to take up racquetball as a way of staying in shape. Despite Elvis's love of physical activity, he'd never been an avid exerciser, but he took to the sport and pretty soon we were renting out the racquetball courts at Memphis State, the Jewish Community Center, and other places around the city for some late-night matches.

Out of the hospital, Elvis had a stretch of a couple months without any work obligations—the first time that had happened for years. When he did get back to work, for his January '74 Las Vegas Hilton shows, he was in particularly strong form. He'd given us all cause for concern, but to watch him enjoying himself at work onstage, you couldn't help but feel that the Elvis we loved so much was back.

I'd come out to see Elvis after my own big gig: I'd just emceed a Three Dog Night/Black Oak Arkansas/Buddy Miles concert at Memphis's Liberty Bowl Stadium that drew twenty-five thousand people. At that event, and all around the city, I heard the same question: Why didn't Elvis ever perform in Memphis? He hadn't performed in his hometown since his 1961 charity concert at Ellis Auditorium, and I didn't have any good answer as to why. In fact, I thought it was about time for a homecoming.

My first night in Las Vegas I found myself in Elvis's dressing room with just the Colonel and Tom Diskin, and I guess I was feeling my oats.

"You know, Colonel," I said, "Elvis really ought to book something in Memphis."

"George," he almost shouted, "you know the old showbiz adage—you don't play your hometown. If you don't sell out, you look bad."

"Colonel, I just emceed Three Dog Night and they drew twenty-five thousand. If they can do that, you know Elvis can sell out eleven thousand seats at the Mid-South Coliseum."

The Colonel chomped down hard on his cigar. "And will you buy every seat we don't sell, George?"

"You know I can't do that, Colonel, but I know Elvis would sell out in a flash."

"Can you guarantee it?"

"I can't guarantee it—I just know it."

"And how many shows have you booked, George?"

"I've booked some, but nothing as big as Elvis."

"Then why are you telling me my business?" he hollered.

"Colonel, I'm just giving you some input," I yelled back. "I'm telling you what I'm hearing all over Memphis, and you can use it or not use it."

Just around then Elvis walked in, and the Colonel and I both shut up.

Not long after I got back to Memphis from Vegas, I got a call from Bubba Bland, the manager of the Mid-South Coliseum.

"Looks like you did good, GK," said Bubba.

"What do you mean?"

"Colonel Parker just called and booked Elvis for four shows."

Those shows sold out in eight hours, and a fifth show was added, which also sold out. The Colonel didn't need my guarantee after all.

It was a hell of a homecoming. The shows were good ones, and the Memphis crowd was crazy for Elvis. All of us around Elvis had learned that we could no longer think of him as some kind of superhero. He was a flesh-and-blood human being, with struggles and disappointments just like anyone else. He could make mistakes, and he could get hurt. He could hurt himself. But watching him onstage back in Memphis, doing what he loved and doing it like no one else could, I still couldn't help feeling awed by this guy.

CHAPTER FIFTEEN

Third and Long

It was an impressive sight, seeing all of Elvis's gold and platinum records side by side up on the wall, alongside the wide variety of honors and awards he'd earned. It really gave a powerful physical presence to his years of accomplishment, and those symbols of achievement now had a home of their own. A patio addition at Graceland—first used to house Elvis's slot-car track, then later used as the site of the Memphis wedding reception for Elvis and Priscilla—was now the trophy room. Elvis really enjoyed this new personal museum, which also contained some of his favorite photos and memorabilia, and for a while every visitor to Graceland got a tour of the trophy room.

I was at Graceland one day when a couple of Hollywood bigwigs came by on a social visit. Elvis led them on a walk through the trophy room, and while the visitors were really excited by the gold singles for some of Elvis's early hits, he wanted to show them something else: the picture of his senior class at Humes High School.

"Look who's up at the top of that picture," he said.

"Uh—who is that, Elvis?" one of the visitors asked.

"That's George Klein," Elvis said. "The man standing beside me right now."

I was sure he was going to make some kind of joke about how I looked back then, or how I looked now. But instead he said, "George was president of our class. And he was one of the few guys that didn't kid me and never gave me a hard time. He was always kind to me and I never forgot it."

The visitors were quiet and didn't quite know how to respond to a moment like that. But I did.

"Thank you, Elvis," I said.

With his health holding steady, Elvis decided to take on a new challenge for himself: film producer. His interest in karate had picked up again, and he decided that he wanted to put together a documentary that would showcase everything he loved about the physical and the spiritual side of martial arts. All of us around him thought it was a great idea that was perfectly timed. When Elvis had first demonstrated karate to us after he came home from his army service in 1960, it was something strange and exotic. But now America had caught up with Elvis, and martial arts had become a mainstream fascination. The Billy Jack films and Bruce Lee's *Enter the Dragon* had been box-office successes, David Carradine's *Kung Fu* was a hit series on television, and soon the song "Kung Fu Fighting" would be a number-one hit single.

Part of the documentary was going to follow the travels of an all-star U.S. karate team as they competed in international tournaments. Jerry Schilling signed on to the project as a coproducer who would run the day-to-day side of the production, and Elvis got additional support from his own karate trainers, Master Kang Rhee and Ed Parker. But Elvis received no support or encouragement from Colonel Parker, whose Hollywood connections and negotiating skills could have definitely made things easier. The Colonel viewed the karate film as distracting foolishness that he wanted no part of.

Elvis wanted his film to include segments of himself demonstrating the basic principles and moves of karate. It had been difficult for him to schedule a time to film those segments, and he'd been trying hard again to lose some weight. But on one September night he felt ready. Red West called to ask me if I could get a camera crew from WHBQ to film Elvis at

Master Rhee's studio and at the Tennessee Karate Institute, a school that Red, with some funding from Elvis, had founded with martial arts champion Bill "Superfoot" Wallace. I got the crew together, and we shot nearly an hour of sequences with Elvis that night. I can't say that Elvis was in absolute peak form, but he was strong and focused and enjoyed sharing his karate insights with a small group of students.

A couple months later, when Elvis was back in Memphis after a Midwestern tour and a run at the Sahara Hotel in Tahoe, I went up to Graceland to view a rough cut of the film. We sat in the TV room downstairs and watched about fifty minutes of team footage and Elvis's demonstration footage that Jerry and his crew had cut together. I'd never been as interested in karate as Elvis or Red or Jerry. In fact, the only time I'd ever been willing and able to punch through a karate board was on one of my visits to L.A., when Elvis and some of the guys built up my interest and confidence by spiking my orange juice with vodka. But I had to admit, the karate documentary footage was really exciting to watch.

That Graceland screening ended up being about as far as the karate documentary went, though. Jerry Schilling did a great job, but problems kept arising with the rest of the L.A.–based production staff. And Elvis wasn't in any condition to deal with the headaches of being an executive producer—he was feeling worn down again. At the end of 1974 he flew off to Las Vegas to go through a second round of a "sleep diet" with a physician who had treated him out there, Dr. Ghanem. I think the concept was that by keeping Elvis sedated and on a low-calorie intake for a couple of weeks, he'd end up rested and slimmed down. But from what I heard, by the end of the treatment he was heavier and feeling even less healthy. He was distressed enough that he had the Colonel cancel his January engagement at the Las Vegas Hilton. I can only imagine that the cancellation brought increased pressure from the Colonel's side to drop the karate film, and by the end of the year, the production had shut down and nobody talked about it much after that.

Elvis was definitely not feeling good about himself on January 8, 1975, his fortieth birthday, and by the end of January, with his body giving out on him again, he checked back into Baptist Hospital. His liver function was off, he was treated for some awful intestinal ailments that had worsened over the years, and he was diagnosed with glaucoma. But primarily, once again, Dr. Nick wanted to wean him off the prescriptions he'd picked up from Los Angeles and Las Vegas doctors, and to try to get his body running well on its own. Previous hospitalizations had brought out a kind of fighting spirit in Elvis, but now he seemed more resigned. When I visited one day, he shocked me by talking openly about his dying, then shocked me more with a quiet announcement.

"GK, I'm going to leave you fifty thousand dollars in my will. I've been in and out of the hospital and Daddy and the Colonel want me to draw one up."

"Elvis, I don't want to hear about that, and I don't want to talk about it. You're not going anywhere. We'll talk about it in thirty years."

"No, I might not be around that long, George. Maybe not."

I'd never heard Elvis talk openly about death like that and it really upset me. I didn't want to hear anything about his will, and I didn't want to hear anything about him dying before his time. I did everything I could to change the subject until he finally let it drop.

When Elvis returned to the Las Vegas Hilton in March, he was visited after one show by Barbra Streisand, who told him that she was planning a remake of *A Star Is Born* and wanted Elvis to play the crucial role of the declining rock-star love interest of Streisand's character—a role that had been played in earlier versions of the film by Frederic March and James Mason. Joe Esposito and Jerry Schilling sat in on the meeting with Barbra, and I heard from them that Elvis was really excited about the opportunity to do some real acting.

I think we all hoped that *A Star Is Born* might do for Elvis's career what *From Here to Eternity* had done for Frank Sinatra when his career was slumping. The opportunity to be taken seriously as an actor would have given Elvis a real incentive to get in shape. But by the time I talked to Elvis about the offer a couple of days later, he already sounded like it wouldn't work out. Pretty soon we all knew why. As soon as Colonel Parker heard about the meeting, he was upset that someone had gone around him to pitch his client directly, ignoring the fact that Streisand was a huge star in her own right who'd just earned a Best Actress Oscar nomination for *The Way We Were*. He demanded from Streisand the same deal he'd gotten on Elvis's movies: top billing, a million dollars up front, and 50 percent of the picture. I think Streisand's people tried to negotiate in good faith for a while, then just gave up. The role went to Kris Kristofferson.

As disappointed as Elvis may have been about *A Star Is Born*, he wasn't giving up entirely on pursuing some new challenges. With hopes of setting up his first overseas concert tours, Elvis bought a Convair 880 jet, which he soon had hangared at Meacham Field, outside of Dallas. There, it would be refurbished, redesigned, and redecorated. One night, we were sitting around talking over possible names for the plane with Elvis. I suggested *Hound Dog*. He didn't like that. A couple of other people came up with suggestions. He didn't like them either. Then Dr. Nick spoke up and said that he thought the plane should be called the *Lisa Marie*. Elvis liked that.

I knew Elvis liked to get things done fast, but I was a little taken aback when he called me out to Graceland one night and announced that he'd decided on a quick way to improve our appearances.

"GK, you and I are going to get face-lifts," he said.

I'd go along with Elvis on just about anything, but this time I put up a fight. Elvis was a little heavy, but he was still an incredibly handsome man, and the idea of using surgery to mess with the face that so many people had admired over the years just seemed terribly wrong.

"Elvis, you've still got the face of a Greek god," I said. "Why in the world would you have a face-lift?"

"If we just have a little bit done now, we don't have to have a lot of work done later." He'd done his homework on the procedure and began to explain exactly what could be done and how it would improve our appearances. I let him go on, and left Graceland telling him I'd consider it. But right away I got in touch with Dr. Nick and told him how upset I was about Elvis having cosmetic surgery.

"He's got the most famous face in the world and he still looks good," I said. "Why would anyone perform surgery on that face?"

Dr. Nick let me know that he'd already had the same argument with Elvis, and said that when he refused to sanction the surgery, Elvis said he'd simply have it done in Los Angeles on his own. Dr. Nick figured it was better to remain a part of the process and have Elvis deal with a surgeon Nick trusted.

So Elvis and I both had mini face-lifts, done by Dr. Asghan Kolyeni of Memphis. Once I consented, I told Elvis I'd run it through my own health insurance, but he insisted on paying for the whole thing up front. Afterward, Elvis felt great about the results, even though the change was minimal. And, all these years later, I have to admit that Elvis was right. The mini face-lift slowed down the aging process, and I probably look better now than I would have without it.

While Elvis was willing to use surgery to improve his looks, he didn't want to rely on anything but old-fashioned showmanship in his performances. That was reinforced for me in 1975, after I'd crossed paths with an old Memphis acquaintance with the unlikely name of Chickaboo Patton. Chickaboo had attended Cal Polytechnic University, and had a scientific mind that seemed focused on the cutting edge of modern technology. He caught up with me at the radio station after work one day and took me out to the WHBQ parking lot to give me a demonstration of something he'd been working on. Using a kaleidoscope-type contraption and some glass prisms, he showed me how he could create 3-D images that appeared to be suspended in the air. He said it was called a hologram.

Chickaboo said he'd thought up a great effect for Elvis. Using an industrial version of what he'd just showed me, he could create an image of Elvis that would appear onstage at the end of a concert. As the crowd applauded, the seemingly real Elvis would rise off the stage, float above the crowd, then vanish. He explained how it could all be done, though most of his science talk didn't mean a thing to me. The bottom line was that the effect could be created with seventy-five thousand dollars' worth of equipment.

It did seem like a pretty cool idea for something new in Elvis's show, and I knew how much he liked being an early user of any new technology. I ran the idea by Jerry Schilling, and he thought it sounded pretty cool, too. One night, after Jerry and I had played some racquetball with Elvis, I decided to run the idea by him. I gave him the full explanation, along with the price tag. Elvis's reaction was quick and to the point.

"Hologram? Holo-shit. What are you talking about, GK? I've never used a gimmick in my act, and I'm not going to start now."

Outside of his own concerts, there was really only one kind of large public event that Elvis was interested in attending, and that was a professional football game at Memphis's Liberty Bowl. Pro football came to Memphis in the summer of 1974 when the city became home to a World Football League franchise, the Southmen. The team was supposed to begin life in Toronto as the Northmen, but the change in city led to the change in name. Memphis fans never really took to "Southmen," however, and the team became unofficially known as the Grizzlies.

The team was owned by John Bassett, a very classy guy who was an entrepreneur with TV and radio interests. I kept running into John at various events around Memphis, and when he heard about my connection to Elvis, he very tactfully asked about the possibility of Elvis coming to a game. It didn't take a hard sell with Elvis—he was excited about seeing the Grizzlies play. So, on the opening game of the '74 season, Elvis and his group were guests in John Bassett's private skybox.

We were back for the opening game of the '75 season, when there was a lot of excitement around town because Bassett had brought three great NFL players to the Grizzlies: Larry Csonka, Paul Warfield, and Jim Kiick, all members of the undefeated, 1972 Super Bowl–champion

Miami Dolphins. For that game, Elvis rented out a city bus to take his group to the stadium, figuring that a limo might get swarmed but fans wouldn't think to swarm a Memphis bus. We got to the stadium just as the national anthem was being sung, and on the radio we heard that it was being performed by none other than Charlie Rich. Unfortunately, as has happened to any number of performers over the years, Charlie had a hard time with the song and muffed a couple of lines of it. As we made our move to the express elevator that would take us to John Bassett's skybox, Charlie was coming off the field, heading for the same elevator. Charlie and Elvis were very happy to see each other, and it was an amazing moment to be standing in a little elevator with two huge talents who had come out of Sun studios.

"That's a tough song to sing," said Elvis.

"It sure is," said Charlie.

"That's why I haven't done it," said Elvis with a laugh. "I've been asked, but I keep saying no."

Elvis and Charlie made some more small talk, then, just before we all stepped off the elevator, Elvis said, "Charlie, I'm glad the rest of the world has finally found out what I've known for a long time."

"What's that, Elvis?" asked Charlie.

"That Charlie Rich is one hell of a singer."

Charlie beamed as if Elvis had pinned a medal on him.

I'd been asked to emcee the halftime show at the stadium that day, and just before I left the box to head back down to the field, I whispered to Joe Esposito and asked if he thought it was okay if I introduced Elvis in my remarks.

"No, no—if people know he's here, we'll never get out," Joe whispered back.

"Are you sure?" I asked.

"I'm sure," Joe whispered.

From the other side of the box, Elvis said, "GK, come over here."

I went over to him. "Yeah, Elvis?"

"Introduce me," he said. Joe just shrugged his shoulders. It was another example of why we said Elvis had "rabbit ears." He heard an awful lot more than you thought he did.

Down on the field, I took my place at a microphone on the 50-yard line, and before I introduced whatever the halftime show was that day, I said, "Ladies and gentlemen, at this time I would like to introduce to you one of the world's greatest entertainers, an incredible talent who calls Memphis, Tennessee, his home. Ladies and gentlemen, he's here today as a guest of John Bassett—Mr. Elvis Presley." I pointed up to the skybox, and Elvis leaned way out of it over the crowd and waved. The crowd went absolutely nuts.

I don't know if Elvis really liked that intro, or if he was just in a good mood, but during the second half of the game he leaned over to me and said, "GK, why don't you go to Hawaii?"

"Go to Hawaii?"

"Yeah—on me. You always use up your vacation time to come to where I am. I want to treat you and Barbara to a trip to Hawaii."

"Elvis, are you serious?"

"Yeah, I'm serious."

After all these years, I knew that one of Elvis's greatest pleasures in life was to give to others, and I knew that turning down his gifts could really hurt his feelings. If sending me to Hawaii was going to make him happy, I was all for it.

We went back to a Grizzlies game the following Saturday, and while we had just as good a time up in the skybox, the outing ended with probably the biggest disagreement that Elvis and I ever had. A big group of us went out to the Memphian for a movie after the football game, then headed back to Graceland to pick up our cars. It must have been past midnight, but Elvis was nowhere near ready to call it a night. In fact, he wanted to fly all of us to Dallas, to Meacham Field, so that we could take a look at how the customizing of the *Lisa Marie* was coming along. He had recently bought a small Gulfstream jet as a present for the Colonel, but the Colonel had returned it to him, saying it was unnecessary and would cost too much in upkeep. Elvis wanted to make arrangements for us to get on that jet and fly to Meacham Field.

There were many, many times when you didn't want a night with Elvis to end, but there were also times when trying to keep up with him just wore you out. He was much more excited about flying to Dallas than any-body else in the group, but we decided we'd go with him. I was particularly hesitant, though.

"Elvis, I've got a big job tomorrow, Sunday night," I said. "I'm booked as a deejay at a club for a 'George Klein Oldies but Goodies' show. It's been advertised and tickets have been sold. It might not sound like a big deal, but I can't blow it."

"Aww, come on, GK," he said. "We'll be right back. You sleep all day Sunday and you do your show Sunday night."

I agreed, and seven or eight of us, including my wife, Barbara, made the flight with him to Dallas and got out to Meacham Field at about four in the morning. Elvis had to wake people up to open the plane area so we could get to the *Lisa Marie,* but all the airfield employees seemed very will-ing to accommodate him. He gave us the full tour of the plane, which still needed a lot of work but already looked like it was going to be a beautiful and luxuriously appointed aircraft. As we prepared to leave the hangar and head back out to the airfield, I thought I detected a familiar twinkle in Elvis's eye—a twinkle that meant he was up to something.

"Look, GK," he said. "We're going to go on to Palm Springs."

I felt my temper rise more than it ever had with him. "Palm Springs? You told me we'd go on back home. I told you I've got this show—it's important to me, Elvis."

"Don't worry about that," he said flatly.

He'd stood up for me and taken care of me so many times in the years of our friendship. But now it felt like I was simply an inconvenience to him. That stung.

"What do you mean, don't worry? I need to go to work, Elvis. And nobody here brought a bag with them—nobody's ready to go to Palm Springs."

"We'll get everything anybody needs in Palm Springs," he said. "We'll just party until the morning and then the jet will fly you back to Memphis in time for the show."

"You're going to fly to Palm Springs, fly me back to Memphis, then have the pilot go back to Palm Springs to bring you back to Memphis? That's five thousand dollars—for what? If you really have to go to Palm Springs, I'll stay here tonight and catch an early flight back for seventy-five dollars."

"Fine. I don't care what you do," he said. He started walking away from me.

It suddenly occurred to me that I didn't have any cash with me.

"Elvis," I called out. "What about some money for the room and the plane?"

"I'm not giving you shit," he said. He didn't even turn around.

"Elvis!" He didn't turn around.

The group quickly took up a collection and pooled their money so that I had enough for a motel room and a flight. Barbara asked what she should do, and since there were some other wives in the group, we decided that she should just go ahead on to Palm Springs. I spent the night in Dallas, flew back to Memphis in the morning, made it back to Graceland, picked up the car, and did my oldies show in a much more frazzled state of mind than usual. Barbara told me that Elvis did indeed buy all the clothes and toiletries that everybody needed out in Palm Springs. They weren't back in Memphis until Wednesday.

The next time I saw Elvis at Graceland, just before he headed out for another Las Vegas Hilton engagement, I half expected that he and I would finally have it out over the incident. But there was probably nothing that made Elvis more uncomfortable than personal confrontation, and I didn't like it either. When I started to mention what had happened, he just shook his head. "We had a good time, GK. You should have been there."

It wasn't much of a reconciliation, but we let it drop and moved on. Then again, it is kind of hard to hold much of a grudge against someone who's treating you to an all-expenses-paid, first-class trip to Hawaii. Barbara and I headed out with Elvis to Las Vegas to see one of the first nights of his run, with tickets to travel on to Los Angeles and then Waikiki.

Unfortunately, Elvis's show was not a good one. He still had an incredible stage presence, but now, to those of us who knew him, he just appeared to be so tired onstage. Performance had once been a source of energy to him; now it seemed to be draining. I'd seen several shows by now that were disappointing, and sometimes Elvis seemed more interested in talking to a crowd than singing for it. Still, I never wanted to be a critic as far as he was concerned. After the Vegas show, Elvis and I and Jerry Schilling were in the hotel elevator together, and I said, "You knocked them out, Elvis." I didn't want to lie to him about his performance—I just wanted to let him know that the audience was happy, and that he could at least feel good about that. Maybe Elvis should have heard some harder truths from us, but I couldn't stop feeling that I wanted to protect him.

Who could protect him from himself, though? A few days into our vacation, Barbara and I were happily checked into a Waikiki hotel when we heard the news: Elvis was in the hospital again. I called Red West immediately. He told me that Elvis had gotten progressively worn down during his shows until he was too weak to continue, and the rest of the engagement had to be canceled. He'd been flown back to Memphis and was checked into Baptist Memorial Hospital. I asked if I should fly back, but Red said that wasn't necessary. Things were under control and Elvis was going to pull through. Dr. Nick was keeping an eye on the liver and intestinal problems that had plagued Elvis before, but mostly he was trying to scale back the massive amount of medication in Elvis's system. Red made the point that Elvis wouldn't want me to mess up a vacation he'd paid for by flying back too soon. I agreed not to fly back, but it became very hard to enjoy the Hawaiian beaches and sunsets knowing that the friend who'd sent me there was not well at all.

When Elvis got out of the hospital this time, he brought some of the staff with him. Since the last hospitalization, Dr. Nick had insisted that instead of having Elvis try to keep track of his pills, they should be delivered to him and administered a couple times a day by Dr. Nick's nurse, Tish Henley. Now Tish and the nurses who had taken care of Elvis in the hospital, Marion Cocke and Kathy Seamon (yes—these were their real names), started doing round-the-clock duty at Graceland. Elvis's variety of medications were given to him by the nurses in a number of daily "packets," and one of the nurses was always around to tend to Elvis's needs as a recuperating patient. Nurse Cocke was a little older, and I think Elvis looked to her as a kind of surrogate aunt. She was a very comforting presence for him, and he enjoyed her backrubs and conversations as much as he appreciated her nursing know-how.

Elvis was not in great condition, but not too long after he got home from the hospital, we got some sad news that let us know just how much worse things could be. While performing in New Jersey, Jackie Wilson had a heart attack onstage, and, as he fell, suffered serious head injuries. The terrible twist was that for years Jackie had been incorporating a fall to the stage in his act—he'd lie motionless and then spring back up again. So when he fell this time, some crucial moments passed before anyone realized he was in serious trouble. By the time he received medical care, he had lapsed into a vegetative state and was being cared for in a long-term care facility. When I told Elvis, he asked me to start calling the hospital every week, to make sure that Jackie got everything he needed. I ended up on very friendly terms with the nurses who cared for Jackie, and while there wasn't anything Elvis could do to add to Jackie's medical care, Elvis had me make sure that fresh flowers were sent to Jackie's room every week, and that the room was always stocked with candy and magazines for Jackie's visitors.

Elvis took delivery of his personal jet, the newly renovated *Lisa Marie,* in November 1975. He was hoping that having his own plane would make it easier to line up international appearances, though for some time now Colonel Parker had been curiously reluctant to pursue any concert opportunities outside of the United States. At the end of 1975, Elvis decided to make up for previously canceled shows by performing at the Las Vegas Hilton for the first two weeks of December. The stretch between Thanksgiving and Christmas was usually a dead time in Las Vegas; not too many travelers made it to the casinos during a time of family holidays, and even the biggest acts often played to half-empty rooms in that period. And yet Elvis sold out every show he had scheduled and set some new Vegas box-office records. Not only was the Hilton ecstatic, but we were happy to see Elvis in better form than he had been in for a while. The shows weren't phenomenal by Elvis's standards, but they were solid, and he stayed healthy through the run.

Back in Memphis, football was still on our minds. There was no more Memphis Grizzlies, as the whole World Football League had folded after the 1975 season. But the NFL announced that it was going to add some expansion teams, and a sports entrepreneur by the name of Mike Lynn was doing all he could to win an NFL franchise for the city. Lynn had lined up enough wealthy investors, but a big part of securing a team was making a great presentation to the meeting of current NFL owners at which new teams would be considered. Those owners weren't swayed just by money—they wanted to be wowed by a city. Lynn figured nothing could add more wow to a Memphis presentation than Elvis Presley.

Lynn had heard that I had access to Elvis and approached me about making a pitch to him. Basically, Lynn wanted to offer 5 or 6 percent ownership of the team to Elvis in exchange for him serving as the team's goodwill ambassador and schmoozing up the rest of the owners. I got Lynn to set down the offer on a single sheet of paper in an official-looking folder and presented it to Elvis at Graceland.

"GK! This is what I was talking about," he said. "This is the kind of deal I wanted you to bring me. This is exactly what I've been looking for. GK, I want it."

"Great," I said. "These people are going to be so happy to have you on board."

"Let me talk to Colonel Parker and get this lined up."

Of course—again—that's where the trouble started. The Colonel told Elvis that the league would have him singing the national anthem for free every Sunday, and that he'd have to do free private concerts for the owners' guests during Super Bowl week. "Elvis," he said, "we're entertainers—not a halftime show. I strongly advise you to stay away from that."

The Colonel could never really tell Elvis what to do. But the Colonel's lack of encouragement and focus on the negatives made it easy for Elvis's interest to wane and for opportunities to slip away. Elvis declined Lynn's offer. And, for the record, Memphis didn't get an NFL team that year.

Elvis and Priscilla kept in touch with each other, and she was usually in Las Vegas to catch a few shows of each of his engagements there. She was as troubled about his health problems as anyone, and I know she did all she could to offer him some emotional support. Elvis still loved being a daddy, and was thrilled whenever Lisa would come to stay at Graceland for a week or so. I remember on one particular visit, I got to be part of the entertainment for Lisa. Richard Davis had worked as an extra on one of the *Planet of the Apes* movies, and he had the mask he had worn in his car. While Lisa played in the back den at Graceland, I went out and put on the mask, then put on my own black raincoat backwards. I came to the back door, marched through in the stiff-legged walk of a zombie, and used my deepest voice to introduce myself to Lisa as Igor the Monster. Some children might have run, but she just stood there wide-eyed and looked me up and down with a little smile on her face.

Elvis loved it. "Now I've got the only kid in the world who has her own personal monster," he laughed.

Linda Thompson remained a great companion for Elvis, and the two of them were extremely well matched in a lot of ways. But Linda began to spend more and more time developing her acting career in Los Angeles, where Elvis leased an apartment for her. Once, while she was away, Elvis—again not wanting to be lonely for too long—asked me if I'd help find him a date. I set him up with another beauty queen I'd had on *Talent Party*, a Miss Ole Miss named Tori Petty. Elvis started seeing Tori quite a bit, which didn't earn me any points with the guys working for Elvis, who had to drive the seventy-five miles back and forth to the Oxford, Mississippi, campus in order to pick her up and drop her off.

Elvis had a gold-plated telephone in his bedroom that only a very few people had the number for. I never had it, but it was the phone that would ring when Vernon, Linda, or Colonel Parker were calling. When Linda was back in town, the gold phone rang one night and she answered it. Tori was on the line. I can only imagine the fight that erupted between Linda and Elvis, but I soon got to see how angry Linda was. Elvis had purchased a house in Memphis for Linda, not far from Graceland, and at a party there she called me aside and confronted me.

"Elvis says it's your fault," she said. "He says you brought that girl around here and fixed them up. I thought you liked me, GK."

"Look, Linda, I like you a lot. You're a good friend. But I love Elvis and he's the best friend I ever had. When he asks me to do him a favor, I'm gonna do him the favor. You shouldn't fuss at me—you should fuss at Elvis."

"Well, he said it's your fault. He wasn't looking for anything and you set him up."

That incident didn't end the friendship between Linda and me, but it certainly put a chill in the air. The next time I was alone with Elvis, I confronted him.

"Damn, Elvis—why'd you tell Linda it was all my fault? I just did what you asked me to do."

"I know, GK," he said with a little smile. "But somebody had to take the blame and it wasn't going to be me."

Linda had always been unusually tolerant of Elvis's relationships with other women. But as dedicated as Linda was to Elvis, she needed to live her own life, too. She remained an important person to him, but slowly they grew apart. As had been the case with Priscilla, while the romance between Elvis and Linda faded away, a great friendship remained.

Some other relationships around Elvis were coming to a rougher end. I wasn't on the group ski trip that Elvis hosted in January of 1976, but from what I heard, the vacation was soured by some of Elvis's wild mood swings and irrational demands. By the end of the trip, Jerry Schilling was angry enough to quit working for Elvis and return to Los Angeles. Joe Esposito was basically in Los Angeles full-time now, too. And old Memphis Mafia members like Richard Davis, Alan Fortas, Marty Lacker, and Lamar Fike were all pursuing their own careers.

In July, Vernon made a couple of calls that broke up the old group even further: He fired Red and Sonny West. He also fired Dave Hebler, one of the newer guys who had been working security. I was shocked when I heard about it. Elvis had never talked to me about being unhappy with these guys, though I knew there were some lingering lawsuits stemming from incidents in which some of Elvis's security guys had gotten carried away in protecting him and roughed people up. (Someone once asked Elvis about the difference between Sonny and Red, and he said, "Sonny will talk to you, then hit you. Red will hit you, then talk to you.")

At first I didn't think the firings would be a big deal. Just about everybody who worked for Elvis had been fired at some point—and was usually hired back right about the time they finished packing their stuff up to leave (though one time Billy Smith, Richard Davis, and Jimmy Kingsley had to be paged at the Los Angeles airport to be told that they were rehired). It wasn't unusual that Elvis would avoid confrontation by having other guys deliver the "fired" or "hired" message, but it did feel wrong this time, especially with Red, who'd been protecting Elvis ever since he'd stopped a bunch of jocks from cutting Elvis's hair in a Humes High bathroom. To have the calls made by Vernon, who'd never really liked most of the Mafia guys to begin with, was cold. And Elvis wasn't even around when the calls were made: He was out in Palm Springs. It was a really unpleasant situation. Two of Elvis's most dedicated employees, one of whom was one of his oldest friends, were cut loose as if it were just a matter of balancing the books. I really hoped Elvis would think twice about this and reach out, at least to Red.

I had a relationship of my own end about the same time. After twelve years, the *Talent Party* TV show went off the air. The show had been moved around to accommodate ABC's broadcast of college football and we lost a lot of audience. More important, styles and music and TV itself had changed enough that the *Talent Party* format just didn't work anymore. I could feel the change in the atmosphere, and realized that the show had come to the end of its run. We didn't do any big final show or grand retrospective. We just stopped, and I went back to focusing solely on my WHBQ radio show.

Big changes had come to Elvis's world and to mine. I didn't know what the future was going to bring for either of us. I only knew that he was still a constant presence in my life, and I wanted to remain a constant presence in his.

CHAPTER SIXTEEN

• • • • • • • •

Unchained Melody

"Good God, I love that car!" Elvis shouted from his favorite seat at the Memphian Theater. "Joe, see that car? I want that one."

A small group of us were out at the theater, watching another of the "blaxploitation" films—movies targeting a young, urban, black audience—that Elvis had gotten very fond of. In one scene in the movie, a huge, white, customized limousine glided into the picture, and shots of the interior of the car showed it to be one of the most luxurious limos imaginable. It was the longest car I'd ever seen and was obviously not a very practical ride, but to Elvis, I guess it looked like a dream come true. Joe Esposito was traveling frequently between Los Angeles and Memphis, and he was with us that night, so the responsibility for tracking down what Elvis wanted fell to him.

"I'll find out what model it is, Elvis," said Joe, "and I'll find out if there's one available around here."

"No," said Elvis. "I want that car right there. The one in the movie. We know how it works in the movie business—the producers rented it from somebody in Los Angeles. Find out who owns it, and let them know we want to buy it."

When Elvis wanted what he wanted, he was going to get it. Joe was on the phone the next day tracking down the movie's production company, then the Los Angeles car-rental outfit. By the end of the day, he had successfully negotiated a price for the car. Elvis sent a couple guys out to Los Angeles on the first plane available. They handed over the check for the car and drove it back to Memphis. Within just a few days of seeing the incredible white limo on screen, he had it parked at Graceland.

Around this time, RCA had been trying to get Elvis to record again. By the beginning of 1976, the label figured that bringing a studio to Elvis might be easier than getting him to a studio. A full-scale professional recording studio was set up in Graceland's den, with banks of gear in a truck parked outside, and Felton Jarvis was there ready to produce whatever tracks Elvis might want to record. In February, this home-recording setup resulted in such strong tracks as the Mark James songs "Moody Blue" and "Hurt," which had been recorded in the fifties by Roy Hamilton.

But during the second Graceland sessions in October, Elvis couldn't keep himself in a performance frame of mind. Nobody was sure whether it was because of mood, illness, or overuse of his prescriptions—maybe Elvis himself wasn't sure either. After just a few tracks were recorded over a couple of days, the sessions ended early. Elvis felt bad enough about it to want to make sure that all the musicians who'd come to the house got home in style. He had the L.A. players flown back to the West Coast on the *Lisa Marie.* And to get J. D. Sumner and the Stamps vocal group back to Nashville in style, he simply handed that long white limo from the movie over to J.D.

While Elvis may have found it hard to get interested in making new records, he was otherwise working relentlessly: His road schedule in 1976 included eight concert tours and a Las Vegas engagement. His health problems continued, and Dr. Nick was working hard to keep his consumption of pills monitored. I thought it was a positive sign that Elvis showed a real interest in racquetball as a way of getting himself in shape. Ever since Dr. Nick had recommended the sport, Elvis had been setting up late-night workouts either at Memphis State, the Memphis Athletic Club, or the same Jewish Community Center that Alan Fortas and I had hung around as kids. These places always had to make special arrangements to keep their courts open late at night for Elvis, and he made a point of thanking them in Elvis style. I remember that he gave the security guys at Memphis State some brand-new expensive shotguns for Christmas. He also donated something like twenty-five thousand dollars to the Jewish Community Center to have a new addition built and dedicated to Alan Fortas's late father.

Elvis always wanted to be the best at what he did, but he wasn't a real natural at racquetball. He'd work hard enough at it to get some exercise, but he could usually be beat by Dr. Nick or Nick's son Dean. I wasn't much good at it myself—I still can't straighten out one of my fingers after having jammed it into the wall at the Memphis State court. Elvis stuck with the sport, though, and eventually, when he got tired of all the driving from court to court, he had his own built out back at Graceland. It ended up being the most beautiful court I'd ever seen, complete with gold fixtures in the showers. But what excited me more was that the building, which was completed in early 1976, could easily be converted into a state-of-the-art recording studio. When I mentioned that to Elvis, he said he was a step ahead of me. Once he got himself in shape, he was planning on making that conversion.

Elvis did talk to Red West again, returning a call that Red made to Graceland. Rumors had been circling for a while that Red, Sonny, and Dave Hebler were going to write a tell-all book, and the rumors had recently been confirmed. The three were teamed with a writer from a tabloid newspaper and had committed to a publishing deal. When Elvis and Red spoke, they were both sad about the way things had turned out, and Elvis let Red know he'd still be there for Red and his wife, Pat, if they needed him. But nothing was really resolved. I believe that Elvis would have liked to have hired Red back, and probably Sonny as well, and would have been happy to put the whole incident behind them. Elvis knew that the guys had not been treated fairly, and he knew how hard it had been for them to find themselves suddenly unemployed. Deep down, he probably understood that they were honestly concerned about him. But the book deal complicated everything.

Toward the end of 1976, Linda Thompson left Memphis for Los Angeles again, and Elvis had a stretch of time at home before he headed out for the last tour of the year and his Vegas engagement. He must have been feeling especially lonely, because he decided that he wanted to meet as many women as possible during that downtime. As usual, I got the call to help him find some interesting people to spend time with, and I started calling up guests I'd had on *Talent Party,* dancers and waitresses from around town, and just about anyone else I could think of who Elvis might enjoy meeting.

Over the course of about two weeks, I arranged for Elvis to have a date with a different girl almost every night, with the dates usually consisting of an evening at Graceland. It was a strange situation, but it still felt nice to be trusted by him as a judge of the looks and personalities he'd be comfortable with. He never wanted to hear exactly what my relationship with the girls had been, though they were in fact all platonic. But I was friendly enough with many of them that I did often hear back about what had gone on the night before. Without fail, I heard that Elvis was a gentleman and had treated his guest beautifully. And most telling of all, every girl I spoke with wondered what Elvis thought of them and when they might be able to go back and see him again. A few tried to guarantee a return visit to Graceland by leaving behind a personal item—a sweater, a purse, even a brassiere.

I know that many nights, Elvis just wanted to sit on his bed and talk with his date. In the early days, we jokingly called Elvis "the silver-tongued devil" because no one was smoother at talking to a girl, or seemed to enjoy it more. Sometimes Elvis just wanted the feeling of companionship—to laugh with someone and have them make him laugh—and whether or not that ended up with physical intimacy didn't seem to be as important to him. Then again, with a beautiful woman in his bed, things could heat up. One of the women I introduced to Elvis then was Gail Stanton, the stunning *Playboy* model I'd first met on *Talent Party*. When I asked Gail about her night at Graceland, she said she had a great time, and that she and Elvis had talked and joked around all night. When I spoke to Elvis, he said, "Yeah, we joked around—we almost broke the damned bed."

Elvis was going through the women I knew pretty quickly, but there were limits to who I'd even consider introducing to him. I knew he wasn't interested in dropping his standards and he wasn't interested in any encounters that were strictly sexual, and I was reminded of that when I emceed a Chicago concert at the Mid-South Coliseum. Backstage, before the show, I met a rock 'n' roll legend of sorts: "Sweet Connie" from Little Rock, the groupie made famous in the Grand Funk Railroad song "We're an American Band." She was usually more interested in spending time with band members than emcees, but I think she approached me because she saw a way of getting to Elvis's circle and perhaps Elvis himself. She looked the part of supergroupie in a long black cape, and, after minimal conversation, she asked if I was interested in her services. (I think that was the first time I heard the phrase "deep throat.") I let her know I had some emceeing duties to take care of and turned down the kind offer. As devoted to her work as Connie was, she wasn't the kind of girl Elvis was interested in.

I was close to running out of women to call for Elvis when I thought of one of the guests I'd had on one of my final *Talent Party* shows: a Miss Tennessee named Terry Alden. She had specifically asked me if she could be invited to a party at Graceland. So one night, when Elvis was having more of an old-style Graceland get-together for a group of us, I told him about Terry, and he said to offer the invitation. She asked if she could bring her two sisters with her, and I said that wasn't a problem. I told her how to check in at the Graceland gate, and that I'd meet her at the door.

The doorbell rang at about ten P.M. that night, and when I opened the door there stood one of the most beautiful girls I'd ever seen in my life—but it wasn't Terry, it was her younger sister Ginger. Terry was beautiful, but Ginger was even more beautiful, and to my eyes she looked like a taller version of Priscilla. I knew Elvis would just about melt when he saw her. I brought Terry, Ginger, and the third sister, Rosemary, inside to the den and introduced them to some of the guys and other guests. Elvis hadn't come down yet, so I went to the private intercom and called up to his room.

"Elvis, the ladies are here, but we've got a problem."

"What kind of problem?"

"Can I come up and talk to you?"

I went up and explained that while Miss Tennessee was downstairs, looking as lovely as I had previously described to him, she had a younger sister who was an absolute knockout. He asked me to describe her. I didn't mention Priscilla's name, but I ran down the list: long dark hair, dark eyes, great figure, great laugh. Elvis wasn't convinced.

"I don't see how a little sister can be prettier than a Miss Tennessee," he said. "But why don't you bring them all up to say hello."

I led Terry, Ginger, and Rosemary upstairs to meet Elvis, and I saw his eyes light up when he caught sight of Ginger.

When Elvis and I had a chance to speak privately, we worked out a little strategy in which I'd give the older sisters a tour of the house while he spent time alone with Ginger in his room. I had stressed to Terry how much of a gentleman Elvis was, and how he really wasn't looking for typical one-night stands, so the girls were very cool about being split up. I gave Terry and Rosemary the Graceland VIP tour, then we rejoined the party.

It was a really nice night, but by about three in the morning everyone had left except me and the Alden sisters, and Ginger still hadn't reappeared from Elvis's bedroom. Terry's protective nature as an older sister kicked in, and she asked me to check on Ginger. I called up to Elvis's room, and he said that he and Ginger were talking about his books and weren't ready to say good night. He asked me to make sure the sisters got home safely, and said that he'd drive Ginger home himself in one of his limousines. The sisters left, and eventually I got home, too. The next day, Elvis told me that he'd driven Ginger home at sunup. And he told me that he was crazy about her. He wasn't interested in new dates anymore: He wanted to see Ginger again.

When Elvis set out on his last tour of the year, he wanted Ginger to accompany him. But there was a complication—Linda Thompson had expected that she would be traveling with Elvis. Linda was smart enough to sense what was going on, though, and when she left Elvis this time, it was for the last time.

Elvis went straight from the last date of his tour to the Las Vegas Hilton. I went out opening weekend and saw a couple of the shows. Elvis's performances were stronger than they'd been in a whi e, and it was pretty obvious that the reason he was rallying was that he wanted to impress one very special audience member: Ginger Alden.

What I remember most about that engagement happened right after a show, when I was walking with Elvis back to his suite, accompanied by some of his security guys and some of the hotel's security staff. We went up the service elevator, got to Elvis's floor, and began to walk down the hallway to his suite when a guy with a camera jumped out of a stairwell and said, "Mr. Presley, may I please take your picture?"

He was a youngish guy, and it wasn't clear right away whether he was just a fan or a professional photographer. That didn't seem to matter to the security guys, though, because right away they grabbed him, pinned him against the wall, and twisted his arms behind him. Somebody got a hold of his camera and was ready to open it to destroy the film.

"Stop, stop, stop," hollered Elvis. "Don't do that. Let him go."

Everybody froze. This guy could just as easily have been a wacko with a gun as a guy with a camera, and security felt they were just doing their job. Elvis signaled for everyone to leave the guy alone and to gather around him. It was almost like he was a quarterback running a huddle.

"Look," he said. "This guy jumped out and surprised us—I understand that. But the words he used were, 'Mr. Presley, can I please take your picture.' He didn't start shooting the pictures and try to run. He asked me, respectfully, and he said 'please.' I don't want you guys being so rough on these people." He stepped from the huddle and addressed the guy from the stairwell. "Mister, are you a professional photographer?"

"No sir, Mr. Presley," the guy answered.

"How many shots have you got in that camera?"

"Twenty-four."

"Look, sir, because you asked me politely if you could take my picture, I'm going to return the favor. Now, what do you want? Action shot? Smile? Karate moves? Let's go."

The guy was grinning like a happy little kid, and he started clicking away for a private photo shoot with Elvis. Elvis struck all sorts of poses, even suggesting the angles the guy should shoot from. When the roll was finished, Elvis gave the guy a friendly handshake and thanked him once again for asking nicely for the pictures. He told the guys around him that he wanted the incident to be a lesson: Most of the people that wanted to get close to him were good people who didn't deserve to be automatically roughed up. I think about that incident a lot, because I think it's a great example of just how much Elvis loved and appreciated his fans.

I never heard Elvis complain about his career, but it must have bothered him that many of the things he wanted had gotten so complicated they just slipped away from him: the karate movie, *A Star Is Born*, the chance to tour internationally. It must have been a relief and a comfort to be involved in a romance that was sweet and simple. Ginger was shy and reserved, certainly not as outgoing as Linda Thompson, and some of the guys around Elvis took that as her being aloof. But I always got along well with Ginger, and she was always kind to me. Considering all of the career plans and opportunities that Elvis hadn't been able to take advantage of, I thought it was nice to see him passionate about something again, and the way he was making plans for a future with Ginger seemed good for him. His passion did come at a small price to me, though. It became common for my phone to ring at three or four in the morning, and when I'd jerk out of my sleep and answer, I'd hear a familiar voice.

"Hey, GK, how you doing?"

"Uh, fine, Elvis. A little tired."

"Ginger's on the extension. Say 'Hi,' honey."

"Hi, GK."

"Anyway," he'd continue, "we just want to thank you for getting us together. We really enjoy each other's company, and we're having such a great time."

They'd go on to talk for thirty or forty minutes about everything going on with them. It was nice to hear, but frankly I just wanted to go back to bed. A couple of times I was struggling mightily to stay awake and listen, when I'd realize that Elvis had fallen asleep on the phone. I'd say good night to Ginger and hope for a full night's sleep the next night.

Despite his newfound romantic happiness, Elvis's health was still an issue. He was going out on tour after tour, but the strong shows were becoming rarer, and the toll his schedule was taking on him was obvious. He may have been depressed or stressed out, but to me one of the main problems was simple—he was bored. Elvis desperately needed an artistic challenge, and I still believed that if he got that, along with a decent amount of rest, he could bounce back just the way he had in the past.

But there were some occasions when I began to wonder about how deep his problems might be. Once, when we were alone in his room at Graceland, Elvis told me about some of the adventures he'd had going out on drug busts with some Denver policemen he'd become very close with. I'd heard some of these stories before, but now Elvis added a new twist—he said that while out on a stakeout, he'd been attacked by a suspect and had ended up killing the guy with a karate chop to the throat. I was blown away by the story and I let him tell it without questioning him too hard about specific details. But when I mentioned it to Joe Esposito, he shook his head and rolled his eyes as if he'd been hearing a lot of these kinds of tales from Elvis.

Another time at Graceland, Elvis wanted me to call up some guy whom he suspected of being a major drug dealer in Memphis. The idea was to set up a buy so that Elvis himself could make a bust. I called the number Elvis gave me and started talking to somebody, but, luckily, I guess I didn't make a very convincing drug buyer, and by the end of the call, no deal had been set up. I thought the call and the stories were peculiar behavior—the kind of stuff that Elvis would have once laughed at but was now deadly serious about. Maybe foolishly, I didn't want to do anything to embarrass him, so instead I dismissed these incidents as side effects from the medication he was taking for his physical problems. I figured he had Dr. Nick watching him every day and nurses living on the premises: Things would get better.

They didn't. While out on the road again, Elvis got so weak that dates had to be canceled, and he was flown back to Memphis and admitted to Baptist Memorial Hospital once again. His heavy appearance now wasn't simply from a poor diet: His gastrointestinal problems had become so aggravated that his body was bloated. Those problems couldn't get the surgical treatment they required because Elvis's system had been too compromised by his overuse of prescription medication. For the first time, I spoke with Dr. Nick about what further treatment might be available to get Elvis clean and healthy. The closest thing to a Betty Ford Center at the time was a special rehab clinic at Duke University. Elvis had told Nick he had no interest in going there, but Nick and I talked about the possibility of sedating Elvis and flying him on the *Lisa Marie* to get him into the clinic. At the time it seemed too great an attack on Elvis's pride, though I see now that we shouldn't have let that be a concern—we all should have been more worried about his health and less worried about whether we'd continue to be welcomed through the Graceland gates.

I do believe that the two people who had the most at stake and the greatest leverage with Elvis were Vernon and the Colonel, and if either one had pushed for Elvis to undergo the treatment at Duke, it might have happened. But that push was never made. Vernon was concerned about his own job security, and the Colonel didn't want anything to interfere with Elvis making money on the road. With Elvis at his most vulnerable, no one stepped up to help.

Elvis didn't get anything beyond the basic care and monitoring at Baptist Memorial, and he didn't even end up getting much rest. Just a couple of weeks after he checked out of the hospital, he was back on the road again.

I was worried about Elvis, but by the summer of 1977 I had some awful worries of my own. Through a strange twist of circumstances, I found myself facing federal charges of mail fraud. Radio station ratings were put together based on the listening diaries distributed and tabulated by the Arbitron service. Listeners kept track of what stations and shows they tuned into in a book, which was sent in to the company at regular intervals. The mailman who handled WHBQ—a guy we knew well enough to have him play on the station softball team—went to the general manager one day and said he had some empty ratings books from people on his route who didn't want to fill them out, and he was willing to sell them. The attitude around the station was that this was a nice piece of luck: You had to figure that not every devoted WHBQ listener was going to fill out an Arbitron book, so filling them out on those listeners' behalf, while not strictly ethical, wasn't much of a stretching of the truth. I ended up filling out several of those books, and while I knew it wasn't something to boast about, I didn't think much of it once it was done.

The problem was that the books hadn't simply been given up—the mailman had stolen them. And before coming to WHBQ, he'd tried to sell them to a competing station. That station had reported him to the authorities, which in this case was the post office. Stealing mail is a federal offense, and the postal service pressed the case forward aggressively. I tried to be as cooperative as I could during the investigation and freely admitted to what had happened, even acknowledging that it was my handwriting in the books. As a result, I was indicted on charges of conspiracy to commit mail fraud. As soon as that happened, I lost my job at WHBQ. I'd been so proud of my career for so long, and now I was feeling as depressed and lost as I'd ever been. There was really only one person to turn to.

Up in Elvis's room, he greeted me with a casual, "GK—how's it going?" and it all poured out of me. I told him everything that had happened, everything I'd done, and how I was now hoping that a lawyer could keep me out of jail. He put a hand on my shoulder and said, "They'll never put you in jail as long as I'm alive."

Elvis couldn't have been more supportive of me, and he said some of the nicest things to me he'd ever said—chiefly that no matter what happened, he'd take care of me. Billy Smith was in the room with us, and Elvis started talking to Billy and me about how he'd hire the finest lawyers he could find to defend me. Then he said that, if it came down to it—if it looked like I was going to have to go to jail—he'd put me on the *Lisa Marie* and fly me out of the country. He was getting worked up, talking about all he could or would do for me, when suddenly he went silent and a strange look came upon him.

"Billy," he said. "Get President Carter on the phone."

It wasn't as crazy an idea as it sounded. Elvis had met and spent time with Jimmy Carter at a concert in Atlanta when Carter was the governor of Georgia. And, after all, Elvis was a guy who had simply showed up at the White House gates and ended up in the Oval Office with President Nixon. I didn't know if having Elvis call the president was the wisest course of action in terms of the troubles I was facing, but I was desperate enough that I wasn't going to turn down any help I could get.

Billy Smith was a real street-smart guy and was someone I had always liked, but Elvis's request to get the president on the phone left him stumped.

"Elvis, what do I do?" he asked.

I knew that the main White House switchboard was a listed number, as I'd seen some jocks at the station call it for a gag. I got the number from information and gave it to Billy. It was about eight P.M. in Memphis, which meant it was nine P.M. in Washington, D.C., and I assumed that the switchboard would not be open. But when Billy dialed, a security guard answered the phone.

"Hello, I'm Billy Smith, Elvis Presley's cousin, and I would like to speak to President Carter," Billy said.

"The president is retired for the evening. You can leave your name and phone number," was the response.

Billy went ahead and gave the information, and I assumed nothing was going to happen after he hung up, as anyone in the country could have called the same number and said they were Elvis's cousin—that's exactly the type of thing the jocks I'd been thinking of would do. The next day Billy did a very smart thing, though. He called the local FBI office in Memphis, told them he had made the call to Washington on behalf of Elvis, and asked if they could do anything to help.

That afternoon, the phone rang at Graceland, and when Billy answered it, he found himself speaking with Chip Carter, the president's son. Chip wanted to speak to Elvis about the matter to be discussed with his father, but when Elvis got on the line, he said that while he meant no disrespect to the younger Carter, the matter was a very private one and could only be discussed with the president. Somewhat remarkably, Chip agreed to have his father call back. Elvis gave him the number to the gold phone in his bedroom. A time was set up for the next day, and it was agreed that the president's people would ask for Billy Smith: That was the code that would get Elvis and the president on the line together.

I showed up the next night, and I could tell from the excited look on Elvis's face that the president's call had come through.

"How did it go, Elvis?" I asked.

"I answered the phone, and a voice said, 'This is the White House calling. Is this Billy Smith?' " Elvis smiled. "For the first time in my life, I got to say, 'No, this ain't Billy—it's his cousin Elvis.' "

He went on to say that he and President Carter had a pleasant conversation, and that he'd run down my legal troubles as best he could to the president. According to Elvis, the president sounded willing to look into the matter to see if there was anything he could do.

"Don't worry, GK," said Elvis. "We'll get this taken care of."

I'm not sure if, from the president's point of view, the matter went any further than the conversation with Elvis. But the case against me kept grinding ahead, and I started trying to get used to the fact that I might have a court date in my future. At the same time, the book by Red and Sonny West and Dave Hebler was about to come out, and the word was that it was a very unflattering look at Elvis's private life. I know Elvis received an advance copy of the book, but I'm not sure if he actually read it. I do know he was extremely upset about it being out there.

I was hurt and confused, and being at Graceland was really the only place where I felt I could relax and forget my worries for a while. I started showing up there probably every other night. And I don't know if Elvis felt any better about his problems having me around, but at a time when his circle of friends had become much smaller, he always allowed me in.

He had a month or so to relax at home before he was to take off on yet another tour, and he and Ginger were together constantly. One night I got another one of those late-night calls from Elvis. This time he wanted to know if I had a copy of the song "Angelica," the heart-rending ballad he'd given away to Roy Hamilton back during the sessions at American Studios. I told him that I had several copies, and he asked that I bring one over to Graceland—he wanted Ginger to hear the song.

"Am I thinking what you're thinking?" I asked.

"Yeah," he said. "I'm going to cut that one. It's still perfect for me."

With the future of my radio career uncertain, I started doing some freelance work over at the Mid-South Fairgrounds, which had been converted into a theme park called Libertyland in honor of the Bicentennial the summer before. One Sunday in August, Billy Smith called me at the park and told me Elvis wanted to do something he hadn't done in quite some time: He wanted to rent out the Fairgrounds for the night. Lisa had come to Memphis for a two-week stay with her father, and he wanted to treat her and Ginger to a private night at Libertyland. I got in touch with the manager, and we arranged to keep a skeleton crew on that night, with strict instructions that the whole thing be kept hush-hush. By midafternoon, all the arrangements had been made for Elvis's night.

A couple hours later, I got another call from Billy. Elvis had changed his mind. He didn't feel up to a night out and wanted to cancel the plans. I got in touch with the manager again, and we undid all the arrangements we'd made. Then, just after closing time at the park, I got another call from Billy. Elvis wanted the party back on. I told Billy it was too late—that the park employees had left for the night. Billy told me that Elvis really wanted it to happen. I knew that a lot of the park staff went to a particular bar after work, so I called over there and was lucky enough to get a hold of the park manager. He was understandably surprised, but said he could get six or seven people together to run the rides and man the games.

I joined Elvis and his group at the park late that evening, and it turned out to be a really wonderful night out. Elvis hadn't seen the park since it had been remodeled as Libertyland, and he really liked the look of it. Lisa was nine years old—just a little younger than Elvis and I had been when we first climbed the cyclone fence to sneak into the Fairgrounds—and she seemed to enjoy the magic of the place every bit as much as we had back then. Elvis himself looked like a little kid again, happily riding with Ginger and Lisa on old favorites like the Pippin and the dodgem cars. I remember standing with them all as we waited for the Pippin cars to come around, and I saw Elvis looking at Lisa with such a sparkle in his eyes, I could really feel the power of his love for her.

At some point, Elvis and I reminisced a bit, recalling a night twenty years before when we'd come to the Fairgrounds in Elvis's newest automobile, a '56 Cadillac Eldorado convertible that he'd had customized. The car had an incredible purple paint job, and the interior was purple and white to match, with custom EP floor mats. The car was so good-looking that we'd really dressed up for the ride in it, and Elvis looked exceptionally sharp in a new gray suit. That night we actually drove right onto the Fairgrounds and used the new Caddy to get from ride to ride and game to game. We were having a good enough time that when it began to rain, Elvis didn't want to leave. The rain got heavier and heavier, and, as we got wetter and wetter, we noticed something peculiar: Elvis's suit started shrinking right on him, until he ended up looking like he'd tried to squeeze into a little boy's Sunday best. When the rain turned into a real downpour, we climbed back into the

Eldorado which, with its top down, had gotten even wetter than us. We tracked an awful amount of mud into the car's gorgeous white interior, and by the time we got back to Graceland, the poor car was a mess.

Elvis and I stood there laughing about how angry his father had been at the sight of the muddied car, and how hard Vernon had to work to get it clean. We didn't have time to share a lot of old stories—he had Lisa and Ginger to look after. But just before we left the park, as dawn was breaking, Elvis surprised me with a comment that reminded me just how sharp that memory of his was.

"GK, you know, you used to make a mistake on your TV show."

"A mistake? What do you mean, Elvis?"

"You used to say that 'Don't Be Cruel' was my biggest selling record."

"I thought it was—'Don't Be Cruel' with 'Hound Dog' as the B-side."

"Nope."

"Well, what was your biggest seller?"

"GK, 'It's Now or Never' sold fourteen million copies."

" 'Now or Never'? Are you sure about that, Elvis?"

He laughed. "I got paid for selling fourteen million records, GK. Yeah, I'm sure."

Early the following week, on August 16, I was back working at Libertyland when the phone rang in my office. It was one of the other deejays I'd been friendly with over at WHBQ.

"I hate to make this call to you, GK," he said, "but we just got a wire story that Elvis passed away."

"Man, you know that's bullshit," I said. "The same story went out last time he was in the hospital, and there wasn't anything to it."

"You sure, GK?"

"I haven't heard a thing."

Almost as soon as I hung up, the phone rang again, and it was a guy I knew from another radio station. We had the same conversation. Then a third call came in, this time from a guy I knew over at CBS television.

"GK, we've got it on reliable sources that Elvis has passed away."

I started to feel uncomfortable hearing this again, but I knew it couldn't be true. "Let me check things out and I'll get back to you," I told the CBS reporter.

I dialed Graceland right away, and the phone was answered by Vernon's girlfriend, Sandy Miller. I could hear some kind of commotion in the background. "Sandy, it's George Klein. I've been getting all these calls about Elvis."

"It's true, George," she said. "You need to get out here as fast as you can."

I felt like somebody had stabbed me with a red-hot knife. I didn't know what to say, what to feel, what to think. I got to my car and started driving to Graceland at about a hundred miles an hour. I just kept hoping and praying that there'd been some kind of terrible mistake. My mind just wouldn't let the bad news take hold, and it raced to come up with alternatives: Yes, Elvis was sick and he'd looked bad, but of course they would be able to revive him at the hospital.

The car radio was on and no matter what station I turned to, I kept hearing the same bulletin: "We interrupt this program with the sad news that Elvis Presley passed away today. . . ." I kept flipping the dial to find the real story—that there'd been a mistake. The news people had really screwed up. Elvis was in the intensive-care unit, but he'd pull through.

It had to be a mistake.

It couldn't be true.

Dear God in heaven, don't let it be true.

I drove through the Graceland gates and up the hill as fast as I could and went in through that back door to the den as I had so many times before. The room was full of people crying and holding on to each other. The one face that stood out to me was little Lisa's. I'd seen her so happy just days before. Now I couldn't imagine how she could make sense of what had just happened to her.

There was one terrible sound that cut through all the other noise in the room, and it took me a moment to figure out what it was: the sound of Vernon Presley crying uncontrollably. He approached me and hugged me.

"We've lost him, George, we've lost him," he said through his tears. "We've lost my dear, dear son."

"Oh, Mr. Presley. No. No, no, no . . ."

It hit me then, and I started crying, too.

Elvis. The boy I'd met at Humes High. The kid who had sung "Old Shep" to our music class. The guy who had welcomed me into his fantastic life. The person who had given me more than anyone I'd ever known. My best man. My best friend.

He was gone.

Someone You Never Forget

The days after Elvis's death passed us by in a haze of tears and sorrow. I felt numb and shaken and could tell that all around me at Graceland, the people who had been close to Elvis were equally stunned and unsure of what to do. In the few moments when grief subsided, I think we all just felt completely empty. And it was strange to look at all the familiar faces I would have been otherwise happy to see—Priscilla, Jerry, Joe, Charlie Hodge, Alan Fortas, Felton Jarvis, Richard Davis, Sam Phillips—and know that every one of these old friends had a broken heart.

The night before he died, Elvis left Graceland for a late-night appointment with Dr. Lester Hofman, a dentist I'd introduced him to way back in 1957. He had some fillings done, then returned to Graceland to play some racquetball with Billy Smith. After the workout, Elvis sat at a piano out in the racquetball building and played some of his favorite songs, including "Blue Eyes Cryin' in the Rain." Back in the main house, he went upstairs to his bedroom with Ginger, and he took some of the monitored mix of sleeping pills, placebos, and medications Dr. Nick had prescribed for him. When Ginger awoke early the next afternoon, she found him on the floor of his private bathroom, already gone. All efforts to resuscitate him failed. His body had just become too weak and too compromised. He was dead of a heart attack at forty-two.

In recognition of the tens of thousands of grief-stricken fans who flocked to Graceland, Vernon Presley quickly made the decision that he would allow a public viewing of Elvis lying in state. That was to be followed by a private viewing in the Graceland living room for friends and family. One of the first phone calls I remember receiving after Elvis's death came from James Brown, who wanted to tell me how broken up he was over the news. He asked if he could come to the house during the private viewing. I checked with Priscilla to make sure it was all right, and late in the afternoon James came up to join us—the first of many major entertainers to pay their respects. I remember being taken aback by how truly distraught James was. I walked him over to the casket, where we both just stood silently. Then he sat quiet and motionless in the corner of the living room for a long while before joining the rest of the mourners in the den.

On the evening of the second day, I took a call from the gate and was informed that a very different kind of celebrity wanted to come up and pay her respects: Caroline Kennedy, daughter of President John F. Kennedy. Elvis and his family had been big supporters of JFK, so hearing that the late president's daughter was at Graceland was like hearing that royalty had arrived. I met Caroline at the door and introduced her to Priscilla, who took her in to meet Grandma Presley (Vernon was too distraught to speak with anyone). Caroline was extremely courteous to the family, and I think we all felt that if anyone understood the kind of loss and grief we were feeling, it was Caroline. Her visit meant a lot to all of us, but we were all shocked a month later when we learned that Caroline, a budding journalist at the time, had turned her visit into a detailed account for *Rolling Stone* magazine, which had Elvis on the cover of its September 22 issue.

It was hard to see so many tears and so many pained expressions, and at one point Jerry Schilling and I stepped away from the group and went downstairs to the TV room. But in that room, the site of so many wonderful times and magic moments, the sense of loss was even greater. I looked at the TVs, the record player, the ice cream bar—all the little things that had given Elvis so much pleasure—and ended up crying harder than I had upstairs.

There was a service at Graceland two days after Elvis's death. Afterward, I was one of the pallbearers who carried his casket out to a white hearse that would take Elvis up Elvis Presley Boulevard to Forest Hill Cemetery. The hearse was followed by a long line of white limousines, carrying all of us who'd been closest to Elvis.

I rode in a limo with Charlie Hodge and Alan Fortas, and as we pulled out of Graceland to begin our slow drive, we were all awed by the sheer number of people lining the road. Every kind of person you could think of, from every walk of life, stood there shoulder to shoulder, paying one final tribute to a man who had meant something special to each and every one of them. On a day of unbearable sadness, that was a beautiful, remarkable sight.

Even on this day, Charlie—always the comedian in the group—had a few wisecracks to make. It was a strange situation, though. Charlie would make a comment or bring up a memory that would get us laughing, but before we knew what was happening, our laughter would turn to sobs. We'd compose ourselves, watch the crowd as we made our procession, then Charlie would say something else and we'd burst into laughter only to collapse into sobs again.

At the cemetery there was another service, then the pallbearers carried the casket to the space in the mausoleum where Elvis would be interred. I stood at the front-right position so I had the chance to be the last person to touch the casket. I kissed my hand, touched it to the casket, and said goodbye.

As many of us talked in the days after the funeral, I began to take note of the many strange occurrences around Elvis's death. Priscilla said she'd been overcome by a strange sense of loss even before she heard he was gone. Almost the moment that Jerry Schilling heard the word of Elvis's death out in Los Angeles, a major drought there ended with a rainstorm. After Linda Thompson heard the news, the power went out in her apartment. As we all gathered around televisions at Graceland the night of Elvis's death to see how the story would be covered on the ten o'clock news, the sound went out on the broadcast. As we carried Elvis's casket out of Graceland, a tree limb fell on Ginger Alden's car. Later, Alan Fortas tried to play a tape of "Blue Hawaii" in his car and it jammed. I tried to play a cassette of *Elvis's Greatest Hits* in my car and the tape broke right after "Can't Help Falling in Love"—the song Elvis ended his concerts with. None of us knew what to make of any of that, but I could never help thinking that all those coincidences added a supernatural twist that Elvis himself would have loved.

Neither I nor any of the Memphis Mafia members were included in Elvis's will. Lisa was the sole heir of Elvis's estate, with stipulations made for the care and support of Vernon and Grandma Minnie Presley. Some in the group had sore feelings about this, but I never felt for a moment that it was even worth thinking about. I had gotten so much from Elvis when he was alive, I didn't need or expect any extra dollars from him after he was gone.

I'd never been a particularly observant Jew, but after Elvis's death I followed the Jewish tradition of *yahrzeit*—a year of mourning marked with daily morning and evening prayers. During that year I did not wear the diamond ring that Elvis had given me, and I don't think I even listened to his music: Those were reminders of the loss that were just too painful.

The years after Elvis's death were unhappy ones in many ways. After many difficult years during which Barbara and I just seemed to grow apart, our marriage ended in divorce. My mother died. And the legal troubles that began with the charges of mail fraud came to an embarrassing end when I was a mandatory "guest" of Shelby County for a couple of months.

Slowly over several years, I managed to put my career back on track. At first I worked hard as a freelancer, doing voice-over commercial work and deejaying an oldies show at nightclubs and private parties. One day, I got a call at home from Knox Phillips, the son of Sam Phillips, who told me that he and his father wanted me to come work at a new radio station Sam had purchased. The format was country rock, something new for me, but they wanted me to be the same on-air "GK" personality I'd always been. The station's call letters were perfect for my return to radio: WLVS.

After I'd been working there a while, Sam had the idea of having me do a regular show dedicated to Elvis, filling it with his music and whatever stories came to mind. I began doing *The Elvis Hour,* and have done it just about every Saturday for the last thirty years. In those years, I've worked a number of jobs at different radio stations, including another stint as a jock on WHBQ when it was relaunched as an oldies station. Today I do *The Elvis Hour* for WMC, the same station that once told me it saw no future in rock 'n' roll.

Eventually, I came to see my memories of Elvis not as painful reminders of a loss but as my most cherished possessions, and I became passionate about promoting and protecting Elvis's legacy. I began to accept offers to speak about him and had the chance to travel all over the world, meeting so many wonderful fans (including one unusual and particularly devoted fan, the comedian Andy Kaufman). I also discovered that talking about my memories of Elvis could be a lot of fun. A big turning point for me came when I was a guest on Oprah Winfrey's show during the first year she had a national broadcast. It was an Elvis-themed show, and I was on with a writer and a fan, speaking to a studio audience full of fan-club presidents from around the country. At one point, Oprah said, "Mr. Klein, I understand that you fixed up Elvis with a whole lot of women."

"That's true," I said.

"Well, what would happen if you and Elvis liked the same girl?" Oprah asked.

I said, "Oprah, are you kidding? Elvis's second and third choices were better than my firsts. Believe me, he didn't have any competition from me."

She broke up and started laughing, as did the audience. For me, it was one of the first times I realized that talking about Elvis didn't have to be a solemn affair. He was the guy I had the best times of my life with, and remembering those times didn't have to be entirely sad—it could also be a celebration.

While my relationships with the people around Elvis could never be the same without him at the center of the circle, I deeply appreciate some of the wonderful connections he made possible. In particular, my friendships with Priscilla, Jerry Schilling, Joe Esposito, Dr. Nick, Scotty Moore, the late Alan Fortas, Sam Phillips, Richard Davis, and Charlie Hodge have made my life that much richer.

I also enjoyed getting much closer to Vernon Presley in the years after Elvis died. He never got over the sadness of losing his son, but when I'd visit him, I think he got some pleasure from sharing stories and memories with a friend who had loved Elvis almost as much as he had.

For a long while after Elvis's death, I considered my long friendship with Red West to be over. He and Sonny's book had created such a painful situation, it was hard to see how that rift could heal. But years after Elvis was gone, I bumped into Red on a Memphis golf course, and he asked if he could talk to me privately. As we started talking, I noticed that Red, a tough guy who hadn't ever run from a fight in his life, had tears in his eyes. He said he wanted to apologize to me and to all the other guys, and said that he hated "the damned book" and wished that he'd never had anything to do with it. He said that since the day the book came out, it had been nothing but a nightmare for him, and he even told me about being attacked in an airport by one particularly angry Elvis fan—an old lady with an umbrella.

Red's words were moving to me. I told him that I accepted his apology and that I'd speak to Joe and Jerry and Richard and Charlie. It took some time, but they accepted Red back as a friend, as we all believe Elvis would have eventually.

I still have my original Snowmen's League card from Colonel Parker, and I had a few interesting interactions with him in the years after Elvis's death. He'd been a bizarre presence at Graceland immediately after the death, wearing loud, Hawaiian-print shirts and looking like he'd arrived ready for a backyard barbecue rather than a funeral. He was very hard to get a read on then, disguising any emotions he may have been feeling by running around to take care of the business arrangements he felt were important for Elvis's estate. It was only in the years after Elvis's death that we all learned something strange about the Colonel's background: He was a Dutch immigrant who, in all his years with Elvis, had never secured a U.S. passport. That went a long way toward explaining why he had never been supportive of Elvis's desire to tour internationally: The Colonel had probably been afraid that if he left the U.S., he wouldn't be allowed back in.

Years after Elvis's death, I was asked to come out to Las Vegas to see an Elvis-themed theatrical production that was aiming for a Broadway run. The producers wanted notes from insiders such as Priscilla and myself and Colonel Parker. When I ran into the Colonel at the Vegas theater, he asked when I was leaving town. I told him, and he said he wanted to be the one to drive me from my hotel to the airport. In all the years I'd known him, this was possibly the most shocking thing I'd ever heard him say: The Colonel never drove anyone to the airport. I thought perhaps he had some bombshell to drop on me during the ride, but we simply made small talk and then said goodbye. Colonel Parker remained a strong character right up until his death in 1997, but it occurred to me after that ride that maybe there were times when he was truly lonely. I really can't forgive him for some of the mistakes I think he made with Elvis, but I also can't deny that he was a brilliant, powerful man, and a trailblazer in his own right.

In 1986, I enjoyed what might be the highest honor of my career. Elvis Presley Enterprises, with the blessing of Priscilla and Lisa, asked me to be the one who would accept the award on Elvis's behalf when he was selected to be a member of the first class of inductees into the brand-new Rock and Roll Hall of Fame. The class included Chuck Berry, Ray Charles, Little Richard, Buddy Holly, and the Everly Brothers, along with several other performers I had personal ties to: James Brown, Jerry Lee Lewis, Sam Cooke, and Fats Domino. The event was held at the Waldorf-Astoria in New York and was first-class all the way. It was also a deeply moving and inspiring tribute to the great performers who had essentially created rock 'n' roll. Every inductee was introduced by a performer with a strong connection to his work, and Elvis was introduced by John Lennon's sons, Sean and Julian—the connection being that John had often been quoted as saying, "Before Elvis, there was nothing." When Sean and Julian brought me up onstage, I noticed one small but striking detail. Julian was wearing an old fifties-style Elvis button on his jacket. He later told me that it was the real thing, and that he'd gotten it from his father.

By then I had accepted the fact that Elvis was gone, and that my life was going on without him in it. But addressing the crowd of music superstars and industry heavyweights that night, I was overcome with a wave of emotion once again.

Another of the greatest honors of my life has come from the opportunity to be a part of the remembrances of Elvis that mark the anniversary of his passing each August in Memphis, during what's come to be known as Elvis Week. I've had so many wonderful moments through the years taking part in the seminars, celebrations, and candlelight vigils. I've made a tradition of hosting a Memphis Mafia reunion at the Alfred's on Beale restaurant during Elvis Week, and for thirty years have produced the memorial ceremonies held in Elvis's honor. One year, Muhammad Ali was the keynote speaker at a memorial. Aside from having the biggest hand I'd ever shaken, he surprised me with the depth of feeling in his remarks, and when he concluded with an impromptu a capella version of "Don't Be Cruel," the audience went absolutely crazy.

For many years now, I've been going back to Graceland every Friday—not to the house per se, but to the exhibition center across the street, which houses among its attractions a Sirius satellite radio studio. From that studio, I host the weekly *George Klein Show* on Sirius's Elvis Channel. As for going up to the house, that's still very hard for me. When I'm called upon to conduct a VIP tour for someone, or need to be there for a special event, I try to treat it as business, but it's a struggle not to be overwhelmed by feelings of sadness and loss. Graceland is still a serene and peaceful place, but I always walk away from there with the realization that today I still miss Elvis as much as the day we lost him.

I'm very lucky to have found a new love in my life: my dear wife, Dara. She's a rock for me, and without her love and support, I don't know how I could have carried on. Needless to say, she's also a big Elvis fan.

Shortly after Elvis died, producer Felton Jarvis told me that in one of their last meetings, he and Elvis had started to plan another recording session. Felton played Elvis a number of demos, and knowing that Elvis had some recent success with Mark James's "Moody Blue," he included another James tune, "Loving You's a Natural Thing." According to Felton, Elvis liked the song enough that he had Felton play it a couple of times.

"That's a Mark James song?" Elvis asked.

"Yeah," said Felton. "But guess who the cowriter is?"

"Who?"

"GK."

"GK? You mean George Klein GK? Well, damn, put that in the A-stack. We're definitely going to cut that one."

He never said a word about it to me, and he was gone before that recording session could happen. But I love to think how much he would have enjoyed handing me a copy of him singing my song, just to watch my jaw drop open.

On an August evening in 2007, I was at the FedEx Forum in Memphis, watching Elvis deliver one more phenomenal performance to a sold-out crowd. The concert was part of the Elvis Week tribute marking the thirtieth anniversary of his death, and it featured giant-screen film clips of Elvis singing, backed with live accompaniment by members of the TCB band. The concert began with a sequence filmed especially for the occasion. From a distant point in space, the camera began to zoom and zoom until it brought viewers inside of Graceland. Jerry Schilling appeared and called Elvis from his room. Jerry and Elvis (played by a very skilled impersonator) walked outside, where Joe Esposito waited next to a helicopter on the Graceland lawn. The helicopter flew over Memphis and landed on the roof of the Forum, where I met them and delivered a line I'd said so many times in the past: "It's time to rock and roll." We walked Elvis down a hallway to the stage entrance, and when the Elvis figure headed for the stage, the real concert began.

I've tried in the past not to get too sentimental at Elvis Week events, but sitting out in the crowd that night, watching that intro and hearing the crowd go nuts, it was impossible not to be moved. And when the real Elvis appeared on that big screen and the band kicked in, it was just like he'd never left. That whole evening, you could feel the love he always had for his audience, and you could feel—even thirty years later—the audience's love of him just pouring forth. It was magical.

I think about Elvis every day. I take great pride in the fact that my friend and I have been honored with "music notes" on Memphis's Walk of Fame, and it means the world to me that my note and Elvis's sit side by side on Beale Street. Missing him hasn't gotten any easier, but I'm delighted that he's become not just a national treasure but a family heirloom: His music has been passed down through a couple of generations now, and it hasn't lost any of its energy or excitement. Elvis was a movie star, an electrifying presence on television, an incredible entertainer onstage, and an almost impossibly handsome man. While all that is still a part of his image, what really carries on is his voice—a voice that could give you goosebumps whether it was singing gospel, country, pop, R&B, or rock 'n' roll. When people listen to Elvis today, that voice can work its magic all over again, and it doesn't seem to matter that we're a long way from 1954.

As sad an ending as Elvis's life had, I take comfort in knowing that he really, truly loved being Elvis. He loved everything about it, from the fans at the Graceland gates to the life on the road to every dream, big and small, that he was able to make come true for himself. I heard him say more than once that he couldn't wait to wake up the next day to see what would happen in the life of Elvis Presley.

Elvis was the most talented man I've ever known, he was the most generous man I've ever known, and he was the smartest man I've ever known. But on a personal level, what I loved most about Elvis Presley was the amazing quality of his friendship. I've never felt as cared for, supported, and accepted as I did with him, and I've never felt as devoted to anyone as I was to him. I only hope he had some sense of how much I loved him as a friend, and how much I appreciated everything he ever did for me. There'll never be another Elvis, and there'll never be another person like him in my life. I just consider myself a lucky, lucky man to be able to say that Elvis Presley was a friend of mine.

I don't think I'll ever really say goodbye to Elvis. But, just like at the end of all my radio shows, I can sign off and send us back to what lives on—his music:

> *"Ladies and gentlemen, the sun never sets on a legend, and there'll always be a TCB on the* Lisa Marie. *The United States of America has had many presidents but only one King, and here he is to sing . . ."*

ACKNOWLEDGMENTS

I'd like to express my gratitude to the people who helped make this book a reality. Thanks to my agent, Scott Waxman, and my friend John Daly and his agent, Bud Martin, who steered me to Scott. Thanks to Jed Donahue and Lindsay Orman at Crown for believing in this book. Thanks to Chris Pfaffman Coffey for her invaluable assistance through the years and on this project. Thanks also to Fred Smith and Flynn Wallace at FedEx for their great help.

Special thanks to Chuck Crisafulli—I couldn't have told my story without you.

A heartfelt thanks to Priscilla Presley and to Jerry Schilling, for your cherished friendship and for all of your support.

Thanks to some dear old friends who offered guidance and assistance through this process: Joe Esposito, Red West, Dr. "Nick" Nichopoulos, Scotty Moore, D. J. Fontana, Jerry Lee Lewis, and Dick Clark.

Thank you to Jack Soden, Scott Williams, and Robert Dye at EPE and Tom Brown at Turner for their help.

Thanks to the great friends who've been there for me through the years: Alan Fortas, Richard Davis, Sam Phillips, Knox and Jerry Phillips, Bill Grumbles, Dewey Phillips, Lance Russell, all the folks at WHBQ , Herbie O'Mell, Chips Moman, Mark James, Felton Jarvis, James Brown, Tanya Tucker, Sam the Sham, Freddie Cannon, B. J. Thomas, Roy Head, J. W. Whitten, T. G. Sheppard, Wink and Sandy Martindale, Kevin Kane, Ronnie McDowell, Bill Morris, Marian Cocke, Larry Geller, John Sisinni, Dean Ranta, Dickie Kline, John Heath, Jim Lockard, Irv Salky, Ted Hansom, "Bardahl," Dr. David Meyer, R. C. Johnson, Beverly Rook, James Burton and the TCB band, Tommy Warren, Ray Walker, Gordon Stoker, Jack Clement, Charlie Van Dyke, Dr. George Flinn, Fred Edmaiston, Gary Rosenberg, Pat Tigrett, Bernard Lansky, Al Ruiz, Sammy Shore, and Tony Gigliotti.

Thank you, Dara, for putting up with me and being the love of my life.

To Elvis—your friendship made the best moments in my life possible. Thank you for everything.

INDEX

ABOUT THE AUTHOR

GEORGE KLEIN is the host of the *George Klein Show,* on Sirius XM Satellite Radio's Elvis Channel, and the weekly *Elvis Hour,* which has aired on Memphis radio for thirty years. In the mid-1950s he was the host of the groundbreaking radio show *George Klein's Rock 'n' Roll Ballroom,* and from 1964 to 1976 he produced and hosted the television program *Talent Party,* which showcased the top rock and pop artists of the day. Klein produced the documentary *Elvis: Memories* and served as narrator and creative consultant for the concert video trilogy *Elvis: The Great Performances.* He has been interviewed by Oprah Winfrey, Larry King, *60 Minutes,* Geraldo Rivera, and the *Today* show, among others. A lifelong resident of Memphis, he has been honored with a musical note on the city's Beale Street Walk of Fame—his note is next to Elvis's.

CHUCK CRISAFULLI is a veteran entertainment journalist and author whose most recent titles include *Go to Hell: A Heated History of the Underworld* and *Me and a Guy Named Elvis,* with Jerry Schilling.